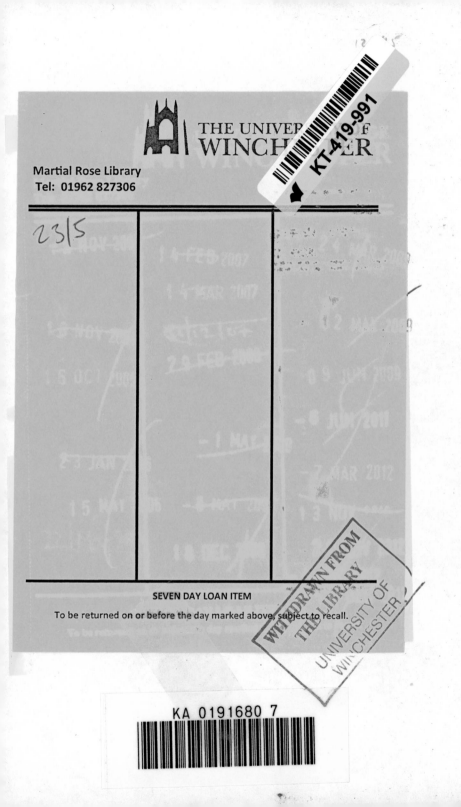

Modern Feminist Thought

From the Second Wave to
'Post-Feminism'

Imelda Whelehan

EDINBURGH UNIVERSITY PRESS

© Imelda Whelehan, 1995

Edinburgh University Press Ltd
22 George Square, Edinburgh

Typeset in Caslon
by Pioneer Associates Ltd, Perthshire, and
printed and bound in Finland

A CIP record for this book is available
from the British Library

ISBN 0 7486 0744 7 Hardback
ISBN 0 7486 0621 1 Paperback

Contents

Acknowledgements

Although completely rewritten in a period of study leave in 1994, this book represents several years of work, and many key shifts in my own feminist thinking. My parents and wider family have experienced the effects of such changes first hand, and yet remained supportive. To them this work is dedicated.

Thanks are also due to Professor Stephen Knight for his practical support for this project, and to De Montfort University, Leicester, for granting me a period of study leave to complete it. Jackie Jones of Edinburgh University Press has awaited the arrival of the long-promised manuscript with patience and good humour.

There are many others who played a crucial part in the development of this work and my research in general. It would be impossible to extend gratitude to all involved, but they include Chitrita Chaudhuri, Carol Edwards, Richard Edwards, Tom Grimsey, Mandy Jarvis, Diana Knight, Nick Lintott, Nick Peim, Nasser Sherkat, Esther Sonnet, Perry Willson and Lucy Zanetti. Special thanks to David Sadler.

Introduction

Feminism embodies many theories rather than being a single discrete theory, and rather than being a politically coherent approach to the subordination of women, is a political commitment – or in some of its forms more an ethical commitment – to giving women their true value. It is not even possible to say that it is a commitment to equality, since some feminists have argued, both in the past and today, for separate spheres of influence, emphasizing difference and complementarity rather than equality.

(Wilson 1986: 8)

GENERAL AIMS OF THIS BOOK

The term 'second wave', applied as a prefix to feminism, implies that it describes a specific moment in history, and signifies a discernible transformation in this body of knowledge – specifically a shifting of boundaries towards a new wave of radicalism. If 'first wave' feminism's chief aim of formal equality between the sexes was regarded as having been achieved through the process of enfranchisement, then feminism should have realized its own demise soon after. But the gains made by the suffrage movements in Britain and the USA were soon to expose more thorny problems for women: formal equality – for whatever sex, race or class – can prove chimerical when civic and political structures which permit such processes of equality already work in favour of the dominant group, and demonstrate that in fact the discourses of power assume relations of inequality at their very roots.

If one considers the achievements of feminism from the perspective of the '90s, feminism appears to be a success story, at least in academic terms. Women's Studies courses are still increasing, and the bookshops appear to be bursting with new publications dealing with issues of gender. Yet underpinning this academic success story is the

reality that feminism as a political movement with a mass following
has waned in both Europe and the United States of America.
Although there remain traces of feminist activism in the actions of
individuals in mainstream politics, isolated groups producing grassroots support for women's issues, or in the production of independent
journals that have remained faithful to the ideals of feminism, the
radical promise of emerging second wave feminism has not been
realized. While feminist debates continue and become increasingly
complex and diverse in the scholarly arena, feminism is constantly
being lambasted in the mass media and is gradually becoming one of
the chief scapegoats for the ills of contemporary life. This tension
between the development of feminist thought in academe, and the
'sins' of feminism as portrayed in the world at large, is one aspect
which this book shall address by outlining, in Part One, the main
features of major strands in contemporary second wave thought, and
then, in Part Two, debating the place of feminism in social, political
and personal life during the '90s.

However, before I embark on a 'survey' of distinctive strands in
second wave feminist thought, I would like to provide a context for
understanding the emergence of the women's liberation movement.
As I hope Part Two will demonstrate, it is not always easy or desirable to divide up feminism into discrete strands; it is clear that feminist thought contains perspectives which sometimes hold polarized
views on the origin and perpetuation of gender difference, and from
thence wider theoretical disagreements can escalate. The purpose of
this Introduction is therefore twofold: to provide a reader unfamiliar
with feminist thought with a basis from which to embark upon this
book; and to offer a retrospective which is also a defence of the radical potential of feminist thought today, in face of detractors all too
ready to dismiss the very real revolution which feminism made on
the consciousness of so many. As I hope this suggests, neither my
Introduction nor subsequent chapters are intended to be objective.
One of the main reasons why I chose to write this book is to offer a
position which strongly refutes claims that feminism threatens to
explode under its own numerous identity crises, or that the term
feminism itself is so semantically overburdened as to be meaningless
or to require a corrective such as 'post-feminism'.

Throughout this work I will blur divisions between feminist politics and feminist academic theory – and indeed between both critical
and creative writings – because to divide the numerous forms of
expression women have used to convey a feminist message is to fragment a body of thought which is entirely symbiotic. Indeed the main

strength of modern feminist thought is its interdisciplinarity, its resistance to easy categorization: to attempt seriously to repartition fragments of feminist thought into discipline-oriented pigeon-holes would be to perform an act of phallocentric vandalism. To understand properly the scope of feminist critiques, it is necessary to appreciate that its resistance to categorisation is a part of its radicalism, and the eclectic processes of feminist thought remind us that for many women being a feminist means that no aspect of their daily personal, social and political life can remain unscrutinized. For this reason some feminist work appears to be resolutely 'non-theoretical', something that detractors put down to feminism's lack of 'rigour'. I hope that my consideration of the so-called 'confessional' aspects of feminism, alongside more sophisticated theoretical speculations, will demonstrate that part of feminism's sustained attraction for readers is its general accessibility. For many, feminism's chief aim ought to be its capacity to involve women from diverse backgrounds, encouraging them to feel that they too can contribute to this immense and ever-growing body of knowledge.

Despite this book's grandiose title, it is not intended to be the last word on feminist thought. Rather, it is an attempt to pull together certain threads in order to support my conviction that feminism remains an exciting and enabling political and philosophical standpoint in the '90s. In Part Two I offer reasons why detractors of feminism must be ceaselessly challenged, and I hope that readers will be encouraged to contribute to a renewed resistance to a forceful and concerted backlash against feminism, which is also a sustained attack on women's basic social and economic rights.

REFORM TO REVOLUTION:
EMERGING FEMINISMS IN THE 1970s

The so-called 'second wave' in feminism is, as the term suggests, a continuation of a movement, that earlier phase of feminism which clamoured for civic equality for women via the vote, achieved in the United States and United Kingdom during the first two decades of this century. Second wave feminism, then, is 'the second peak of a feminist movement that has existed for more than 100 years' (Dahlerup 1986: 2). Second wave research has also foregrounded those earlier female thinkers who put forward views on women's social and political status which we might in retrospect identify as 'feminist'.[1] Arguably the most important of these was Mary Wollstonecraft, whose *Vindication of the Rights of Woman* was first published in 1792, and whose ideas have helped shape the women's

movement ever since. But feminism's 'first wave' signalled the beginnings of a mass movement, and this synthesis of ideas resulted in
calls for collective action in the fight for women's equality through
lobbying and reformist campaigns.[2] The first wave succeeded in
achieving a significant victory – that of enfranchising women within the political and legal system, and facilitating the possible future
reform of the most inequitable aspects of social life. The second
wave, however, became a response to the lean years after the achievement of putative equality; the result of a dawning recognition that
the system itself seemed to have an inbuilt propensity for institu-
tionalizing gender (as well as other) inequality. The second wave is
therefore distinct in recognizing the possibility that there might not
be a solution to women's continued oppression short of a revolution.

It is impossible and therefore probably inadvisable to pinpoint one
year to mark the beginning of feminism's second wave; however,
1968 carries a certain symbolic resonance – not least as the year of
public manifestations of New Left radicalism in Europe and the
USA.[3] In the United States, many women, disenchanted by their
involvement in male-dominated left-wing politics, were defecting to
localized, non-hierarchical women's liberation groups. Such groups
were established in order to interrogate the social and material conditions of individual women's existence, often with the longer term
aim of creating an agenda for political transformation of the social
and economic status of women. Women's participation in left-wing
politics, which often involved performing largely menial and 'feminine' tasks – such as typing and clerical or domestic support work
– alerted them to the stark fact that existing political groups and
theoretical positions did not take the issue of women's subordination
seriously. Furthermore, radical men appeared to be quite happy to
exploit a 'natural' sexual division of labour in order to service their
own cause, unaware or unconcerned that they might be themselves
perpetuating oppressive power relations. Because mainstream political and social theories focused on 'male' experience in the public
sphere of work, women found themselves, paradoxically, 'outside'
analyses of class and relations of production, while being nominally
contained within such a perspective. Left-wing analyses of social
injustice focused on class as the central determinant of power relations, assuming that male and female experiences were identical; and
if women's oppression was considered at all it was regarded as an
effect of capitalism.

In a speech given at the Free University in New York City on 17

February 1968, Anne Koedt articulated a sense of collective female disillusionment:

> Within the last year many radical women's groups have sprung up throughout the country. This was caused by the fact that movement women[4] found themselves playing secondary roles on every level – be it in terms of leadership, or simply in terms of being listened to. They found themselves (and others) afraid to speak up because of self-doubts when in the presence of men. They ended up concentrating on food-making, typing, mimeographing, general assistance work, and serving as a sexual supply for their male comrades after hours. (Koedt et al. 1973: 318)

Women began to reflect upon feminism's past, and to reconceive the potential for women's liberation outside the parameters of a political discourse which afforded little space for women as a distinct, though unwieldy, category. Their disenchantment with the radical political movements of the '60s led them to believe that female subordination was more than just an effect of dominant political forces; it was endemic in all social relations with men. Once women began to scrutinize such effects collectively within consciousness-raising groups, they found their suspicions that a socialist revolution would rapidly metamorphose into a white bourgeois male revolution, all too well founded. As a consequence revolutionary strategies themselves had to be reviewed: going beyond merely militating for material changes, women recognized the need to challenge the dominant ideological representations of femininity.

This overt resistance to conventional definitions of what 'being a woman' means came to characterize second wave feminist activism. In 1968 the first widely reported example of such activism occurred when feminists staged a demonstration at the Miss America contest in Atlantic City, 'protesting, among other points, "Women in our society are forced daily to compete for male approval, enslaved by ludicrous beauty standards that we ourselves are conditioned to take seriously and to accept"' (Brownmiller 1986: 9). The demonstration itself offered a visual spectacle but one which directly challenged the ethos of a beauty industry exemplified by an event where women were 'rewarded' and valued purely on the basis of their looks. The demonstrators also attempted to force spectators to make a connection between this beauty pageant's criteria for establishing female worth, and similar assumptions current in society at large. Such demonstrations were not just intended to draw people's attention to a particular aspect of social injustice against women. Rather they invited the participation of other women as an early consciousness-raising exercise. A 'freedom trash bucket' was set up at the event, into which were thrown bras and girdles – items which symbolized women's enslavement to unrealistic standards of beauty. This receptacle assumed the proportions of a major controversy in the media's reporting of the event: 'Imaginary flames were added later by a news agency reporter, and the idea caught on in a big way. The media loved it. Sexy and absurd, it neatly disposed of a phenomenon which would otherwise have proved rather awkward to explain' (Coote and Campbell 1987: 3; see also Castro 1990: 187–9).

Thus the image of feminist as rabid 'bra-burner' was born, as was the beginnings of a media witch-hunt against feminism which is still evident today. Whatever attempts were made to dismiss such protests as attacks from bitter, unattractive females who could never become Miss America themselves, nonetheless, no one could fail to see that the event importantly signalled a new phase of feminist direct action. Here was a tactical departure from mainstream political lobbying: now the target was an entire system of ideas. The Miss America protest also taught its organizers that demonstrations of sisterly solidarity could too easily be construed as vicious attacks on other women (the contestants in the beauty pageant in this case). Later protests were unambiguously directed at the men responsible for parading women as sex objects. The primary site of struggle, as characterized by these early demonstrations, was the female body itself, and the restraints imposed upon it by contemporary Western notions of femininity.

In Britain, 1968 marked fifty years of women's suffrage; a landmark viewed increasingly as at best a Pyrrhic victory. The First World War had, of necessity, drawn women into the workforce as the 'reserve army' of labour, and enfranchisement for women at the war's end seemed to be at one level an acknowledgement of their crucial role on the home front. The Second World War again demanded the massed presence of women in the workforce. These women found that, for them, the cumulative effect of both wars with their consequent economic and social turmoil was a degree of liberation from the constrictions of their dominant domestic role. For the state was forced, temporarily at least, to assume a far greater responsibility for childcare and other support services. The wartime housewife was positively seduced into performing the dual role of carer and worker – roles which had previously been cast ideologically as mutually in conflict – and many women, having recognized a potential they were previously persuaded was biologically impossible, would be reluctant to return to the home full time.[5] World events had transformed the lives of working-class and bourgeois women alike, and it seemed possible that this transformation might be permanent.

However, the years after the Second World War produced a retroactive ideological shift: a revivified 'cult of the housewife' was effectively a consolidated attack on women's new-found freedom, devoted as it was to recreating and redefining the domestic space as women's space. Domestic labour was construed in capitalist terms; the housewife of the 1950s and 1960s was constructed and mythologized as a competent businesswoman surrounded by a wealth of labour-saving devices, so that housewifery could be ideologically packaged as a skilled, highly technologized industry of its own. The housewife's role was one of autonomy and responsibility; as the major purchaser of commodities in the family household, she was intensively targeted through commercial advertising. The image of the housewife as the purveyor of high standards of domestic organization was fed back to individual women though the media – where it had become increasingly glamorized and correspondingly difficult to live up to. Unless, that is, the role was adopted as a full-time occupation.

Undoubtedly the twentieth century saw substantial improvements in the quality of women's lives. The wife and mother of the 1950s and 1960s no longer resembled the 'Angel in the House' of Victorian popular mythology. Nevertheless, the home was once again regarded as the proper haven for the 'whole' woman. For 'normal' women – women who married and had children – maintaining the household was to be their proper destiny; indeed it became an identity in itself, to the exclusion of all others. Careers were supposed to be temporary launch pads, abandoned when the 'career' of motherhood was embarked upon. Women who wanted both a family and a career had a difficult time juggling work with their domestic and 'true' identity. Career women who eschewed the path of maternity and matrimony confronted the inequities of a labour market where they were neither properly paid for doing the same work as men nor rewarded with promotion to senior positions for showing equal competence. As Betty Friedan observed in her pathfinding book *The Feminine Mystique*, 'It is more than a strange paradox that as all professions are finally open to women in America, "career woman" has become a dirty word' (1965: 60). Yet, for all the marketed glamour of the passive, pure and contented homemaker, there was a clear disjunction between this ideal and the material realities of the daily drudgery of most domestic labour, which afforded little glamour and less intellectual and social stimulation.[6]

Until the emergence of second wave feminist activism there appeared to be no means by which women could express a sense of their own subjugation that did not conjure up treacherous images of unnaturalness and perversity. The galvanizing effect of the women's liberation movement was achieved by a transformation of feminist notions of political intervention, signalling a significant departure from the mainstream political arena altogether and extending the parameters of feminist discourse beyond recognition. Feminists of the later '60s onwards broke all the 'rules', both of traditional lobbying tactics and to some extent of left-wing oppositional politics; they communicated in women-only cadres, preferring non-hierarchical formations where all group members shared tasks equally. Here women attempted to create a political philosophy which paid little heed to founding fathers of modern democracy, but might rehabilitate female antecedents where available. While the media attempted to portray such women as petty latter-day hyenas in petticoats, they betrayed a fear that feminists who did not lobby or present petitions through figure-heads offered a more sinister threat to the status quo – they could not be contained by the requirements of political appeal because they denied the entire political process any credence. How could one really identify those numerous but invisible militants who, for example, festooned advertising posters with stickers in the London Underground, declaring them offensive to women?[7] In their early public appearances, feminists declared their solidarity, not as adherents to any party line, but as women.

Emergent feminists of the late '60s and early '70s were inclined to be more reflective in their extensive analyses of 'what it means to be a woman', and ready to question the foundations of existing social/familial relations. One significant reason for this more radical manifestation of feminism was that more women were gaining access to further and higher education and consequently finding it less easy to settle into domestic quietude. Many women had been involved in radical left-wing politics; and though they might have become disaffected with the rigidly hierarchical, phallocentric nature of such organizations, they had learnt important political lessons. The radical movements of the late '60s inspired the hope that direct action and attacks on the all-pervasive Establishment might eventually cause substantial material and ideological shifts in the social formation. The central problem for modern feminists remained, however, the unassailable fact that while women could now to some extent redefine their social identity by pursuing a career, they could not shake off the timeless and naturalized association of women with the home.

CONSTRUCTING THEORIES/FINDING AN ORIGIN

Betty Friedan's *The Feminine Mystique* (1963) appeared to herald the new dynamism of feminist thought, as it tackled many of the issues that were to characterize second wave politics in the latter part of the '60s. The scope of her analysis of the 'problem that has no name' – the alienation felt among US housewives dehumanized by the drudgery of domestic labour – confirmed Friedan as one of the pioneers of modern feminism. One reason for her book's resounding success lay in its focus on the experiences of white middle-class women – the very group that were to form the majority in the new women's movement. Over thirty years later the problem still has no name; or rather, the problem itself has diversified into numerous equally intractable problems. For contemporary feminist theorists the act of naming is almost as complicated as the problems themselves: landmark feminists of the past, such as Mary Wollstonecraft, Virginia Woolf and Simone de Beauvoir all observed that 'woman' in Western culture is defined only in negative terms by what they lack – status, independent income, education, history and most of all, the discrete qualities associated with 'masculinity'. 'Man', so often used as a generic term to signify 'humanity' only emphasizes the cultural and social exclusion of women where men are the 'norm', and where seemingly 'universal' values are in fact men's values. Perhaps Virginia Woolf most cogently expresses the resulting sense of alienation so often felt by women: 'if one is a woman one is often surprised by a sudden splitting off of consciousness, say in walking down Whitehall, when from being the natural inheritor of that civilization, she becomes, on the contrary, outside of it, alien and critical' (1977: 93). Simone de Beauvoir, writing some twenty years after Woolf, further demonstrates that the power to describe/define essential characteristics peculiar to the female of the species has always been the male preserve: 'it is civilization as a whole that produces this creature, intermediate between male and eunuch, which is described as feminine' (1972: 295). In *The Second Sex* de Beauvoir locates the category 'woman' as lying uneasily between the concepts of 'male' (phallic) and 'not-male' (castrated), offering a critique of male-oriented discourses, such as Freud's, which typify women as essentially the representation of lack. Woman's 'lack', in de Beauvoir's view, is not anatomical, but cultural and ideological – gaining credence from the fact of woman's unique role as reproducer of the species.[8]

Perhaps de Beauvoir's notion of woman as eunuch inspired the title of Germaine Greer's *The Female Eunuch* (1970) – although it remains an unacknowledged legacy. Greer locates the cultural status of woman as equivalent to the eunuch, interrogating Freud's representation of the child's perception of herself as castrated: 'in traditional psychological theory, which is after all only another way of describing and rationalizing the status quo, the desexualization of women is illustrated in the Freudian theory of the female sex as lacking a sexual organ' (1971: 68). Here Greer ponders the psychoanalytic exploitation of a definition of woman as 'lack', or obverse of the male; as she observes, such a definition facilitates a slide into a conception of woman as lacking a sexual organ and thus sexual feelings altogether. For radical feminists generally, Freud's concept of penis envy endorses patriarchal power by foregrounding the phallus as the symbol of culture and civilization; while affirming a view that 'normal' women have no demonstrable sexuality at all. Feminists generally were insulted by the assumptions behind Freud's theory. Rather than inspiring envy, de Beauvoir argues, a young girl's first view of 'this outgrowth, this weak little rod of flesh can in itself inspire them only with indifference, or even disgust' (1972: 73). Nonetheless, what Freud identified was the centrality of the phallus in Western culture so that by the mid-'70s Juliet Mitchell, in *Psychoanalysis and Feminism* (1974), could argue that Freudian theory might be appropriated by feminists as an aid to the understanding of the perpetuation of patriarchal processes. Freud's work might be interpreted as symptomatic of the existing social organization, describing the effects of culturally oriented gender difference rather than prescribing them as absolute.[9]

During the late '60s and '70s the focus for analysis of the central sites of women's oppression was constantly changing; the Freudian legacy offered a compelling case for seeing the central problem as lying in the characterization of the female sexual response and its traditional conflation with reproductive imperatives; yet this did not in itself explain the institutionalization of social and economic inequalities. Once feminists had discovered that 'woman' could only be defined as 'not-man' – outside or invisible in mainstream forms of knowledge – the chief difficulty lay in finding a language which could articulate the specificity of female experience as both critique and manifesto for change. Modern feminists were more likely to have access to higher education than their forbears, but they nonetheless remained marginalized – as women – within such privileged and phallocentric discursive networks. At times, early theoretical explorations of the subject seem nebulous and diffuse, especially as modern feminists were less likely to have faith in the efficacy of change through lobbying and modification of existing social institutions. De Beauvoir's suspicion that 'civilization as a whole' is irredeemably constructed along male principles, required further exploration, given that male-oriented discourse remained resistant to the inclusion of female experiences. Confronted by the absence of available academic /political space for the development of a 'discourse of feminism', women would have to forge that space; but there could be no simple agreement about how, and by what means this should be done.

During this period of innovatory and ground-breaking analyses, publications appeared seemingly independent of each other; although at a rhetorical level it was commonplace to talk of feminism in the singular, differing political 'strands' were beginning to consolidate their own specific positions and visions of the future. It seems likely that a great number of the most common conceptions (and often misconceptions) about feminism derive from the '70s when feminist militancy was at its peak. Some commentators have even suggested that, 'the history of the women's movement in the 1970s . . . was marked by bitter, at times virulent, internal disputes over what it was possible or permissable for a feminist to do, say, think or feel' (Delmar, in Mitchell and Oakley 1986: 9). But despite evidence that the second wave was founded upon active tensions, feminists of the early '70s did construct networks of communication, conferences, demonstrations and newsletters, which crossed boundaries and emphasized aspects of feminism's commonality. There may not have been one dominant definition of feminism, but all strands were rooted in the belief that women suffer injustice because of their sex; and the emergence of women's liberation as not only a movement but an intellectual tendency too proved attractive to many women.

Emphasis on consciousness raising and direct action meant that feminist politics emanated from the individual and private sphere of experiential and emotional responses to oppression. This dictated the shape of early feminist agendas – concentrating on issues such as paid housework, abortion, contraception, the family, and the sexual division of labour. There appeared to be no clear-cut divide between theory and practice within the nascent movement which – by virtue of its broad-based structure – implicitly conceived of itself as a theory in perpetual process, rather than a doctrine to be disseminated to willing converts. Writings from this period devote most of their energy to pinpointing gaps in contemporary knowledge, rather than offering authoritative solutions or dogma. In this sense all strands were constantly in a state of transformation and modification – to identify oneself as a radical, for example, would not guarantee a consensus among radicals as a whole as to how radical feminism could be defined.

The women's liberation movement remained loosely structured and decentralized in its determination not to produce 'stars' or leaders to speak for its 'members'. This was one of the most striking and positive features of sexual politics, as well as being, arguably, the cause of its later decline. The feminist 'cells' which sprung up independently throughout the United States and later in Britain, produced tentative manifestos focusing on issues of particular concern to women, but tended on the whole to shy away from 'theory' – anything which seemed to invest heavily in the structures and constraints of 'male' thought. It was not until later that the need for some kind of theoretical framework, some way of reflecting upon feminist past and present achievements, as well as negotiating the conflicting philosophies which comprised second wave feminism, was recognized. The popular consciousness was of feminists as terrorists, trading in dogma which threatened the fabric of social life, and which would therefore take something from 'ordinary' women, rather than give them something, and this alienated women who might otherwise have profited by identifying themselves with the women's movement. Personal memoirs confirm that feminism changed the lives of individual women (see Rowbotham 1989; Wandor 1990), but it had not succeeded in disturbing the foundations of Western democracy which resolutely centred upon 'public' man and 'private' woman. When women collected to talk about problems affecting women they found themselves to be curiously and ambiguously outside language, and it was relatively easy for (male) commentators to suppress some of the most cogent feminist arguments by dismissing them as lacking the 'correct' discursive apparatus. From its beginnings second wave feminist discourse was outlawed from pre-established intellectual theories because they could not conceptualize a discourse whose difference primarily hinged upon its gender specificity, and which effectively destabilized or conflated existing academic disciplinary frameworks. At the same time, however, feminism was already contained within such frameworks – there being no 'outside', no neutral women's space – just as the term 'woman' was contained and compressed legally and philosophically within generic 'man'.

What made the women's movement distinct from other radical movements of the late '60s can be summed up by one of its most famous slogans, 'the personal is political'. The more this simple statement has been reiterated, with various applications, the more power it seems to yield. It indicated the concentration of feminism upon women's experiences of femaleness, particularly their individual accounts of the pressures brought to bear by contemporary concepts of ideal-type femininity, and it helped propound the conviction that the private was of very public concern. Consciousness raising was a central process in politicizing the personal: not only was it intended to awaken women to the injustices of their secondary social position, but they were encouraged to reassess their personal and emotional lives, their relation to their families, their lovers and their work. Not only might this allow women to express their dissatisfaction with occasions when they felt that they had been exploited or coerced in the name of duty, love or guilt, but it was hoped that it might also permit women to negotiate an autonomous identity beyond those associated with family duties. Although this initial process focused very much on the individual, and could be seen therefore as politically naive or regressive, or tending towards personal therapy, the ultimate aim of consciousness raising is an analytical one, enabling the members of a group to view women's oppression in more abstract, even theoretical terms (see Castro 1990: 20–5). Although the term consciousness raising (CR) has become associated with radical feminist politics in particular, one could argue that all feminist positions utilize such a process; particularly effective in feminist politics because it necessitates the scrutiny of one's private life and therefore gives the lie to the notion that this area of human experience is, or should be, beyond the purview of political intervention. The evasion of 'domestic' issues in politics had excluded women for centuries.

Yet the concentration on 'personal' politics meant that the actual status of feminism as perceived by other political groups became problematic. Left-wingers felt that a focus on gender-specific issues acted as a diversion from the main business of a consolidated attack upon the ruling classes. At the US National Conference for a New Politics in 1967, New Left men denied women's issues any political currency (Castro 1990: 20): it remained a commonplace thereafter to argue that a revolution in class consciousness would liberate both women and men from the oppressive effects of a capitalist social organization. To liberal and conservative eyes the views of feminists represented the views of the unrepresentative few; and it is also true that feminists alienated many potentially sympathetic women by what was viewed as their extremism – especially by their questioning of one of the most central institutions of society, the family.

POLITICAL AGENDAS OF THE SECOND WAVE

There was generally substantial agreement between different feminists about the main issues for feminism. However, clear splits are evident in their analyses of the roots of female oppression: while they were quite certain of the effects of female subordination, there tended to be sharp disagreements about where the origins of male power were located. Nonetheless, certain terms became common feminist parlance, and specific issues came to reflect shared concerns among all feminists. Further, feminist activism, in addition to the development of various communication networks, came to represent women's liberation at its broadest and most vital base. Conferences were one means of collecting together groups of women in order to attempt agreement on some fundamental issues, although the main difficulty in doing this was to avoid any implication that any one group of individuals had the right to lead or hijack the progress of the women's movement.

If the 1968 Miss America protest in Atlantic City brought feminism out into the public gaze, the stirring of the British consciousness was far more sedate. In February 1970 Ruskin College, Oxford, saw the first Women's Liberation Conference in Britain, attended by at least six hundred people. It is viewed by many as a moment of political awakening (see Wandor 1990), yet regrettably, just as the Miss America protest is most memorable for initiating the myth of feminists as bra-burners, the Ruskin conference is remembered for the graffiti daubed over the college walls (see Rowbotham 1989: 13). This conference was followed by a protest on 20 November 1970 at the Miss World Competition at the Albert Hall, as a means to communicate to other women directly and publicly – beyond the distorting effects of the mass media. Unfortunately, in common with the Miss America protest, the reasons behind the disruption were hostilely misrepresented by the press as a destructive act by the disaffected few.[10]

However, a major success of the Ruskin conference was its establishment of a National Women's Coordinating Committee which encompassed all the vying feminist positions, rather than appearing to stand for one party line. A structure of small autonomous groups was adopted:

Our first priority isn't to get over information, but know what everyone in the room thinks. We believe in getting people to interact, not to listen to experts. We want them to *themselves* make an analysis of their situation, which will lead them to action . . . . (quoted in Coote and Campbell 1987: 15)

In this spirit, a great deal of feminist energy was expended in creating centres and groups which would help women, as well as promote the consciousness that such support networks were essential and were precisely what was unavailable in state provision of female welfare. Women's centres with various facilities were set up in both Britain and the United States, and in 1972 the first British refuge (and indeed the first in the world) for battered women was established in Chiswick by Erin Pizzey. This refuge spawned many others and resulted in the establishment of a Women's Aid Federation (Coote and Campbell 1987: 36). Women's health centres prompted self-awareness about the female body and female sexuality, and Rape Crisis Centres began to emerge in Britain from 1976. The Women's National Coordinating Committee in Britain had tabled four basic demands: equal pay, equal education and job opportunities, free contraception and abortion on demand, and free twenty-four hour nurseries (see Wandor 1990: 242–3). These demands themselves provoked a reinterpretation of the reasons for women's special or unequal treatment in such areas – not least a re-evaluation of what 'patriarchy' could mean. The term often rather loosely connoted the universal and timeless oppression of women by men, even though it is clear that certain groups of men have unequal access to dominant power networks. The conventional view of patriarchy as connoting the rule of a dominant elder male over an extended kinship network which included servants, and entailed control of all economic production of the household no longer holds sway, since the family itself has refigured into a smaller nuclear unit. But feminists have argued that our society still bears the vestiges of patriarchal organization. In particular, male dominance has become such a naturalized aspect of social life that man's rule of both the household and its economic resources is perceived as the norm.

It was Kate Millett, in *Sexual Politics* (1971), who did much to popularize the feminist adoption of the term 'patriarchy' for feminists. Millett perceived patriarchy to be the fundamental oppressive force, despite differing class and ethnic origins embedding individuals in various relations of power, and causing local distinctions between forms of patriarchy. She argues that it is a system of power which encompasses and underpins all other forms of social relations:

> If one takes patriarchal government to be the institution
> whereby that half of the populace which is female is controlled
> by that half which is male, the principles of patriarchy appear
> to be two fold: male shall dominate female, elder male shall
> dominate younger. However, just as with any human institu-
> tion, there is frequently a distance between the real and the
> ideal; *contradictions and exceptions do exist within the system.*
> While patriarchy as an institution is a social constant so deeply
> entrenched as to run through all other political, social, or eco-
> nomic forms, whether of caste or class, feudality or bureaucracy,
> just as it pervades all major religions, it also exhibits great vari-
> ety in history and locale. (Millett 1977: 25; my emphasis)

Although Millett has been frequently criticized by latter day feminists for her ahistoricism, I think that this passage demonstrates that
she takes both historical and cultural concerns into account. What
she draws to our attention most strongly is some of the more pervasive effects of patriarchy – that its effective operation at the level of
ideology contributes to a sense of its naturalness and inevitability.
Following Jaques Lacan, Juliet Mitchell describes patriarchy in
psychoanalytic terms as the Law of the Father – meaning that entry
into civilization (via language, or the Symbolic Order) necessitates
entry into a pre-defined patriarchal system. This position is analogous to Millett's in her suggestion that patriarchy informs our
perception of social reality by being entrenched in knowledge itself,
and her powerful evocation of the fundamental power of patriarchal
ideology in our society helped to shape second wave debates. The
cavalier usage of the term to signify male domination sometimes
obscures the possibility of a more detailed examination of the ubiq-
uitous nature of female subordination in contemporary Western
societies. Patriarchy is undoubtedly a confused and confusing concept: certainly one is able to identify vestiges of patriarchal power in
familial structures, similar to those which predate capitalism, but
capitalism has exaggerated the observable differences of biological
sex in order to maintain its own conditions of possibility. Even if
patriarchal rule does not operate explicitly as a perceivable material
reality, there is a need to invoke the concept at the level of representation, as Michele Barrett does, by allowing that a 'patriarchal ideology' is still effective (Barrett 1988: 19).

For feminists, the effects of a patriarchal ideology are most keenly
felt within the family environment – which is precisely the sphere

most often ignored by political theorists. Feminist critiques have made it clear that it is the wife who generally plays the instrumental role in the socialization of children, and as the emotional cushion to protect the (male) worker from the psychological damage caused by the alienation of the workplace (two of the main functions of the family according to functionalist sociologists), while the husband/father's position in the public sphere determines the family's class status. The women's role is most often theoretically obliterated beneath considerations of status and husband's occupation, even though it could be powerfully argued that it is the woman's role which guarantees the existence of the familial form – hence the feminist identification of a need to question the traditional demarcation between the public and private spheres. Since this elision operates most effectively at an ideological level, feminists tend to emphasize the effects of a familial ideology upon women's domestic role and the sexual division of waged labour, which naturalizes woman's place in the home, and ignores her social contributions in the public domain.

The family, although in definition fluid and changeable to suit the ideological demands of differing epochs and cultures, is valued as an institution, indestructible despite the vicissitudes of time. More than that, it is accepted as part of the natural order of things, strengthened by ideologies of religion, the law and popular morality. If patriarchy is conceived as synonymous with civilization, then the family is viewed as civilization's cornerstone. This naturalization of the family has led the majority of feminists to pinpoint it as the crucial site of women's oppression, particularly since mainstream analyses of the family tell us little about its complex and indirect relationship to dominant networks of power. The concept of the family seems, therefore, to function most effectively at an ideological level – even though there is an increasingly marked disjunction between the family 'norm' and most people's lived experience of family life. This ambiguity around what 'the family' really means produces a situation where 'much of the pressure exerted on individuals to conform to various indices of behaviour relate more to fear of social disapproval of "the family" than to strictly internal family demands' (Barrett 1988: 205). Adherence to gender identity, for instance, is something endorsed and reinforced by schools, media, peers and other ideological agencies outside the household domain.

It was therefore logical for feminists to devote much attention to the structure of the family, and attempt to uncover the real conditions of ordinary women's lives; after all, the affairs of the domestic sphere had been marginalized to the extent that little was actually known about how people conducted their so-called private lives. Feminists also had to tackle the myth that women belonged to the private, affective and nurturant sphere of human relationships to the exclusion of being participants in the public domain, demonstrating that women's naturalized association with the home and with domestic labour effectively occludes their social and economic contributions at both a micro and macro level. In the process of interrogating the public/private division, feminists fruitfully questioned the foundations of such a divide, and in whose interest this distinction was maintained. In the search for moments of origin and incidents of perpetuation of gendered inequalities, some working definition of 'patriarchy' appears to be indispensable, however problematic such a notion may be to hold today and use theoretically. It is very difficult to site the locus of male power in one place, or to argue that the socially deprived male can still have access to a form of legalized tyranny over his partner; yet feminists have largely had to resort to such unpopular polemic. Many feminists would still agree that the only viable solution to the current state of affairs is a major ideological revolution, in order to shatter the general complacency around the immutability of gender differences and corresponding social experiences. Yet as this book testifies, the means by which 'patriarchy' is characterized is infinitely various, and the conclusions and utopias formulated may conflict; but such tensions and contradictions seem to echo above all the contradictions and tensions lying at the heart of an ideology of gender or patriarchy. Although this has been a source of much anxiety, particularly in recent years, what makes feminist politics seem virtually unique is its refusal to lay down doctrinal givens – instead all feminist research is offered as work in progress, often as part of a commitment to continued consciousness raising.

Any political movement will face internal power struggles which threaten to destabilize and undercut its vitality. Moreover, as I shall further explore in Part One, second wave feminism did not emerge from a common political base – its philosophical roots lie in diverse schools of thought, and there has been substantial disagreement over the extent to which any 'patriarchal' roots (such as Marxism) should, or could, be shed, and what the place of men within the movement should be – if indeed they should be allowed a space at all. The politics of feminism was, therefore, heterogeneous from the outset, and far from being simply destructive, this was part of the dynamism of women's liberation and ultimately inevitable, since 'Women, in a sense, are feminism's greatest problem. The assumption of a potential identity between women, rather than solving the problem, became a condition of increasing tensions' (Delmar, in Mitchell and Oakley 1986: 28). Part of feminism's success has been to establish woman as an object of study, by freeing her from the distortions of male-oriented knowledge. But since the chief proponents of early second wave politics were white, middle-class, educated women, there was always a grave risk that female identity would become as homogenized as it is in male discourse, and that countless women would be marginalized by a movement which claimed to champion their rights.

bell hooks has argued that the majority of white feminists have done little but pay lip service to the idea of the diversity of women's lived experience, even though she agrees that the political interrogation of the personal is enabling for all women 'because it challenges each of us to alter our person, our personal engagement (either as victims or perpetrators or both) in a system of domination' (hooks 1989: 22). Latterly many feminists have taken up black women's critical challenges, and investigated how sex, race and class function as factors which together structure the social meanings of femininity, and in which women themselves constitute hierarchies of power and privilege, in order to develop perspectives which account for the shared experiences of all women as well as acknowledging their differences. hooks cautions that white feminists' (sometimes well-meaning) refusal to 'speak for' black women serves to reinforce the polarity between black and white female experience, and could itself result in a perpetuation of racism, in that 'it helps . . . take the burden of accountability away from white women and places it solely onto women of colour' (hooks 1989: 47).

At first sight lesbians in the women's movement have fared better than black women; since the late '60s they have been visible as activists and contributors to second wave writings. Indeed, there are accounts of the early years in which lesbian feminists are characterized as about to wrest feminism from its heterosexual 'guardians'. It is still a commonplace to associate radical politics with lesbian feminists, even though this scarcely appears to be the case.[11] One method by which the mass media has consistently attempted to undermine the power of feminist discourse and alienate potential 'recruits' is to characterize all feminists as lesbians. It is disturbing, therefore, that many early feminists propagated homophobic sentiments – in the fear of being found 'guilty', by association, of being a lesbian. Ginette Castro's account of these formative years of second wave militancy suggests that lesbians were commonly seen as a disruptive force, suspected of using the movement as a vehicle for proselytization. She further recounts rumours that lesbians were used by the FBI to discredit feminism; and that an anonymous force 'outed' Kate Millett as bisexual.[12]

The strength of early feminism was its commitment to alternative forms of political organization, summarized in the following statement from the (British) Women's Liberation Workshop (1970):

> We reject a structure based on the concept of leaders and led. For this reason, groups small enough for all to take part in discussion are basic units of our movement. We feel that the small group makes personal commitment a possibility and a necessity and that it provides understanding and solidarity . . . As a federation of a number of different groups, Women's Liberation Workshop is essentially heterogeneous, incorporating within it a wide range of opinions and plans for action. (reproduced in Wandor 1990: 241)

Feminism studiously avoided the pitfalls of leadership by making it an explicit policy to allow a voice to every woman who joined at a local level. One negative side-effect of this, however, was that no one could veto the views of women who were foregrounded by the media as spokespeople. This allowed the creation of an unofficial star system, including such figures as Betty Friedan and Germaine Greer – who have since recanted their earlier feminist views – and more recently, figures such as Camille Paglia.

I shall return to this problem of 'ownership' and feminism later in this book, and hope that this introduction emphasizes my own conviction that feminism's heterogeneity is its greatest strength and the key to its survival and perpetuation in the face of forces which try to erode its credibility in increasingly devious ways. Feminism has undeniably developed to accommodate differences within gender, even if such accommodation still has a long way to go. Interventions by black and lesbian feminists into what threatened to become a white heterosexual female stronghold (particularly at an academic level) have been instrumental in extending the purview of feminist politics, contributing to an ideological war waged against the homogenized representation of women offered by the mainstream. It would be nothing short of offensive to suggest that such interventions have disrupted feminism's putative unity; instead they remind us that to lay claim to the title 'feminist' is not to adhere to a certain orthodoxy. The existence of active debate confirms the richness of feminist discourse which is constantly diversifying and shifting ground in an effort to undercut the hegemony of male discourse. Feminism today may still be guilty of allowing privileged space to the privileged; but its strength lies in its commitment to creating a politics which offers a form of knowledge where 'women are its subjects, its enunciators, the creators of its theory, of its practice and of its language' (Delmar, in Mitchell and Oakley 1986: 27). Women's issues are common media currency these days, and it is essential that feminists challenge the extent to which these issues are being resolved in women's favour. Arguably there is less room for despair or pessimism about the future of a chameleon-like organization which, in Drude Dahlerup's words, 'has been declared dead many times' (Dahlerup 1986: 3).

Part One

Generating
the Second Wave

Chapter 1

Liberal Feminism:
The Origins of the Second Wave

As feminists we need to reclaim our history and understand
the complex construction of what we now know as feminism.
It is also necessary to analyse those ideologies which have
shaped our thinking and structured our experience of gender
and our explanation of women's oppression. It seems to me
that all of this is part of the project of building a feminist
political theory.

(Hunt, in Evans et al. 1986: 47)

Before I embark upon a critical account of feminism's 'strands', I
should reiterate that the term feminism is itself problematic, because
the theories that inform it are heterogeneous. Although I shall often
use 'feminism' and 'feminist' as if they can incorporate a collective
vision of political change, the use of these terms is always accompanied by a certain degree of anxiety. I do believe that there is a body
of knowledge which can be described as 'feminist' and that this
knowledge has no pre-inscribed boundaries. Yet I also believe that
there are times when the term is misused, or stretched beyond recognition, and I shall pursue this particular argument in Chapter Ten. It
may therefore be useful to being by positing a very basic description
of the feminist endeavour which embraces all the 'strands' to be discussed in this and the following chapters – a description which suggests a minimal requirement for the broadest definition of feminism.
All feminist positions are founded upon the belief that women suffer
from systematic social injustices because of their sex and therefore,
'any feminist is, at the very minimum, committed to some form of
reappraisal of the position of women in society' (Evans, in Evans et
al. 1986: 2). One of the major sites of difference, however, is in defining the 'oppressor' and locating the source of oppression – indeed,

the term 'oppression' itself might be exchanged for something more moderate, since it conjures up images of tyranny which are unpalatable to liberals. The sometimes conflicting positions within feminism tend nonetheless to foreground the same substantive issues: it is when it comes to isolating 'causes', or posing 'solutions' that there seems to be little or no agreement.

An initial problem lies in the definition of 'politics' itself – a term most memorably appropriated and extended by radical feminists as 'sexual politics'. Since politics and political theory are usually defined as the science of government and civic order, there can be no obvious critical space for feminist commentators, if we accept that this is a public sphere still largely closed to women. As many feminists have insisted upon grounding feminist analysis in female experience and therefore contesting male meanings, it seems reasonable to view all feminist positions – even the most entrenched in liberal orthodoxy – as transgressing such a definition. Despite the fact that since the seventies most feminists have determined their stance to be political, they have been regularly excluded from the corpus of political theory. The fear is, presumably, that politics, as it is dominantly defined, will lose some of its academic 'rigour' if it were to be tainted by sexual politics; and institutional political agendas would have to be stretched beyond recognition if they were to incorporate feminist considerations. As a consequence, it is likely that the boundaries of democracy as we currently understand them would break down rapidly, or require transformation, were feminist critiques to be given any serious attention.

I begin my survey of the dominant 'strands' of feminism with liberal[1] feminism because it is one of the oldest forms of feminist thought, and arguably the most difficult to define. In common with Marxist feminism, it depends upon a degree of analytical investment with male-oriented meanings of politics and social transformation. As will be seen, however, the insertion of gender-based issues into pre-established bodies of knowledge of necessity extends the limits of such knowledge and places both liberal and Marxist feminists in a degree of conflict with the original analytical framework of these political positions. The hegemony of liberal philosophical positions in Western society, which stretches back to at least the seventeenth century, and looks for the origins of liberalism in 'natural laws' (such is Thomas Hobbes's position[2]), makes it an extremely diffuse and unwieldy socio-political stance. A high liberal position is most generally associated with commonsense moderation – often a viewpoint that eschews its own political consequences altogether, and instead

puts forward ideas as the most 'natural' and 'logical' ones; and contemporary liberal feminists also tend not to identify their position as
'political' but rather as a sensible, moderate and reasonable claim for
formal sexual equality.

THE LIBERAL FEMINIST TRADITION

It is often argued that the origins of liberal philosophy are co-existent
with the rise of capitalism, so that the language of autonomy and
self-improvement becomes inextricably linked to the property
interests of the middle classes.[3] Liberal investment in a concept of
metaphysical dualism separated man (and I am using this word
advisedly for reasons which will become rapidly apparent) from other
animals as distinct because of their ability to reason, conceptually
resulting in a mind/body split – the mind associated with rationality,
and the body with all things base, physical and shared with other
living creatures. The ability to reason and the consequent capacity for
humans to conceive of themselves as unique individuals, and therefore the basic constituents of all social groups, is foregrounded by
classic liberals, such as John Locke and Thomas Hobbes. This guiding notion of abstract individualism immediately creates fissures in
the liberal political perspective, since:

> logically, if not empirically, human individuals could exist out-
> side a social context; their essential characteristics, their needs
> and interests, their capacities and desires, are given indepen-
> dently of their social context and are not created or even
> fundamentally altered by that context. (Jaggar 1983: 29)

Liberal philosophy sets out to prove man's nascent desire for society,
yet insists that each individual is a creature shaped by nature and not
by social conditioning. The problem for liberals lies in justifying
man's natural desire to become a social animal, particularly when
their model of the ideal organic society is a hierarchical one where
many members have to accept their lack of privilege as natural and
immutable. Liberal thinkers have to bridge a central contradiction in
their thinking – that is to portray civilization as a natural progression
in the evolution of man, whilst allowing that man predates civilization and could, strictly speaking chose another means to exist in the
world. Thomas Hobbes, writing *The Citizen* in 1651, projects a view
of man in the bare state of nature (before civilization) as constantly
in conflict with all other men and therefore requiring contracts of
citizenship and rules of morality and government to prevent the logical conclusion of total conflict (death), thus satisfying the citizen's

nascent self-interest. Society, therefore, facilitates the institutionalization of rules for competition within the state. All individuals obey
such rules which permit them to pursue a truncated form of self-
interest in exchange for the hope of self-preservation. Hobbes thus
asserts that though 'nature hath given to *every one a right to all*'
(Hobbes 1978: 116), for the sake of the protection offered by civic
rule, 'the right of all men to all things ought not to be retained'
(Hobbes 1978: 123). Although Hobbes maintains that in their natural (uncivilized) state all men would be equal, in terms of their right
to pursue their own self-interest, this right is relinquished under civil
laws in the name of higher reason:

> I know that Aristotle, in his first book of Politics, affirms as a
> foundation of the whole political science, that some men by
> nature are made worthy to command, others only to serve; as if
> lord and servant were distinguished not by consent of men, but
> by an aptness, that is, a certain kind of natural knowledge or
> ignorance. (Hobbes 1978: 143)

Hobbes, in common with other founding liberal philosophers, seems
to utilize two conflicting views of nature: one which avers that man,
abstracted from society and forced to thrive upon his instinct for
self-preservation, would need to be esteemed equal; one which
espouses rationality as itself a natural human quality engendering a
recognition within all humans of the need for social groupings governed by rules and contracts, which some enforce and some have
enforced upon them. Although later writers conceive of individuals
acting upon principles of moral impartiality as opposed to naked
self-interest, liberal thinkers tend to picture social cohesion as based
upon individual competitiveness, governed by limited powers of the
state to enforce mutual respect and civic rights and counter likely
conflict. Moreover, government is portrayed as a process achieved by
universal consent.

The rhetoric of naturalness conjures up images of biological and
social determinism simultaneously, especially in the liberal belief that
there are timeless and universal principles which inform the regulation of harmonious society. But in the above summary of the classic
liberal position, I have deliberatedly retained the use of the word
'man'; liberalism tends to cast female nature as separate, an adjunct
to the male principle, which derives its meaning only as different
from masculinity, yet notionally contained within such a category
(the generic use of 'man'). Because a distinction is made between

male and female nature, women are not always encompassed under generic man, and indeed their claim to the status of rational beings alongside men cannot be assumed in liberal thought. The concepts of the public and private sphere are used to identify the limits of state intervention in individual existence. The 'public' comes to mean aspects of social life where state intervention is legitimate; whereas the 'private sphere' is the realm of abstract individualism – where 'man' maintains his dominion free from the fetters of civic intervention. This is where the term 'man' is manifestly gendered: male nature becomes the paradigm of social interaction by default; female nature belongs to the home and to the irrational side of human nature, associated with qualities such as nurturance and emotion.

Accordingly the chief aim of liberal feminism – a tendency whose history is almost as long and as chequered as the history of liberal thought – has been to accord to women the rights that men hold 'naturally'. Liberal feminism has a long tradition of gender-based interventions in Western thought, and we have the legacy of such writers as Mary Wollstonecraft, and later John Stuart Mill and Harriet Taylor, who set out to show that all social categories are structured by the fact of gender; and that 'femininity' is a prison rather than a quality of healthy femaleness. The language of liberty, rights and legal equality is the currency of liberal feminism, witnessed clearly in the works of the Suffragists; but few, perhaps, have argued more passionately than Wollstonecraft that femininity is a condition akin to slavery.[4] The seemingly neutral and inclusive term 'human nature' needed to be re-examined to demonstrate that while it obliterates social/biological difference by conjuring up an impression of collectivity, it in fact marginalizes female experience by characterizing men and women as quite different and of conflicting 'natures'. This essential contradiction between an overarching but simultaneously bifurcated concept of human nature which is summoned by early liberal feminists, reflects wider tensions within the liberal notion of human nature altogether. It is perhaps worth emphasizing that 'human' powers of reason did not unequivocally extend to women; rather, the liberal concept of female nature appears to assume women's innate irrationality.

Enlightenment feminists such as Wollstonecraft asserted that women too possessed the innate capacity for reason, and should therefore be granted equal citizenship. In *Vindication of the Rights of Woman* (1792) she powerfully argues that women's capacity for rational thought has been suppressed by their lack of education:

> Women are everywhere in this deplorable state; for, in order to
> preserve their innocence, as ignorance is courteously termed,
> truth is hidden from them, and they are made to assume an arti-
> ficial character before their faculties have acquired any strength.
> Taught from their infancy that beauty is women's sceptre, the
> mind shapes itself to the body, and roaming round its gilt cage,
> only seeks to adore its prison. Men have various employments and
> pursuits which engage their attention, and give a character to the
> opening mind; but women, confined to one, and having their
> thoughts constantly directed to the most insignificant part of
> themselves, seldom extend their views beyond the triumph of the
> hour. But were their understanding once emancipated from the
> slavery to which the pride and sensuality of man and their short-
> sighted desire, like that of dominion in tyrants, of present sway,
> has subjected them, we should probably read of their weaknesses
> with surprise. (Wollstonecraft 1975: 131)

Wollstonecraft is perhaps the earliest feminist thinker to challenge
essentialist notions of femininity – qualities which seemed neatly to
oppose those rational virtues of human (or male) nature. She demonstrated that women were commonly viewed as ruled by the pull of
their bodily functions (notably reproduction) and physical attributes,
and therefore mentally incapacitated. Though wary of asserting that,
given the opportunity to realize their full potential through the discipline of education, women could achieve full equality with men,
Wollstonecraft firmly posits what will become a vital distinction
for latter-day feminists; that the bare physical facts of biological difference should not be unquestionably extended to create distinctions
between the mental or rational capacity of men and women.

Wollstonecraft's arguments remain firmly within the chief precepts of high liberalism; she wanted women to be included within
the category of autonomous individuals who freely engage in a social
contract, and where their natural aptitude will dictate their social
standing. Significantly (although again unsurprisingly, given that
liberalism affects a disregard for class politics) her book charts in
detail the experience of middle-class woman trapped both in the
private sphere of domesticity and incumbent moral/ethical ignorance. Even though she emphasized the social effects of women's
incarceration in the home – their lack of access to formal education,
their gendered socialization into the trappings of femininity – her
text focused implicitly on the realm of the personal relations between
a woman and her father or husband. As Ursula Vogel argues:

> Discrimination against women differed from the treatment suffered by other under-privileged groups in the eighteenth century ... in that the reason for exclusion cannot easily be rendered transparent. They are sunk in, and obscured by, personal relations which resist identification as forms of domination and subjugation. (Evans et al. 1986: 17)

Wollstonecraft heralds later feminist practice by emphasizing the personal within her political discourse, but the liberal sanctification of the private sphere meant that she immediately transgresses the parameters of liberal political debate by questioning the power structures of man's private space outside the dominions of the state. In other ways, too, Wollstonecraft's critique undermines some of the givens of liberal thinking. The institutionalization of gender difference is grounded in the summoning of natural and immutable differences. And if the 'natural' is used by liberal philosophers to legitimate existing civic and social order, as it is by Thomas Hobbes, then to argue for change is to summon up images of unnaturalness and irrationality. Wollstonecraft's case, it seems, is *a priori* denounced by the epistemological foundations of liberalism. Looked at another way, Wollstonecraft arguably exposes basic contradictions within liberal thought itself – in that its universal moral principles of liberty, justice and citizenship cannot be applied equitably to all human beings. Worse, certain institutions are formalized as sites within which certain inequities such as hierarchies of privilege operate, thereby informally sustaining the private sphere so that qualities of justice or liberty cannot properly be gauged within its purview.

Wollstonecraft appeals to reason – an inclusion of women within the 'Rights of Man' – which is effectively an appeal for women's inclusion as part of the human species, to eschew the worst effects of biological reductionism. She argues that women have lacked the capacity to engage actively in political processes purely because they have been denied opportunities to develop their intellectual faculties (she accepts the possibility of greater physical frailty, but dismisses its relevance to the case). More than this, in her concluding remarks to *Vindication of the Rights of Woman*, Wollstonecraft forcefully relocates much of the blame for women's enslaved state; it is not the result of her nature but of man's tyranny: 'From the tyranny of man, I firmly believe, the greater number of female follies proceed; and the cunning, which I allow makes at present a part of their character, I likewise have repeatedly endeavoured to prove, is produced by oppression' (Wollstonecraft 1975: 318). The language here is more unequivocal than that used by twentieth century liberals: here the relationship between men and women is clearly situated as a power relationship, where men hold sway, not by virtue of their greater ability to rule, but by maintaining tyrannous subjection over women in their homes and marriages.

I have argued briefly in this section that liberal philosophy is predicated upon a basic conceptual contradiction, where natural qualities are summoned to: (a) endorse man's superiority over the rest of the animal kingdom by virtue of reason; and (b) legitimate existing forms of social order in Western capitalism as most properly compatible with the human temperament – perceived to be governed by self-interest and competitiveness. There is evidently a degree of slippage between these two uses of the term 'natural', which occlude the nature/culture divide. To some extent this usage is adopted uncritically by liberal feminists in order to argue in similar rationalistic terms for women's right of access to fully determined qualities of human nature. If man can transcend his animalistic, instinctual origins to create a world of reason, culture and social order, then surely women should also be credited with the faculty of mental transcendence, rather than being conceived as trapped inside their bodies which are traditionally seen to dictate the limits of their cerebral responses; so like animals, they too must be kept under restraint.

On the whole Wollstonecraft's plea for the rights of woman, is a plea for the chance for women to fulfil their socially endowed functions as wife, mother and moral guardian with self-control, freed from the emotionalism she sees as endemic to the female sex in their present enslaved situation. While rationality, then, is conceived as potentially genderless, she still accepts that fundamental sexual divisions determine differing social roles for men and women, but that given the opportunity for proper education, women would be able to discharge their duties more effectively. In terms of 'natural' human instincts, Wollstonecraft seems to subscribe to the view that women, properly educated into their moral and civic responsibilities, would be able to curb men's unbridled and corrupt sexual appetites – in this, central features associated with masculinity and femininity remained unexamined. Yet her primary demand – for the same education to be provided for women as is provided for men – necessarily gestures towards a future where women, equal in intellectual attainments, might deserve, as individuals, the right to enter the civil domain and to be economically autonomous. Her underlying argument that the inclusion of the rights of woman within civic rights would enable women to be truly useful members of society belies the fact that a 'revolution in female manners' (Wollstonecraft 1975: 317) might pave the way for a more groundbreaking form of revolution.

The work of Wollstonecraft and other Enlightenment feminists was to influence the writings of abolitionists and Suffragists in the USA and Britain in the mid–nineteenth century. The liberal faith in reason and the natural and inalienable rights of man to life, liberty and the pursuit of happiness that had informed the American Declaration of Independence (1776), were sentiments shared by nineteenth century feminists, who wanted the rights of woman formally inserted into civic processes, rather than question the validity of those processes at all. Nineteenth-century campaigners challenged the way in which women had no legal presence, simply becoming an adjunct to men in marriage, arguing that liberal thought itself accorded all rational creatures the right to self-determination, whereas women have neither custody over themselves, their children, or property and income. Of course liberalism's value on private property and inheritance meant that women's role as reproducers of legitimate heirs was crucial, and such legitimacy could only be consolidated through the formal social and legal control of women. Even so, the American feminist Elizabeth Cady Stanton, among others, attempted to extend the natural rights doctrine to embrace women in her Declaration of Sentiments issued in Seneca Falls, New York, on 19–20 July 1848. The Declaration, in open imitation of the Declaration of Independence states: 'We hold these truths to be self-evident: that all men and women are created equal; that they are endowed by their Creator with certain inalienable rights; that among these are life, liberty and the pursuit of happiness . . .' (cited in Donovan 1992: 6). Not only does this rephrasing remind us how the term 'man' was used to exclude, but it paves the way for the political agendas of American and British Suffragists whose claims would culminate in the demand for suffrage, but would include demands for access to employment and higher education, the right to own property, and pressure to liberalize divorce laws. Nineteenth-century liberals also believed in women's role as the guardians of a nation's morality, and in advocating male chastity, it is clearly assumed that women are untrammelled by sexual feelings of their own. This conviction, that it is the duty of women to be the moral conscience of humankind – to the point that they are in some sense responsible for the control of male sexuality – remains in evidence in liberal feminist thinking during the second wave.

Just as liberal feminism provided the impetus for the most significant transformation in women's status for centuries – the acquisition of the vote – their faith in liberalism prescribed the limits of their radicalism, limits which informed the moderate arm of second wave thinking in the sixties and seventies. The emphasis of liberal politics upon the bourgeoisie also influenced liberal feminist agendas. It explains their prime focus on the value of education, on lobbying (acquiring rights through rational argument), and on the importance for women as individuals (rather than as militant groups) to pursue their potential – accepting personal responsibility if they failed. It also meant that 'a strictly liberal analysis left the private sphere untouched' (Donovan 1992: 27).

THE LIBERAL ELEMENT OF SECOND WAVE THINKING

Modern liberal feminists have reaped the benefits of two centuries of liberal feminist writings, and in a sense, all current feminist positions derive impetus and inspiration from such writers, so that this tradition lies at the heart of feminist knowledge. But this legacy also brings with it certain tensions that lie at the centre of liberal thought. These tensions are particularly evident in attempts by feminists to posit a model of female equality within a system of beliefs that operates on the assumed right to participate in the free market economy, despite the fact that for many women, free engagement in the economy is not viable. The liberal perspective on state intervention in people's lives also proved problematic, since state support was crucial to many women's lives, and any shrinkage of its services would probably mean that their living standards deteriorated. Most important, liberal feminists were still caught in the double-bind of appealing for women's right to personhood, whilst attempting to expose the means by which women were victims of dominant meanings extrapolated from biological sex differences which continually threatened to deny this right. In the United States of America, NOW (National Organization for Women), founded in 1966, still felt obliged to declare in its Statement of Purpose that 'NOW is dedicated to the proposition that women, first and foremost, are human beings . . .' (cited in Donovan 1992: 25). Nearly 120 years after the Declaration of Sentiments, feminists still had to plead entry to humanity. Also underpinning modern liberal feminist thinking is the implicit affirmation that 'women's work' – mothering, domestic management and nurturance – is still just that – women's work, but at the same time women should be encouraged to realize their true potential in public spheres, not instead of but in addition to these commitments. This conviction was to contribute to the 'superwoman' myth which has come under fire from detractors in recent years, as feminists are blamed for encouraging women to over-extend themselves to the point of mental and physical collapse; although, of course, the intention of feminists other than liberals was to socialize domestic labour and remove the naturalized association of women with the home.

Writings on individuality, the state and the constraints of femininity, reflect the continuing bourgeois bias of liberal feminism. Betty Friedan's portrait of the bored housewife, who having given up higher education for domesticity finds herself trapped in self-absorption and neurosis, echoes Wollstonecraft's vain, frail and ignorant domestic angel. Both only have resonance in their particular cultural /historical contexts as representations of privileged middle-class existence. The liberal belief in the universal and static qualities of human nature meant that the direction of liberal feminist energies is towards reform; and education reform, as in Wollstonecraft's day, is high upon the agenda. A concept of equality is clearly central to liberal feminist thinking, although given that equality in liberal terms means equal access to a meritocracy, the concept demands further scrutiny.

Betty Friedan is an important writer in the feminist tradition not least because of her crucial role in the formation of NOW. Writing *The Feminine Mystique* in 1963, she was to characterize the effect of nurture rather than nature upon women as 'sex role conditioning'. Friedan's analysis of The Problem that has No Name that beset countless middle class American housewives, illustrates that despite increased opportunities for higher education and entry into rewarding careers, women were turning back to the hearth in their droves. Further, this urge to return to domesticity might have deeper resonances than the superficial 'answers' that were proffered by the American popular mass media – that women had been encouraged to transcend their 'natural' aspirations through education, and other 'masculine' goals. Friedan terms this chimerical problem the 'feminine mystique', which she characterizes early on in her book:

> The feminine mystique says that the highest value and the only commitment for women is the fulfilment of their own femininity. It says that the great mistake of Western culture, through most of its history, has been the undervaluation of this femininity. It says this femininity is so mysterious and intuitive and close to the creation and origin of life that man-made science may never be able to understand it. But however special and different, it is in no way inferior to the nature of man: it may even in certain respects be superior. The mistake, says the

mystique, the root of women's troubles in the past is that
women envied men, women tried to be like men, instead of
accepting their own nature, which can find fulfilment only in
sexual passivity, male domination, and nurturing maternal love
. . . Beneath the sophisticated trappings, it simply makes certain concrete, finite domestic aspects of feminine existence
. . . into a religion, a pattern by which all women must now live
or deny their femininity. (Friedan 1965: 38)

Friedan's description of the feminine mystique has disturbing simi-
larities to Wollstonecraft's analysis made over one hundred and sev-
enty years earlier. Yet many of the women that Friedan interviewed
had received an education that Wollstonecraft would have envied.
Where the two women differ is that Friedan, in common with many
feminists of the period, pinpointed a subtler, less tangible oppressive
force at work, which, while having a profound effect on such
women's material existence, seemed to stem from and operate effectively and semi-autonomously at an ideological level. Eva Figes, a
British feminist who published *Patriarchal Attitudes* in 1970, concurred with Friedan arguing that 'woman, presented with an image
in a mirror, has danced to that image in a hypnotic trance' (Figes
1970: 15). Nonetheless Friedan does not pursue the ideological
factors at stake to anything like the degree that radical and Marxist
feminists do. Liberal feminists, like all liberals, concentrate on individual autonomy and the right to self-determination with the result
that although, on the face of it, Friedan is attacking the patriarchal
status quo which exhorts women to give all their efforts to childcare
and housewifery, there is a subtext to her writing that seems to be
blaming the women themselves.

The book is in some sense a part of the consciousness raising
tradition, in that she charts the reasons behind this problem that has
no name and poses solutions which are largely related to the efforts
of women to reconstitute their own identities. But unlike radical
feminist efforts which focus upon individual female identity and
experience as the first step to collective revolution, Friedan's revolution remains largely an individual one; if not achieved, she implies,
women only have themselves to blame. While she entreated women
to find creative work outside the home, she assumed that they would
find methods to continue their domestic responsibilities as well.
Rosemarie Tong offers a cogent critique of Friedan's argument,
observing that:

> *The Feminine Mystique* failed to consider just how difficult it would be for even privileged women to combine marriage and motherhood with a career unless major structural changes were made within, as well as outside the family. Like Wollstonecraft, [Harriet] Taylor and [John Stuart] Mill before her, Friedan sent women out into the public realm without summoning men into the private domain. (Tong 1989: 24)

Eva Figes' *Patriarchal Attitudes*, although in many ways a more comprehensive examination of the religious, philosophical and psycho-analytical reasons that women have been oppressed in the past, is fairly uncompromising when she scrutinizes the contemporary woman in the final chapter, 'Today and Tomorrow'. She argues that since achieving the vote there has emerged a generation of neurotic, lazy and idealistic women, concluding that it is men's interest to effect social change since they shoulder the substantial economic burden! Here we see that domestic labour is swiftly overlooked since worth is only calculated in terms of paid work. Figes, like Friedan, can only countenance social change and not transformation, and that burden for progress lies primarily with the actions of individual women. Moreover, it is characteristic of liberal feminism that while adept at cataloguing the institutional and ideological means by which women have been oppressed for centuries, they tend to fall short of offering any solution that implies a lack of confidence in current socio-political processes.

Liberal feminist thought commonly displays a wariness to affirm women's full potential for total equality, while maintaining that this potential has never been fully realized. Here we can identify traces of male-oriented liberal thought; that while the rights of the individual are sacrosanct in liberal philosophy, it is up to the individual to pursue success through 'merit'. This construction quite blatantly chooses to ignore the existence of other social or cultural factors which might make it quite impossible for an individual to acquire the means to realize such potential. This concept of 'abstract individualism' – that essential human qualities belong to the individual regardless of social context – reifies notions of freedom and autonomy and tends to assume, among other things, that people always act in their own best interests. In the case of women specifically, it is clear that they often – for social, economic or ideological reasons – put the interests of partners or children first. What modern liberal feminists have been anxious to point out is that liberalism's mind/body binary opposition has become correlative with male/female distinctions contained within the blanket term 'human nature'. In such an equation women become synonymous with nature and physicality (and as such are conceived as trapped within the fact of their biology), whereas men are equated with the mind and rationality, and are therefore construed as the progenitors of culture. Unless such oppositions are fully interrogated and deconstructed the logic of liberalism dictates that women straddle the man/beast divide, recreating the necessary epistemological conditions for female subordination.

Since liberalism has been a highly influential Western philosophical position, it is unsurprising that it has played an important part in the formation of a specifically feminist discourse. In fact, it is Alison Jaggar's conviction that feminism owes a great deal to the liberal tradition: 'indeed, it owes so much that some Marxists characterize feminism as an essentially bourgeois phenomenon' (Jaggar 1983: 47). In order to establish a specifically liberal feminist political perspective it is evidently necessary to call into question some of the most fundamental precepts of liberalism – notably the slippage of the mind/body divide to connote discrete qualities of sexual difference. In addition, something which potentially sets classic liberal feminists in opposition to socialist and radical feminists is the notion of the inviolable 'private sphere': in theory this would disallow them from any thorough politicization of women's existence in the home environment, including issues such as marital rape and domestic violence. In practice, critics since Betty Friedan have found it necessary to exhibit the tensions present in women's domestic and sexual lives in order to bring issues of gender inequality to the surface. There is, however, a limit to how far liberal feminists will 'pry' into individual's private social/sexual choices: for example, by virtue of their commitment to freedom of expression they are unlikely or unwilling to take a hard line on issues such as pornography.[5]

Because of liberalism's long history of links with industrial capitalism, liberal feminists tend to be reluctant to pose any direct challenge to capitalism, which effectively leaves the option of a limited intervention in the institutions which maintain it. This might well preclude detailed analyses of the family – not only as an institution which functions effectively for capitalism, but also as belonging to the sacred 'private sphere'. The liberal feminist's strategy for social change is hence tightly restricted by the desire not to overturn the status quo; they prefer the tactics of reasoned argument via noncoercive demonstrations and lobbying for legal and civil reforms. Since liberals have always staunchly protected the individual's right to self-advancement, liberal feminists would generally assert that a meritocracy is not sexist as long as women acquire the same social and legal status as male citizens. Inevitably, as Friedan's work readily illustrates, liberal feminism is centred on the needs of middle class women, and would possibly not accept class or racial difference as a significant handicap in the path to self-advancement.

The above overview suggests that liberal feminism's powerful links with classic liberalism prevent any productive discussion of the root causes of women's oppression, since the guiding structures of contemporary Western society are not really questioned. Indeed, there is little evidence that liberal feminists of the past have wanted to achieve a significant break with traditional liberalism by calling any of its central precepts into question, even though their stance as feminists effectively does just this. But liberal feminism has had an abiding effect, particularly on American feminist politics; through NOW it has achieved a substantial degree of success with its policy of 'soft' lobbying. It has never become such an overtly influential political stance in Britain or in the rest of Europe, in terms of mainstream political engagement (although representatives of women's issues in mainstream politics tend to offer a broadly liberal feminist position), though this is not to underestimate the impact of its writings upon the embryonic stages of the second wave.

LIBERAL FEMINISM AS 'SCEPTICAL FEMINISM'?

In Britain in 1980 Janet Radcliffe Richards' *The Sceptical Feminist* was published. Offering a stance that derives its impetus from the liberal philosophical tradition, she adopts the guise of an objective commentator on contemporary feminism, appraising the flaws in its logic and arguments that render it an unpopular and therefore 'failed' movement. Although she does not announce herself as a liberal thinker, her mode of argument assigns her to such a position. Moreover, her repeated use of the first person plural indicates that to some extent she perceives herself as a feminist, however sceptical. Richards sees her task as a corrective one – upbraiding the more 'extreme' and unattractive aspects of feminism, notably lamenting many feminists' refusal to train their powers of reason and logic in debate. Richards assumes that the mode of reasoning she utilizes is universally accepted as the only way to solve a philosophical problem – she ignores many feminists' contention that reason is itself compounded upon a patriarchal logic which has as a central premise the intellectual/moral inferiority of women.[6] Her alarm at a tendency to celebrate 'unreason' within the women's movement, is based on her suspicion that such a stance merely reinforces existing masculine and feminine divisions.

However, other feminists might interpret such a perspective as a means by which to redefine what constitutes reasonable argument within a social order which denies women any such capacity. Effectively, she argues that rather than engaging in our own peculiar brand of 'unreason', we should take time to learn the forms of philosophical and discursive enquiry that are usually the male preserve. She implies that feminists' 'eccentric' mode of argument is the result of poor education rather than design. Yet many feminists might well respond by observing that women are already steeped in such knowledges which have inscribed within them precepts inhibiting a thorough investigation of the particular experiences of the female, and that one of feminism's victories has been the provision of the opportunity to question the production of such knowledge systems.

Richards is concerned that feminism's belief in female intellectual and social equality ignores the possibility that, since we cannot know women's true potential at present, there may be a necessity in the future to allow for the existence of inherent sexual difference:

> There may be very few feminists, for instance, who would even admit to considering the *possibility* that women might on the whole be less capable of works of genius than men: for most feminists, the inherent equality of the sexes in all such matters is part of the official doctrine. (Richards 1982: 60)

If it is the case that women are handicapped in certain matters (through childbirth and so forth), she argues that it would be foolish to try to obscure these facts, since they need not prevent women from occupying positions of power in a feminist utopia. Feminists might agree: but her chief rhetorical gambit – that of the possibility that women may be less capable of works of genius – reminds us of the limitations of liberal thought, blind as it is to the possibility that the definition and scope of 'genius' automatically excludes women. Her overall argument is that feminism needs to be more flexible in the alternatives it offers to women, in order to encourage a flowering of as yet unknown potential – a criticism many contemporary feminists might accept. But she is uncomfortable with feminism's primary focus upon injustices against women, arguing that 'to fight with nothing in view but the good of women is to fight for an *unjust society*' (Richards 1982: 24). Much of her discussion is underpinned by fairly conventional discussions of the nature of justice, based on the rather inaccurate premise that feminists spend little time considering other forms of social inequality and their relation to gender. Justice is of course a thorny problem for feminists, and clashes between differing strands are most manifestly felt in debates around class, race and sexual orientation. Richards recognizes that feminism's primary intention is to hold up to question all existing social institutions and customs, but underestimates the scope of that intention, which assumes that projected social transformations incorporate a changing status for men as well. Feminist utopias are necessarily woman-centred in their concerns, since one of their most important functions is to reflect upon the present – to gesture at ways in which things could be otherwise.

Richards criticizes the women's movement for what she perceives as its indeterminacy,[7] whereas others might more positively charac-terize its non-doctrinal aspects as evidence of its rich diversity. She attacks what might be regarded as the 'stereotypical' face of feminism, and argues that a feminist 'style' – characterized as a total rejection of all conventional standards of feminine beauty and sexual attrac-tiveness – leads to a repression of individual self-determination: 'the fact is that women who dress in a conventionally feminine way, or give the impression of caring about their appearance however little effort it actually takes, are regarded by many feminists as enemies' (Richards 1982: 226). She trivializes feminists' endeavour to politi-cize issues of representation and female sexuality, conflating debates about the imposed sexualization of the female with sexual pleasure itself, and asserting 'it can be no part of a serious feminism to argue that there is anything inherently wrong with the sensual enjoyment of sex' (Richards 1982: 233). For her, feminist personal politics denies individual women their personal preference – although of course feminists would want to debate the extent to which such 'choices' are made freely. She defends the sanctity of the private sphere, and therefore refuses any credence to feminist problematiz-ations of the public/private divide, or analyses of a dominant ideology which positions women in an object relationship to men – in fact she appears to condone such a view – 'there can be no reasonable feminist principle which says that women ought not to want men, and if women want men they must be willing to be pleasing to them' (Richards 1982: 230). The thrust of the book, in its attempt to rescue feminism from its worst excesses, addresses a reader who has always been the focus of liberal feminism – white, middle class, heterosexual – ignoring women who do not inhabit what is a relatively privileged social position.

One might wish to dismiss *The Sceptical Feminist* as to some extent anti-feminist, but what it does is to try and create a rift between 'normal' women and 'extremists', and widens the gap by attempting to make less moderate feminists appear naive and even stupid. It typically appeals to the readers' common sense – assuming them to be women who may wish to assert their right to equality under democracy, but have no wish to radically transform their current status quo. However, Richards' reappraisal of feminism fails to take account of how such 'common sense' opinions come to be entrenched in our consciousness, not necessarily because they are the most effective wisdom available. The underlying assumption is that women largely want what is now available to them, although with a little more freedom to exercise certain choices. In fact Richards assumes, in common with Wollstonecraft and Friedan, that right-minded women still wish to be in sole charge of domestic arrangements and childcare. She concludes that feminism is an 'unpopular movement'(Richards 1982: 320), and largely blames feminists themselves for creating exclusionary practices, and advocating alternative social arrangements which antagonize other 'reasonable' women. Just as the liberal view of a meritocracy enables the evasion of 'blame' for poverty and deprivation, so Richards' 'reasonable' pro-feminist elite would be those with the money and status to buy certain privileges, such as childcare, with or without a feminist consciousness.

Liberal feminists' constant recourse to reason, and commitment to a recognition of the rights women already theoretically possess, is its most problematic feature for other feminist perspectives. Nonetheless its historical impact as a corrective to dominant political thought cannot be ignored, since its fight for equality created the conditions whereby dissenting feminist stances could emerge. It still remains popular and influential, and as Andrea Nye postulates is often the first form of feminism that women encounter: 'When a woman in the United States or Western Europe first identifies herself as a feminist, it is often as a liberal feminist, asserting her claim to the equal rights and freedoms guaranteed to each individual in democratic society' (Nye 1988: 5). A woman who is a liberal feminist might rarely define herself as a feminist, although she may be happy to declare her support of women's equality in the workplace and in law. She might be quick to dissociate herself from any hint of 'extremism', and have confidence that, if most of women's demands have not already been met, that they will be achieved by lobbying and reason. In its investment in a social hierarchy that allows nominal equality on the basis of merit and effort, it reminds many feminists of early second wave errors in assuming that women's collective experience of oppression was a bourgeois one, since it addresses women who have the luxury of making choices which they often mistakenly assume are available to everyone. It is also too often a position from which the women's movement is undermined, its politics trivialized, and made indistinguishable from an anti-feminist wave, which assumes the title of 'post-feminism', and urges a reconsideration of the 'facts' of human nature – as something which 'extreme' feminism has rather too precipitately rejected. When I discuss the new 'feminist' detractors in Chapter Ten it will become clear that the most powerful quality of their rhetoric is its reasonableness, its appeal to 'normal' women, and particularly women who believe that an investment in feminism is a necessary rejection of relationships with men.

Chapter 2

Marxist/Socialist Feminism: Reconstructing Male Radicalism

> Both reformists and revolutionaries have to contend with the
> fact of a class antagonistic society; and feminists must simi-
> larly realize that the oppressive social division between men
> and women, though not a class division, at the very least rep-
> resents a fissure in the groundplan of human society which
> must be charted before it can be bridged.
>
> (Oakley and Mitchell 1976: 15)

AN UNEASY ALLIANCE:
THE MARXIST-FEMINIST ENCOUNTER

In the previous chapter I suggested ways in which liberal feminism
can seem to become ineluctably entrenched in the terms of its host
discourse, and in effect emphasize its own exclusion. It could be
argued that Marxism yields greater possibilities as a model which
potentially exposes the dependency of Western civilization upon
perpetuating class distinctions, and therefore might be 'stretched',
following Engels' argument in *The Origin of the Family, Private Property and the State* (1884), to expose the utility of gender difference to
capitalist social relations.

The terms Marxist and socialist become relatively interchangeable
when describing those feminists who have endeavoured to form
alliances with the political Left. However, critics such as Rosemarie
Tong argue that they represent two distinct tendencies within feminist
thought – socialist feminism having superseded Marxist feminism
and being 'largely the result of Marxist feminists' dissatisfaction with
the essentially gender-blind character of Marxist thought' (Tong
1989: 173). Marxist feminists, she asserts, see class as the ultimate
determinant of women's current social/economic status, whereas

socialist feminists view gender and class as equally powerful oppressive mechanisms. In addition, socialist feminists focus upon areas of sexuality and reproduction. I do not agree, however, that such a clear distinction can be made, and would concur with Alison Jaggar that 'socialist feminism is unmistakably Marxist, at least insofar as it utilizes the method of historical materialism' (Jaggar 1983: 125). The adoption of the broader term 'socialist feminist' seems to be largely a response to Marxist hostility and a move towards involvement with mainstream left-wing politics, rather than a symptom of theoretical fragmentation. The very addition of gender to the Marxist theoretical equation prompts scrutiny of areas of female sexuality and procreation, so that a maintenance of class as the central determining factor of contemporary power relations seems untenable. Since much of the following is concerned with the appropriation of Marxist thought for feminist purposes, I shall use the term 'Marxist feminism' in the initial stages of this discussion, and then proceed to use the term 'socialist feminism' in the successive sections – to indicate the growing split between feminist analyses and Marxist orthodoxy.

Marxists do not, of course, share the liberal investment in maintaining the social status quo, since the condition of social life for the oppressed and exploited under advanced capitalism is the primary subject of their critique. Feminists hoped to develop Marxist perceptions of a socio-economic system based on class divisions and fuse this with a revolution in consciousness. In their attempt to merge second wave radicalism with Marxist analyses of the capitalist social formation, Marxist feminists encounter a major difficulty: the concept of patriarchy – often regarded as suggesting the existence of a universal and transhistorical system of power relations between the sexes – seems incompatible with class analysis, which is historically and culturally specific, but elides the gender question almost entirely. Where liberal feminists still tend to regard the domestic sphere as the focus of women's lives, Marxist feminists are concerned with the fate of women workers in the labour market, as well as with examining how women's perceived natural function as carer and domestic labourer affects notions of her 'value' within the workplace. They share with radical feminists (see Chapter Three) a commitment to politicize the personal and private, by arguing that women are held in the thrall of a patriarchal system of relations, which may work as functional for capital, but predates it and therefore might be regarded as having a certain degree of autonomy. However, their attempts to forge an alliance with Marxism meant that they expended a great deal of their energies challenging a political agenda which tenaciously

obscured the fact of women's oppression, and might therefore perpetuate it outside a capitalist social formation.

Feminists exposed the fact that class-based analysis either assumes
that women enter the class system on equal terms with men, or that
they are of no relevance to either its maintenance or destruction. Just
as a liberal concept of rationality presupposes a male model of reason,
so Marxism presupposes that male experience of inequities under
capitalism will be the motivating force behind a revolution, and
therefore the building block upon which to construct an alternative
social formation. Marxists, unlike liberals, ostensibly repudiate purely
essentialist notions of human nature. The Marxian notion of *praxis*
posits human activity as social activity – that there is a dialectical
relationship between human biology and human society, which is
constantly undergoing modifications through the process of history
– yet this concept is not interrogated in relation to particular social
roles of women. In theory, Marxist analysis of historical flux
appeared to facilitate a consideration of the social construction of
gender roles, which could dispense with the biologistic assumptions
that lay at the heart of liberal philosophy; but in practice, women's
'natural' social functions were assumed as givens.

Marxist thought proved attractive to feminists because of its
eschewal of universalizing notions of human nature; but more pragmatically, such a mode of analysis was familiar to many women who
found their political awakening in left-wing radicalism. Both movements are, after all, seeking a total transformation of social institutions
in order to end the exploitation and oppression of specific social
groups. The Marxist consideration of the function of ideological
processes is particularly conducive to feminist appropriation, as a
means by which individuals' 'collusion' in their subordination can be
critically reappraised. Nonetheless, Marxist feminists faced a substantial hurdle to their project, which is that the basic tenets of
feminism and Marxism – a resistance to patriarchy versus a resistance to class – appear to be mutually incompatible. And Marxists
have at times been hostile to feminists, characterizing the women's
movement as constructing an abstract and ahistorical case of special
pleading – in that grouping together all women as an analytical category is not compatible with social delineations exposed by class
analysis. Feminism, it is argued, homogenizes female experience
from a wholly bourgeois perspective, creating a political diversion
which forestalls revolution rather than facilitates it.

Such attacks primarily resulted from feminism's focus upon
women's private lives as the crucial site of unequal patriarchal power

relationships, a sphere which plainly has no place within Marxism's economistic framework. Feminists responded by arguing that the Marxist analysis of labour relations is inadequate so long as it ignores how other forms of unpaid, 'unproductive' (in traditional Marxist terms) labour – such as procreative and domestic labour – contribute to the stability and viability of industrial capitalism. Certainly Utopian socialists of the nineteenth century such as Saint-Simon and Fourier (viewed by Marx and Engels in the 'Manifesto of the Communist Party' as forming 'mere reactionary sects' (Marx 1973: 96)) examined the effects of gender oppression under capitalism. Nevertheless, 'women's position is increasingly marginalized in socialist work by a focus on paid labour and class relations. This occurs with the rise in importance of Marxism and a male-dominated organized Left' (Johnson in Gunew 1990: 305). The increasing dominance of Marxist ideas which gradually subsumed an older socialist tradition meant that feminist concerns were lost in the diminution of Fourierist, Owenite and other utopian positions, which, deriving impetus from the legacy of Mary Wollstonecraft's *Vindication of the Rights of Woman,* had as a central concern women's liberation and sexual freedom.[1]

A central problem for Marxist feminists was that women seemed to be governed by two semi-autonomous but mutually strengthening power mechanisms – the operation of a patriarchal ideology of immutable sexual difference within the family, and a sexual division of labour in the workplace. Both had received little attention in the Marxist tradition. In the development of a Marxist feminist theory, Friedrich Engels' *The Origins of the Family, Private Property and the State* was a crucial text. However, Engels' position on women's place under capitalism is ambiguous: he assumes that women independently acquire class status by virtue of the same economic determinants as men, but also infers that all women are proletarianized within marriage – where male power is regarded as analogous to that of the bourgeoisie. The family, therefore, represents a capitalist system of relations in microcosm, and it is assumed that once class is abolished, so sexual inequality will disappear. In this way women's particular experience of oppression is absorbed and obscured under a description of class antagonism, with a result that 'there is therefore no theoretical space to develop any understanding of patriarchy, as either a separate or a related system, for sex oppression has in effect been rendered invisible' (Hunt in Evans et al. 1986: 53).

Feminists needed to untangle the conjoined threads of patriarchy and capitalism in order to determine how far capitalism can be blamed for women's oppression – a state of affairs which manifestly existed in earlier social formations. Engels locates the phenomenon of the 'pairing marriage' (following broader incest taboos within previously polygamous tribal cultures) as heralding 'the capture and purchase of women' (Barrett's introduction to Engels 1985: 78). He presupposes the existence of a primitive matrilineal social organization that is at some point overthrown by a patrilineal one, and the historical landmark he selects for this transformation is the creation of wealth and private property. He argues that the possibility of the transfer of capital from one generation to the next requires the male head of the family to be able to identify his legitimate heirs; but in common with other nineteenth-century commentators on the 'mother-right' debate, Engels admits that we cannot trace the approximate moment in history when such an overthrow was achieved, other than to claim that it falls within prehistoric times.

Engels implies that despite the 'prehistoric' origins of the patriarchal family form, it had become an instrument for capitalism. If patriarchy is held to have merely become functional for capitalism, then one might argue that analysis of capital and its reproduction negates the need for an analysis of patriarchy *per se*; and for this reason feminist scrutiny of women's specific status in the spheres of the family and in commodity production were held to obscure the more 'important' questions raised by class analysis. The calculated avoidance by classic Marxists of gender issues creates a theoretical slippage whereby women's oppression predates and yet becomes organic to capitalism. From feminists' perspective, women's subordination is in danger of implicitly becoming linked to biological destiny. Women's realms as reproducers, carers and nurturers within a monogamous family relationship are largely left untouched by Marxism's concentration on the public sphere of waged labour and the accumulation of capital. The 'private sphere' – the obverse of the labour market – becomes hermetically sealed as outside the framework of materialist analysis, outside the relations of production and, ultimately, given Engels' vague interrogations into the field of prehistory, beyond history itself. In common with liberalism, woman's social role was by implication seen as rigorously bounded by her biological identity and nature; while males' superior rationality or thirst to transform nature by the action of *praxis* was the key to civilization.

A central feature of contemporary Marxist feminist thought has been to construct a viable theoretical framework that could at once incorporate female experience outside the labour market, a framework that acknowledged women's unique relationship to familial and ideological forces, and yet could counter what was regarded as ahistorical tendencies within radical feminist politics. A starting principle was that female domestic labour – reproducing and maintaining the workforce – should be considered an aspect of production (or reproduction), which worked to the benefit of capital. In addition, it was asserted that women's role in the labour market was hugely influenced by this domestic identity, and made their relationship to production distinctly different from men's. Although Marxist analysis concentrated on relations of production within the labour market, 'no Marxist theory provides a satisfactory historical account of the sexual division of labour' (Jaggar 1983: 72). This concept of a sexual division of labour brought to the fore the effects of both ideological and material processes upon women at work. Feminists observed that female labour is concentrated in low paid bands, such as cleaning, nursing and childcare; whereas Marxists assumed that it was women's exclusion from the public sphere which was the primary source of their oppression – even though this oppression was deemed unworthy of further inquiry. What is most problematic for contemporary feminists is that women have always been present in the labour force; and now more women enter full-time occupations, a sexual division of labour still prevails.

The supposed propensity of women for domestic and caring roles influences dominant attitudes to women within the labour market, and informs the 'choices' women have in employment, to the point where one can identify an area of 'women's work', deemed to be qualitatively different from men's. Women who undertake paid labour still tend to suffer the effects of low pay, or the insecurity of part-time or outwork, which they often endure because of additional commitments of housework and childcare. Recent equal pay legislation (in the UK, the Equal Pay Act of 1975) has had a negligible effect on women's pay conditions, primarily because the majority of women workers are concentrated in a handful of jobs containing very few male workers. Since the legislation stipulated that women should receive the same wage as men for comparable work, it was a simple matter for employers to 'regrade' jobs held by women in cases where they were similar to those done by men. So the act became self-defeating – perhaps only serving further to entrench the ideology of the sexual division of labour within the sphere of employment.[2]

Feminists have observed that the concentration of women within 'service' jobs (a trend increasing with the technologization of labour) seems to reflect the division of labour in the household, where women are still primary carers. It is only possible fully to examine the feminization of certain forms of waged labour by an investigation of the ideology of family life and domestic responsibility, which feeds upon biologistic assumptions about natural sexual divisions. A good example of such a tendency is the case of the medical profession, where the doctor-nurse-patient relationship might be seen to mimic the father-mother-child hierarchy of the home (see Gamarnikow in Kuhn and Wolpe 1978: 96–123). Historically, the nursing profession has been regarded as suitable women's work, requiring care and similar domestic skills which are the desired moral attributes of the 'good woman' in the home. Since domestic labour has no exchange value, women's domestic skills gain low financial rewards when transferred to the labour market. The masculine ideal of a 'woman's place' perpetuates and covertly justifies the unequal value ascribed to men's and women's work, and in the case of medicine, 'the occupational ideology of nursing thus genderised the division of labour: it associated science and authority with doctors and caring – putting science into practice – with women' (Gamarnikow in Kuhn and Wolpe 1978: 114). Similarly, in lower and middle schools where most women teachers are to be found, the caring and socializing aspects of the work take precedence over the educational role. In addition to the ideological representation of the 'natural' divisions in domestic labour, we might also identify an 'ideology of naturalism' informing the structures of waged labour itself, where the 'patriarchal' relations of the family are recreated to similar effect, and gendered patterns repeat themselves.

The concept of a 'family wage' – where a man's earnings are presumed to be sufficient to support an entire household – provides further material justification for retaining women's pay at a lower level: their wages are deemed an additional 'luxury' despite the fallacy of the breadwinning wage in today's society:

> Although few families have in fact depended upon the male wage, the belief that they do underlies our present sexual division of labour in a fundamental way and has, furthermore, been influential in determining the attitude of the labour movement to women's wage work. (Barrett 1988: 78)

As Barrett suggests above, the chief paradox of the 'family wage' is that a relatively low proportion of families fit the ideological 'model': single female parents are left close to the poverty line, or a woman's wage may be the sole or main support for a family with an unemployed or casually employed male partner. Yet the logic of the man's 'right' to a breadwinning wage still carries enough weight to be summoned by political parties and the labour movement alike.

The fact is that for working-class families the sexual division of labour is potentially divisive – if, for example, lower-paid women are regarded as taking away men's 'rightful' jobs in a time of recession. This is an important area of analysis for feminists. It profoundly affects the utility of a Marxist model of labour relations when it is working-class men themselves who are brought into direct conflict with their fellow women workers. This situation is ultimately sustained by the notion that women are secondary status workers, able to undercut the higher wage demands of men. The labour movement has compounded such conflict by consistently defending the male labourer's unquestioned right to earn his family wage. For this reason women's wage labour tends to be viewed as a disruptive, competitive element in the labour market, instead of grounds for legislating for wage parity in real terms across gender (or indeed racial) divides.

The history of gendered labour conflict stretches back at least as far as the nineteenth century, when trade unions attempted to close their ranks to a growing female labour force, and effectively quashed the efforts of women to campaign for emancipation in the workplace.[3] Given the predominance of male labour concerns in the trade union movement, equal pay was never a high political priority, and gender issues are still treated as relatively unimportant. Marxism and the labour movement tend to fuel the common misconception that women normally remain in the home, sustained by a single male breadwinner. Women are thereby consigned to a secondary labour status, which conceivably remains unchanged even after a Marxist socialization of relations of production. In this context it is obvious that the Marxist analysis of wage relations is grossly inadequate for feminist purposes, not only because it disregards the hidden economic functions of domestic labour, but also because it denies any importance to questions of sexual/racial division at work.

Marxist feminists have concluded, therefore, that in a very real sense the patriarchal/familial ideology permeates the wage labour structure as effectively as it polices women's private lives: 'In assessing the factors which might account for the position of women as wage labourers it is impossible to escape the conclusion that family structure and the ideology of domestic responsibility play an important part' (Barrett 1988: 157). The power of social representations of the family cannot be underestimated, especially if they are reaffirmed by Marxists through the absence of such considerations in their theoretical frameworks. Legislation will remain particularly ineffective so long as trade unions decide it is in their members' interests to militate for the inalienable rights of the man to earn a family wage. In this atmosphere of gendered conflict, capital will continue to reap the benefits of exploiting cheap female labour, when a dominant familial ideology confirms that in the 'natural' order of things, women belong to the home.[4] Women workers are predominantly viewed as the 'reserve army' of labour, to be drawn upon in times of economic buoyancy or national crisis, and expected to return to their homes in times of mass unemployment – despite the fact that since the eighties women 'had become the regular troops' (Coote and Campbell 1987: 79). The sexual division of labour is perpetuated most effectively at an ideological level, since women ostensibly can make the choice to engage in a full-time career. But unlike the male experience of work, women's choices often have to, at the least, be informed by a recognition of their 'natural' obligations to their families. Marxist feminists urged an awareness of the effects one's personal life can have upon one's social existence, and such a stance demanded further investigation of the family and patriarchal power.

Marxists tend to assume a 'universal history of the family' (Coward 1983: 257); the family is subsumed within the economic framework of capitalism as a pre-given structure, hinting at acceptance of the notion of fundamental, eternal differences between the social functions of men and women. A distinction between waged labour ('exchange value') and domestic labour ('use value') is made, where waged labour is almost exclusively defined as 'work', thereby obscuring the question of the economic value of domestic labour. Any crucial link between the processes of domestic and waged labour is effectively blurred by locating domestic labour within the realms of 'personal relations', where marriage is conventionally viewed as allowing a husband access to his wife's labour free of charge. Marxist feminists set out to show how the family – a form which predates capitalism – does in actuality fulfil an economic role within capitalism in the relations of production and human reproduction.

From a feminist perspective, there is clear evidence that economic relations of production overspill into domestic labour: 'Since the production and reproduction of labour power take place substantially within the family through the labour of the housewife, then it is clear that her labour is in one way or another crucial to the generation of surplus value' (Kuhn and Wolpe 1978: 57). In other words, domestic labour underpins capitalist profit margins by recreating the availability of labourers, and providing a haven from the alienating effects of waged labour. Thus, it reinforces the separation of the two 'worlds' of public and private. It would be impossible in our present social arrangement to calculate the value of such a service in monetary terms. The public/private divide also strengthens capitalist relations if one sees the private sphere as containing the vestiges of patriarchal power relations, where male dominance is endorsed by society, presumably to defuse the powerlessness experienced by the male worker in the public domain. An account of patriarchal power relations facilitates a revisionary critique of Marxism's contradictory assumption that the family is at once functional for capital in some indirect way, while having a degree of autonomy by virtue of historically preceding capitalism. Accordingly, Marxist feminists would argue that a reduced form of patriarchal relations still functions within the family, which determines and controls women's procreative functions as well as strengthening justification for the sexual division of labour in the workplace.

While Marxist feminists highlight the economic importance of the household, in common with other feminists they simultaneously explode the popular biologistic myth that 'home-making' is something to which women naturally aspire. In order to do this it is important to consider the family form in an historical context, to show how flexible it is to the needs of dominant social forces, and how it reproduces itself most effectively through ideological representations. These may or may not correspond to people's lived realities, 'since the structure of the household, definition and meaning of kinship, and the ideology of "the family" itself, have all varied enormously in different types of society' (Barrett 1988: 199). In order to avoid the mystificatory and emotive connotations of the term 'family', Marxist feminists have tended to refer to the 'family-household system' or a 'familial ideology'.[5] The ideological and material relations influencing the family-household system are apparently mutually strengthening and not easily separable. For the working class, the household might be the site of major divisions, where all men benefit from the privileges bestowed upon them by the fact of their masculinity. Women, then, are subordinated both at work and in the home.

Much debate has been generated around the problems of relating gender divisions directly to class structure, and upon adjudicating between the relative importance of either. For feminists, the conception of the family unit, headed by the (male) breadwinner, tends to obscure and *a priori* deny women an independent social status in public life. The institution of the family itself provides an obstacle to female self-determination, as class is primarily designated by the family breadwinner's earning potential, and since it is assumed that the breadwinner is male, it is a correspondingly gendered analytical division. This, of course, ignores the material conditions of women, who constitute an increasingly significant proportion of the labour market. To expose the chasm between the ideological representation of women versus their perceivable material conditions of existence requires a shifting of the theoretical paradigms which assume the legitimacy of the public/private distinction. Particularly since, as Michele Barrett observes, 'an aspect of women's relationship to the class structure is that it is mediated, to some extent at least, by the configuration of the family, dependence on men, and domestic labour' (Barrett 1988: 135).

If, in fact, few women spend all their adult life in the home dependent upon a male breadwinner, it must be the case that in a family with both a male and female earner, a woman's wage – even if it is supplementary to a larger wage – improves the whole family's standard of living. By virtue of her involvement in waged labour, a working woman ought to be regarded, at least on an abstract level, as independent of her relationship to the family. It is clear that not all people deemed to be members of the same social class do have equal access to comparable jobs at equal rates of pay, but gender and race weaken bargaining power, constituting an internal hierarchy within given class positions. Class, after all, does not imply an homogeneous status for all its occupants: it must be seen as divided into age, skill, ethnic group and sex. This awareness facilitates a feminist materialist investigation which accepts that some women are more privileged than others.

It is certain at least that women's social position is affected by their often dual role as domestic/wage labourer – especially by the fact that the importance of the latter is ideologically suppressed. Within the labour force women are likely to have less upward mobility because of the ties of mothering/caring. Even if these 'ties' can be resolved by full-time childcare, they are still perceived as 'natural' by employers, who may be prejudiced against women who do not regard them as such. So, in a sense women are proletarianized by virtue of the fact that they proliferate in low status jobs (as do racial outgroups). In common with men, a woman's projected position in the labour market is influenced by her education and (father's) class background; but unlike men, a woman's actual labour status can also be determined by the way her relationship to the labour market is mediated through her dependence upon a husband and her assumed domestic responsibilities – not to mention how gender socialization affects her own view of her career potential. In view of the numerous complex factors which may restrict women's entry into full employment, it seems inevitable that any feminist discussion of class must also consider factors such as race and sexual orientation – those effaced by traditional 'class-based' analysis.

The difficulties confronting feminist analyses of class, the family and the sexual division of waged labour expose how crucial an examination of ideology is to all these theoretical strategies. Marxist feminists were not alone in a growing conviction that the perpetuation of a society divided along gender lines is primarily assisted by the action of ideological apparatuses which naturalize such social divisions as essential for the personal happiness of its members. Marxist feminist debates consequently came to focus on representation in addition to the economic base, and upon the effects of gender socialization and the construction of female sexuality. These issues reconnect Marxist feminists to other feminist political strategies, and the concept of ideology thus requires further exploration.

IDEOLOGY AND FEMINISM

Marxists, feminists, and in particular Marxist-feminists, have attempted to strengthen their analyses of oppression – whether perceived as class or class/gender oriented – by developing a more complex theory of the functions of ideology, in an endeavour to account for its problematical interrelation with material 'social reality'. When confronting the fundamental problem of how to account for the tenacity of gender differentiation and its subtle and diffuse operation in societal structures, feminists have summoned ideology to mean anything from 'false consciousness' to an 'unconscious' internalization of dominant social values. An exploration of the relationship between infrastructure and superstructure is, however, crucial in the elaboration of a political stance which retains a sense of the role of feminism in grassroots, issue-based struggle as well as its discursive role within an abstract theoretical battleground. Since the 1970s feminists have encountered mammoth problems in their efforts to locate and identify the mechanisms by which desired and distorted images of femininity are perpetuated in society. It is a complex matter to assess the means by which such images become equated with 'fact' or common sense, as they are communicated through schools, the law, the media, literature; and inform an individual's conceptions of, and attitudes to sexual difference.

Prior to feminist approaches to ideology, Louis Althusser had already identified problems with the Marxist theory of the maintenance of relations of production under capitalism. In his essay 'Ideology and Ideological State Apparatuses' (1969), he attempts to modify the classic Marxian account of the status of superstructure (law and the state/ideology) as subordinate to the infrastructure (economic base), which is viewed as the determining instance for superstructural processes. The initial proposition of Althusser's thesis is that in order to maintain its existing relations of production, capitalism needs to reproduce the conditions of production, and that this reproduction cannot simply happen at the localized level of each individual 'firm', or productive unit. At the very least, capitalist enterprises depend upon one another for raw materials, new machinery and so on; in addition each unit requires other 'raw material' such as labour-power, whose 'reproduction' takes place outside the sphere of production. In order to reproduce itself, labour power not only requires sufficient wages for food, clothing and child-rearing, but also an appropriate form of education.

This model of conditions of reproduction moves us beyond the scope of the Marxian economic base to the meta-level of the state itself. This not only provides the skills, via schooling, appropriate for labour power to reproduce itself in a way that functions for a capitalist society, but also imparts 'rules' of good behaviour to its citizens: 'rules of morality, civic and professional conscience, which actually means rules of respect for the socio-technical division of labour and ultimately the rules of order established by class domination' (Althusser 1984: 6). In other words, the state intervenes in the reproduction of labour-power at a crucial level 'outside' the realms of production 'proper', and enforces submission to a code of behaviour which serves the interest of capital and also naturalizes the division of labour in its present form. The state guarantees reproduction of the status quo 'in forms which ensure subjection to the ruling ideology or the mastery of its "practice"' (Althusser 1984: 7), dependent upon the class status of the individual. We can observe that Althusser identifies a profound interrelationship between the economic base and superstructure, where the material conditions of production are reinforced actively and coercively by a dominant ideology which simultaneously reproduces its own ideological framework as inevitable and immutable.

Althusser points out that the relationships between infrastructure and superstructure have, in traditional Marxist terms, been construed as either a relationship of 'relative autonomy' on the part of the superstructure, or in terms of a 'reciprocal' action of superstructure upon the base. Departing somewhat from these interpretations, he considers the superstructural elements of power, whose component parts comprise the state, in terms of the way they consolidate a particular (capitalist) status quo, which represents to itself and its subjects a desired social reality realized in material practices. Primarily, Althusser distinguishes between the effects of state power and the state apparatus – state power being analogous to that 'class' which maintains dominance via an abstract power network (the state apparatus), which could conceivably remain intact after a seizure of power by another social group. In addition to the State Apparatus – described as repressive since it ultimately 'functions by violence' (Althusser 1984: 17), whether physical or non-physical in form – he distinguishes Ideological State Apparatuses (ISAs) that emanate from and feed back into the Repressive State Apparatus (RSA). These are diverse, plural and operate as 'a certain number of realities which present themselves to the immediate observer in the form of distinct and specialized institutions' (Althusser 1984: 17), and which function by means other than active or tangible repression:

> If the ISAs 'function' massively and predominantly by ideology, what unifies their diversity is precisely this functioning, insofar as the ideology by which they function is always unified, despite its diversity and its contradictions, beneath the ruling ideology, which is the ideology of 'the ruling class'. (Althusser 1984: 20)

It is evident that Althusser is thus establishing close links between the RSA as a centralized unit of power containing components such as the government, the administration, the army, the police, the courts and prisons, and the mediatory processes of the ISAs, which consolidate the unity of state power whilst containing and repressing contradictions that are the effects of ongoing class struggle. He maintains that no class could hold state power for long without transforming both the RSA and the ISAs. Both are instrumental in replicating specific relations of production, and therefore more fundamental than the acquisition of dominance. Consequently, each ISA contributes to the perpetuation of the RSA, which clearly implies that ideology has a direct interventional relationship with people's material conditions of existence. In this respect it is apparent that Althusser's model moves towards a definition of base/superstructure as inseparable in practice, or as effects of each other – in that material reality is itself mediated and subject to transformations by the effects of ideology, and changing economic needs dictate subtle ideological shifts (the effects of a wartime economy upon the 'reserve army' of female labour would be a case in point).

A vital distinction for feminists is Althusser's account of the creation and maintenance of separate private and public spheres. The RSA is seen to function primarily in the public domain, whereas a large part of the ISA's effects are felt in the private sphere of the family-household system. The ideological processes which function most effectively in the private sphere inform those institutions which are seen to pre-date capitalism, such as the family, property relations and the sexual division of labour. Further, Althusser avers that it is the state (the ruling class) which determines the very boundaries between 'public' and 'private' – boundaries which are left intact by analysts such as Marx and Engels. And he cites the family and education ISAs as the most effective ideological apparatuses in a mature capitalist formation. This parallels feminist endeavours to bring to the fore the effects of these two institutions on the positioning of women in the private sphere, where it is argued that it is in the 'natural' apolitical site of the family that ideology most successfully effaces its own effects.

Feminists, in order to construct a viable oppositional ideological strategy, have first to recognize that Marxist theories of ideology themselves operate within what Michele Barrett vaguely terms an 'ideology of gender'. The recognition that all Marxist theories of ideology situate ideology as 'determined in the last instance by the class struggle' (Althusser 1984: 35), prompts feminists to find new means to conceptualize the effects of a social formation which they perceive as equally determined by the perpetuation of notions of gender and racial difference. Perhaps Althusser's concluding thesis is the most engaging for feminists. In his assertion that ideology interpellates individuals as subjects – in other words that our notion of individuality and selfhood is, in fact, socially constructed – in a way that profoundly affects our material existence, he offers a position which echoes that of poststructuralist theorists. Ideological processes, in the way they mediate and negotiate the repressive aspects of the State Apparatus are perceived as achieving a 'materiality' of their own. In other words, ideology does not just operate at the level of 'ideas', because ideas exist within and are given meaning by our actions, which insofar as they are 'social actions' are themselves ritualized in ways that are delineated by a particular ISA. We are already 'hailed' or interpellated as subjects by means that allow us to be 'identified' in the social formation by the 'double-mirror effect' of an ISA which implicitly contains at its centre the Subject par excellence (e.g. a projection of God in the religious ISA, or the idea of the model family which is summoned in the functions of the welfare state) to which we are subjected. We recognize our 'self' reflected in these processes because, it is argued, the notion of the self emanates from the social formation, and not from within the individual. From this 'Subject' we obtain our meaning in relation to all other subjects – accordingly, individuality itself is viewed by Althusser as an effect of the operation of ideology.

Althusser's model of interpellation – which necessitates the mutual recognition of subjects, (central) abstract Subject, and the subject's recognition of her/himself – requires extension to accommodate the view that women operate in the present social formation as subject/object in a paradoxically unstable subject position. Althusser's observation of the dual effects of ideology – upon consciousness and as dictating a range of actions – has proved attractive to Marxist feminists who have recognized that a feminist revolution requires not only equal access to material power processes, but also a sustained attack upon dominant ideological mechanisms, by demythologizing their perceived 'naturalness'. From such a perspective the quasi-biological account of patriarchy's 'universality' might be countered, and its success as a dominant ideological force examined and undercut. Following Althusser, feminist theorists have rejected the prevailing Marxist notion that ideology constitutes a distortion of reality by the ruling class, or indeed that ideology acts as a direct reflection, in ideas, of the determining economic base. Emphasis shifts instead to the relationship of ideology to lived experience: as the representation of the imaginary relationship of individuals to the real conditions of their existence. The gendered subject is constructed and reproduced in ideology and 'reality' is therefore perceived as a series of intersubjective social situations and relations.

Procreation, and its differing consequences for men and women, are often summoned as the eternal root cause of female oppression. The essential problem is the way gendered difference appears to be inscribed at every level of the social formation – in its material practices and ideological processes – giving the impression that the 'reality' of that difference is as inevitable as the anatomical distinctions which give credence to it. Notions of the naturalness of sexual difference clearly filter into Marxist discourse, where the status of women in the domestic sphere, and the configuration of the bourgeois family form is virtually removed from any historical context. In opposition to this view, Sheila Rowbotham categorically states that 'the nature of female subordination is as subject to social change as any other kind of subordination. Women were oppressed before capitalism. But capitalism has changed the nature of female oppression' (Rowbotham 1973: 57). Barrett, in common with Althusser, denies ideology in itself any materiality, while acknowledging the material effects of ideology as it is realized in social practices:

> It is impossible to understand the division of labour, for instance, with its differential definitions of 'skill', without taking into account the material effects of gender ideology. The belief that a (white) man has a 'right' to work over and above any rights of married women or immigrants has had significant effects in the organization of the labour force. Such a belief has therefore to be taken into account when analysing the division of labour, but its location in material practices does not render it material in the same way. (Barrett 1988: 89)

The phallocentricity of the Marxist analytical model presents such a difficulty, but one could agree with Althusser that 'what happens at the level of the firm is an effect, which only gives an idea of the necessity of reproduction, but absolutely fails to allow its conditions and mechanisms to be thought' (Althusser 1984: 3). In other words, modes of production themselves need to be considered at a macrolevel, whence their conditions of existence are perceived to thrive upon a sexual/ethnocentric division of labour, where women and racial outgroups are concentrated in low-paid, low-status jobs in relation to their (white) male counterparts. Take the example of the clothing industry which involves the production of commodities by (mainly non-white) female outworkers or women working in sweatshop conditions. It is crucial to acknowledge that it depends upon the exploitation of cheap labour. The conditions under which these women work – lack of trade union collectivization, low pay etc. – are a result of their femaleness – they might become outworkers because of childcare and other domestic responsibilities – and their ethnic status which might make access to better-paid jobs difficult.

If ideology operates by connoting the 'natural' order of things, it is vital that feminists renew their efforts to expose its distortions and contradictions. It is, of course, crucial that feminists do not lose sight of the issue-based struggles confronting women but tackle these problems by action against the perpetuation of such material practices. However, they must be wary of attempting to broach such prejudice exclusively on an issue basis, when an 'ideology of gender' is constantly perpetuating the 'reality' and 'naturalness' of inequitable sexual and racial divisions. The meta-level effects of dominant ideological processes can successfully defuse the 'victories' gained in localized spheres, such as equal pay and anti-discriminatory legislation. A revolution in consciousness is crucial to the socialist feminist agenda and therefore the critique of the ideological frameworks of contemporary social formations is vital. The first steps to such a revolution are to expose the contradictions inherent in the dominant ideologies of contemporary life because, 'an analysis of gender ideology in which women are always innocent, always passive victims of patriarchal power, is patently not satisfactory' (Barrett 1988: 110).

MOVING AWAY FROM ORTHODOXY: PROBLEMS IN MARXIST-FEMINIST ANALYSIS

Marxist/socialist feminism has always been a stronger tendency in Britain than in the US, where radical and liberal politics proved more popular.[6] According to Ginette Castro, Socialist Worker's Party women in the USA tried to hijack radical and liberal women's groups for their own purposes, capitalizing upon the unstructured formation of many of such groups (Castro 1990: 122). Whether or not she exaggerates the case, commentators on feminist activity on both sides of the Atlantic chart serious tensions between radical and socialist feminists, leading in Britain to a destructive split in feminist politics around 1978 – the year of the last National Women's Liberation conference, held in Birmingham. An important and recurring point of dispute was the question of whether to include or collaborate with male political sympathizers, prompted by radical feminists' doubts that men had anything to contribute to women's liberation in its developmental stages (see Wilson 1986: 100). The very fact that left-wing feminists endeavoured to accommodate gender issues within a pre-existing male-oriented framework seemed to suggest to radicals a symbolic collusion with the enemy, and a consequent dilution of feminist politics by the addition of class considerations.

The issue of men's involvement in feminism has of course been a contentious one, and radical feminists are most often characterized as operating separatist strategies – at least at a political level – in order to create a movement sustained and expanded by women alone. Socialist feminists' theoretical alliances with Marxism were viewed from other feminist quarters as not just a political engagement with men, but as an affirmation of male discourse, which others had discredited as exclusionary at its core, and therefore irredeemable for feminist purposes. Many feminists have additionally recorded the practical difficulties of forming liaisons with male activists who tend to dominate and structure discussion to their own purposes. But the problem for socialist feminists seemed to be primarily in getting Marxist men to take their revisionary materialist model seriously, as well as countering entrenched male prejudices about female political participation – a prejudice that seems to have existed within socialist organizations since the nineteenth century, where women were regarded as naturally tending to conservatism.[7] It appears to be the case that socialist men were interested in matters of gender, but that they seemed to be drawn to forms of feminist analysis removed from a Marxist framework. As Lynne Segal observes, radical feminism has proved more popular to socialist men.[8] Ironically this suggests that contemporary left-wing men prefer to characterize feminism as an autonomous bourgeois movement, which devotes its energies to specifically 'female' issues surrounding sexuality and domesticity, rather than responding to its critiques of current male-dominated political positions. Socialist feminists nonetheless encouraged male/female discussions on the grounds that patriarchal structures will never be abolished while men retain an investment in their perpetuation.

In the past decade socialist feminism has striven to produce more adequate methods of defining the nature of oppression, and counteract the abstract ahistorical connotations acquired by the term 'patriarchy', and 'by the end of the decade many if not most socialist feminists were convinced that patriarchy was at least as basic a structure as capitalism' (Segal 1987: 49). An historical perspective could demonstrate that patriarchy is inscribed in both the economic and ideological structures of contemporary Western society, illustrating a degree of shared experience between women, that cut across class and race boundaries:

> Women share common experience of oppression which, though they may be mediated by class, race and ethnicity, nevertheless cut across class lines. All women are liable to rape, to physical abuse from men in the home, and to sexual objectification and sexual harassment; all women are primarily responsible for housework, while all women who have children are held primarily responsible for the care of those children; and virtually all women who work in the market work in sex-segregated jobs. In all classes, women have less money, power and leisure time than men. (Jaggar 1983: 77–8)

Socialist feminists do take class divisions seriously, rather than claiming, as radicals tend to, that all women form part of an oppressed underclass. In this their work proved attractive to working-class women, who had generally felt alienated by the middle-class dimensions of radical and liberal feminism. Their appropriation of Marxism's commitment to historical specificity meant that they were able to unpack the unwieldy concept of patriarchy, and make connections between this seemingly timeless system of domination and a capitalist social reality. Although the rhetoric of shared sisterhood is beguiling as a slogan, it can be offensive to those women who do not have access to the privileges of their more prosperous and enlightened 'sisters' who themselves tended to gloss over the day-to-day material hardships of women's lives in favour of concentration on representations of femininity.

Feminist questions are at odds with the class-based nature of Marxist critiques; to set women apart as a class (or classes) of their own was perceived by classic Marxists as introducing divisive and diversionary debates to a political framework which depended on unity within class regardless of gender. A revolution in the material conditions of existence would supposedly achieve liberation for working-class men and women alike. Furthermore, because of feminism's tradition as middle-class defenders and thinkers, any attempt to pursue a feminist perspective within socialism was seen as bourgeois treachery. It was largely a question of a clash of priorities between socialist feminists and classic Marxists, where feminists' foothold in Marxism was compromised by their aim to forge links between gender and class oppression in the recognition that, 'an autonomous or semi-autonomous body of theory needs to be developed to explain the domination of women by men' (ten Tusscher in Evans et al. 1986: 66). Feminists highlighted the conceptual problems of classic Marxist analysis and showed that women's relations to class were at best equivocal; they probed the so-called 'private sphere' of the home in order to assess the extent to which domestic labour (including reproduction of the workforce) might be viewed as functional for capitalism, and exposed the prevailing sexual/racial inequalities within the labour market itself. It was in a real sense impossible for classic Marxism to assimilate such critiques of its own analytical structure unless it was prepared to transform its own definitions of the real source of oppression.

An editorial in *Feminist Review* (No. 23, Summer 1986) reflects a sense of identity crisis among socialist feminists, in the face of left-wing allegations that feminism has lost its political commitment and steadily drifted nearer the Right. The editorial collective of *Feminist Review* attribute this partly to the existence of a 'generation gap' in contemporary feminism:

> The women involved in the formative period of socialist feminism in Britain were nearly all highly educated, white and middle class, their politics indebted to the 1960s student revolt and its legacies. Young feminists' formative experiences are of chronic unemployment, a massive dismantling of public services and provision, and a more right-wing, embattled and confrontational political culture. In this history gross social divisions have been given new and painful meaning. (*Feminist Review*, Summer 1986: 4–5)

Feminists were aware that they may have rested on their radical laurels and not kept abreast of changing political realities – leaving them both incapable of challenging New Right assaults on women's rights, and rendering their work unattractive to many politically-aware women since the '80s. There has been an increased recognition that socialist feminism can no longer give precedence to matters of class and production at the expense of important issues such as racial difference, homophobia, sexuality, ideology and culture. More than ever feminists have to fill the analytical gaps in political theory, which still resolutely ignores the specific needs and demands of women. Socialist feminism has political resonance, asserts the *Feminist Review* collective, precisely because it perceives Western society as containing more than one system of domination:

> In contemporary Britain we can identify capitalism as an economic system based on the exploitation of the labour of the working class. We can identify imperialism, based on the exploitation and subordination of whole peoples, races and ethnic groups. And we can identify the system, call it sexism, patriarchy or a sex-gender system, based on the power of men over women. (*Feminist Review*, Summer 1986: 7)

In practice the clashes between questions of class, race, gender and sexual orientation are still prevalent in the women's movement, where different priorities create differing analyses of patriarchal/imperialist power. There has been some important appropriations of Marxist analysis to explore race and gender (see Davis 1982), but rarely from white women. Further, it has been argued that some white feminists' more recent acknowledgement of their ethnocentrism, tends to sidestep the deep-rootedness of racism in society and in feminism itself.[9] Perhaps it is socialist feminists' growing interest in matters of female sexuality and identity that announces the most significant rift between their work and that of Marxism, despite their attempts to demonstrate how such factors are fundamental to the economic base of society. At this end of the socialist feminist spectrum, we can witness a strong link with radical feminism, where personal politics warrant closer materialist analysis, in order to show that the public/private distinction maintained in all phallocentric political discourses is founded on the ideology of male dominance, and contributes to a maintenance of the equilibrium of such dominance.

It seems, then, that classic Marxism, in common with classic liberalism, is of strictly limited use to contemporary feminist thought, in that fundamental to both positions is the assumption that woman is socially subordinate to a politically, materially and ideologically dominant man. If deeper scrutiny of such theories as Marxism bears witness to the fact that woman is persistently associated with a transhistorical, all-consuming notion of nature, it is at times difficult to see the benefit of attempting to 'tack on' feminism to such monoliths, when it seems that the question of women's social position can at best remain a supplement.[10] However, many feminists would still defend the necessity to appropriate and reappraise 'masculine' discourses, if only to subvert them so as to be better able to question and criticize existing patriarchal political structures. As Annette Kuhn points out, this often results in the 'woman question' being clumsily inserted into the bedrock of academic disciplines as a side-issue, but never fully assimilated as an integral feature (Kuhn and Wolpe 1978: 1–2).

Although there are clear links between socialist and radical feminist politics, socialist feminism acquired a reputation for having 'ghettoized itself from interaction with non-socialist-feminist debates' (Phillips in *Feminist Review*, Summer 1986: 29). Meanwhile, the women's movement suffered some intra-feminist disputes:

> Arguments between socialist and radical feminists shook the women's liberation movement at times. Yet feminists on both sides saw eye-to-eye and campaigned together on a number of specific issues, and for most of the time, the movement managed to remain a singularly heterogeneous body, in which radical and socialist feminism co-existed. (Coote and Campbell 1987: 25)

A major criticism was of socialist feminism's apparent collusion with men and male-oriented discourse; but in their recognition that issues of sexuality, ideology and reproduction are fundamental areas for the investigation of women's oppression, they were fairly close to radicals, although the terms of their analysis differed.

Socialist feminism highlights a recurring problem for all feminists – the clash between a notion of 'sexual politics' and the necessary redefinition of 'politics' itself. Political analysts assert that politics deals with power relations at a macro level only, leaving such institutions as the family uninvestigated. Barrett, writing her new introduction to *Women's Oppression Today* in 1988, confesses that her attempt to integrate Marxism and feminism is informed 'with a much greater sense of the desirability of this at a political level than I would now express' (Barrett 1988: xxiii). Her changed stance reflects the growth and diversity of the feminist enterprise in recent years, where the emergence of increasingly heterogeneous feminisms have provoked related investigations into the nature of oppression by race and sexual orientation. The nature of feminist discourse is thus transformed even further beyond the scope of classic Marxism. Barrett's recent pessimism about the place of feminism in relation to Marxist analyses of class struggle is an acknowledgement that it cannot simply be slotted into a preconceived theoretical enterprise which denies it any intellectual or epistemological credibility. Feminism potentially destabilizes the tenets of Marxism: once theories of ideology are held up for examination, no tool of political enquiry can be left unscrutinized.

Barrett has concluded that feminism and Marxism are epistemologically poles apart: 'I would tend now to locate feminism even more firmly within a liberal, humanist tradition' (Barrett 1988: xxiii). One might well equally conclude that Marxism, which cannot by its own formulation conceive of itself as 'outside' the coercion of dominant ideological processes, has imbibed much of the liberal tradition of abstract thought, notably in its characteristic blindness to the operations of sexual/racial divisions in society. Feminism, at least by its theoretical 'unorthodoxy', has taken steps to question the epistemological roots of Western phallo(/ethno)centrism.

Chapter 3

Radical Feminism: Redefining Politics

> Where liberal angels and Marxist cadres have hesitated to tread, radical feminists have marched. While inadequate thought on the reasons for action, and the location of targets, have undoubtedly posed problems for the remainder of the movement, radical feminism has alerted us to many wrongs. Moreover, it is a virtue that, by its very existence, it keeps the issue of the politics of sexuality and sexual preference alive.
>
> (Evans in Evans et al. 1986: 112)

Although radical feminism is very much a new departure of the '60s, some aspects of its philosophy might be seen to have their roots in the American cultural feminist tradition in the nineteenth and early twentieth centuries. There seem to be particular links with the work of Charlotte Perkins Gilman, and her woman-identified utopia *Herland* (1911). Cultural transformation is a dominant aspect in the work of such feminists, although many would emphasize women's essential difference from men to a greater extent than later radicals did.[1] Another important legacy for radical feminists of the late '60s was that most were defectors from the New Left and civil rights movements, and 'much of radical feminist theory was therefore forged in reaction against the theories, organizational structures, and personal styles of the male "New Left"' (Donovan 1992: 141). In this sense, radical feminism summons up the spirit of the second wave, symbolizing the rage of women against the shackles of male power, a rage which became channelled into numerous acts of militancy and direct action against patriarchy. This rage, distorted, trivialized and depoliticized, was seized upon by the media and parodied in the mainstream, and still informs the popular (mis)conception of a 'feminist' today. Radical feminists eschewed existing

political structures or male-oriented philosophies, in favour of creating a space for women to lay claim to – to write, to think or to speak
as their feelings and personal experiences dictated. Its almost wholesale departure from an older tradition of feminism was particularly
evident in the stance adopted towards sexuality and the representation of women in the mass media.

Radical feminism, therefore, attempts to create a discursive arena
freed from the tyrannies of male-oriented political discourse. This
can be set in opposition to much of the work produced by socialist
and liberal feminists which in part endeavours to wreak something
from the bare bones of existing phallocentric forms of knowledge.
The radical stance is often inaccurately taken to be synonymous with
lesbian feminist politics; in truth the dominant issues brought to the
fore by radical feminism were often subjected to heterosexist or ethnocentric analysis, and both lesbian and black feminists were critical
of what they perceived to be significant gaps in radical theory.
Nonetheless radical feminism's ground-breaking work in investigating
the spheres of female sexuality and female socialization, provided the
impetus for the creation of a new kind of feminist theoretical space,
facilitated by radicals' negation of phallocratic political hegemony.

In a sense radical, black and lesbian feminisms might all be
dubbed 'radical' if we take the word to signify going to the root or
foundation of established thought. All three loose groupings, to a
greater extent than any feminist movements which predated them,
were prepared to rock the foundations of contemporary philosophical
and political thought. In this they share certain features with other
developing oppositional political movements of the '60s and '70s:

> In addition to the CND, the emergence in the 1960s of other
> social reform and environmental groups – including those cam-
> paigning for the legalization of abortion and homosexuality,
> and against capital punishment – helped to create a climate of
> reform in which feminism could flourish. (Gelb in Dahlerup
> 1986: 106)

Nonetheless, radical feminism found little hope for coalition with
such groups, which were deemed to be founded on sexist (and racist)
principles; in addition radical feminists favoured the small group
formation, rejecting firm links within or outside feminist politics. On
the whole, radical feminist politics announced the transition from
earlier twentieth-century women's rights movements, with a liberal
or socialist legacy, to the new women's liberation movement, characterized by its decentralized, localized and anti-elitist organizational

principles – something which liberal and Marxist feminists have also integrated into their political practice.

Before embarking on a closer investigation of the politics of radical feminism, it is perhaps necessary to reiterate that there is 'a common misconception that the radical-socialist divide reflected a split between lesbians and heterosexuals' (Coote and Campbell 1987: 22); yet these associations have made radical feminism 'a scarecrow with which to frighten women away from feminism' (Castro 1990: 124). It would be equally preposterous to assert that black and lesbian tendencies operate on the grounds of exclusive consideration of either race or sexual orientation.[2]

RADICAL FEMINIST POLITICS

Radical feminism emerged as a powerful oppositional discourse during the late '60s. It flourished during a period of marked upsurge in radical political agitation – for example the student and civil rights movements – and challenged the epistemological basis of both Marxism and liberalism. Radical feminists, possessing no single core doctrine which informed their theories, were fragmented from the start, a process exacerbated by their preference for small group formation, where each individual woman could find a voice, and where all tasks could be shared out equally. The groups devised their own consciousness raising strategies, and produced manifestos independently of one another, operating as distinct political 'cells' who might or might not forge coalitions in cases of direct action. One result of such discrete and free-floating political activity was that it provoked a degree of criticism from more centrally organized feminists – such as the liberal tendency that comprised the membership of NOW in the States[3] – and also a large amount of parody from the mass media.

Radical feminism's 'invisibility' as an 'organization' with no identifiable leaders and centres was perceived to be a major strength by its adherents: they do not subscribe to any one tradition in political thought and are therefore at liberty to constantly reinvent themselves. Although it would be fair to assert that radical feminist politics has been most broadly influential in its work upon issues which closely affect women's personal life and physical and mental well-being, it is much more difficult to isolate a central governing principle informing radical feminist work than it is with other strands. Perhaps anthologies such as Robin Morgan's *Sisterhood is Powerful* (1970) and Koedt, Levine and Rapone's *Radical Feminism* (1973) most effectively do justice to the sheer range and heterogeneity of radical feminist perspectives, although it is difficult to identify a

representative range of radical feminist writings still in print.[4]
Especially in its embryonic period, radical feminist writing showed a
commitment to the experiential, and it is rare to find proponents
debating or contesting the meaning of their radicalism among themselves, or explicitly announcing a radical feminist tradition – since
they rarely credit the sources of their ideas (Douglas 1990: 23).

Radicals appear to pride themselves on being notoriously difficult
to define, and this is in part an effect of their commitment to denying that one voice can speak for the many. However, Bonnie Kreps
provides a useful characterization of radical feminism as a tendency:

> which chooses to concentrate exclusively on the oppression of
> women as women (and not as workers, students, etc.). This
> segment therefore concentrates its analysis on institutions like
> love, marriage, sex, masculinity and femininity. It would be
> opposed specifically and centrally to sexism, rather than capi-
> talism. (Koedt et al. 1973: 328)

Much of their energies were focused on discussions around gender as
a social construct from which permeate all other forms of material
and ideological female oppression. In order to explore the nature of
such oppression more thoroughly, radicals concentrated on the experiences of the individual woman in society, often using writing as a
vehicle to communicate their own narratives of pain, and to convey
their passionate belief that sexism lies at the heart of women's
oppression. From their perspective the problem for women is quite
categorically men. Even male sympathizers to the women's movement are treated with suspicion, on the grounds that they still wield
the power to be potential oppressors existing with the privileges such
power bestows whether they acknowledge it or not. In any case,
radical feminists had to confront the arrant sexism of certain left-
wing men. As late as 1969, The American Student Democratic
Society pamphlet declared that, 'the system is like a woman; you've
got to fuck it to make it change' (cited in Echols 1989: 120). Since
every aspect of women's social and private lives is deemed to have
been latently infected by the curse of male domination, all forms of
male-oriented knowledge, including the use of language, is liable to
scrutiny. This necessarily includes all male analyses of oppression
including Marx's characterization of capitalism which, in common
with Marxist feminists, radicals recognized could not account for the
tenacity of female exploitation across history and cultures. Accordingly, they tried to confront the seeming universality of female
oppression by positing a universalizing notion of patriarchy.

Such feminists were convinced that a female revolution in consciousness was the most crucial primary step towards a social revolution, and their wholesale commitment to consciousness raising is testimony to this. Consciousness raising was conceived as the most effective means of encouraging all women to acknowledge their entrenched secondary status, by accepting that no aspect of their lives – particularly their personal lives – was innocent of patriarchal influences:

> Everything, from the verbal assault on the street, to a 'well-meant' sexist joke your husband tells, to the lower pay you get at work (for doing the same job a man would be paid more for), to television commercials, to rock-song lyrics, to the pink or blue blanket they put on your infant in the hospital nursery, to speeches by male 'revolutionaries' that reek of male supremacy – everything seems to barrage your aching brain, which has fewer and fewer protective defenses to screen such things out. You begin to see how all-pervasive a thing is sexism – the definition of and discrimination against half the human species by the other half. Once started, the realization is impossible to stop, and it packs a daily wallop. To deny that you are oppressed is to collaborate in your oppression. To collaborate in your oppression is a way of denying that you're oppressed – particularly when the price of refusing to collaborate is execution. (Morgan 1970: 1)

This is part of Robin Morgan's impassioned introduction to *Sisterhood is Powerful*, and demonstrates the emphasis of radical feminism on enlightenment and from thence revolution; but it also seems to carry an explicit threat to women who perhaps do not conceive of their oppression in quite the same terms. This is a fairly common tendency in some radical feminist writings and has regularly antagonized women, since it implies that all who do not agree with this perspective on women's oppression are living in a state of false consciousness or colluding in their own oppression by active means. I think, however, that the spirit of the message in context becomes clearer; that is that radicals often exploited the rhetoric of urgency in order to rally large groups of women under the broadest of political agendas possible, in order to convince them that total social change was possible with massive collective support through a refusal to sustain and perpetuate male power in their personal and working lives.

Consciousness raising in particular added a new dimension to the growth of feminist politics, which gave momentum to the conviction that all women should become involved in political activity, and the development of strategies to counter oppression. Consciousness raising offered women the opportunity to share and analyse experiences which were previously discredited as having no currency in wider political debates. The smallness of such groups encouraged this sense of a personal touch, which was and remains the trademark of the radical endeavour.

It is difficult to generalize about the range of activities or debates that took place by means of CR methods, but the anonymous essay, 'Consciousness Raising', in *Radical Feminism* (Koedt et al. 1973: 280–1), offers some insights into typical aims of the process. These guidelines suggest that a period of three to six months should be devoted to the articulation of members' personal experiences, before these are analysed in 'feminist' terms. This is then followed up by establishing activities and self-help groups, such as reading groups, childcare centres, and organized protests. There are of course problems with a structure which relies upon individual self-knowledge, not least that it is eminently compatible with the dominant ideology of abstract individualism, which deflects from collective activity – a clearly stated end result of CR. Carol Williams Payne is just one writer who expressed her dissatisfaction with the CR project, pointing out that although discussions centred on personal problems, 'we never tried to relate these problems to the structural problems of women in society nor did we think about how they could be dealt with beyond the personal level of these particular women in their particular situations' (Payne in Koedt et al. 1973: 283).

A democratic 'structureless' group does not of course guarantee equitable discussion, and can just as easily allow the most vocal members to take over and create an unacknowledged internal hierarchy, where power relationships hold sway more tenaciously for being denied: as 'Joreen' (Jo Freeman) remarks, 'there is no such thing as a structureless group' (in Koedt et al. 1973: 286). Writing in 1972, she conceived feminism's 'structurelessness' as itself tyrannical, in that after the exhilaration felt by individual women in small 'rap groups' there is a sense of aimlessness and anticlimax. She also claims that a denial of organizational structure enables elite groups of women to gain power by subterfuge – 'The more unstructured a group is, the more lacking it is in informal structures, and the more it adheres to an ideology of "structurelessness", the more vulnerable it is to be taken over by a group of political comrades' (in Koedt et al. 1973: 296). Her solution to this problem is to institutionalize modified democratic procedures, on the assumption that 'structures' are instituted unofficially in any case. One 'invisible' structure was that of membership criteria, where certain groups could hold sway over the range of issues discussed in their cell, by means of blocking the entrance of, for example, heterosexual married or partnered women. Such a quota is established in the 1969 manifesto of 'The Feminists', a New York 'Organization to Annihilate Sex Roles', who state that 'no more than one-third of our membership can be participants in either a formal . . . or informal . . . instance of the institution of marriage' (in Koedt et al. 1973: 374). Not surprisingly, this quota was controversial at the time and antagonized many potential members and 'made married women feel as though they were the enemy' (Echols 1989: 179).

While socialist and liberal feminists embarked primarily on a discussion of social structures and women's unequal position within them, radicals tended to focus on the personal lives of women, an area to which consciousness raising inevitably directed their attention. Important aspects of women's lives such as marriage, childcare, sexuality, health and work could not be readily considered within a mainstream, sociological framework, and the radical slogan, 'the personal is political' sought to elevate these issues to a matter of urgent political concern. This resulted in a concentration on grassroots mobilization, rather than on refining a coherent political theory. Many radical activities focused on the development of a 'woman's culture' through explorations into literature, art, music, and health, although it could be argued that such endeavours risk leaving the dominant culture uninterrogated. But such quests for a pre-existing authentic woman's culture affected radical 'theoretical' positions, which were expressed in diverse forms, ranging from what might approximate to a mainstream theoretical stance, to fiction, art and music, in the quest for a body of knowledge and tradition freed from the shackles of male interference.

Perhaps more than any other branch of modern feminist thought, radical feminism's activities transformed the foundations of what could be defined as 'political', not least because 'our theory is that practising our practice is our theory' (Chester in Feminist Anthology Collective 1981: 69). In other words, radical feminist writings are consciously deemed inseparable from group tactics, rather than as a discrete contribution to an abstract philosophical position. Theory and practice, personal and political combined were to be the means by which women might transform their lifestyles, at the same time as militating for social transformation. The belief that radical feminism needs 'to question every single aspect of our lives that we have

previously accepted as normal/given/standard/acceptable and to find
new ways of doing things' (Chester in Feminist Anthology Collective 1981: 68), resulted in a search for alternative lifestyles removed
from the stifling effects of patriarchy. Communes, businesses, women's
festivals and other women-only concerns were established to allow
women to pursue and construct their own identities unfettered by
pre-given social institutions such as the family, marriage and domestic labour. The negative aspect of this emphasis on politicizing the
personal is that individual women felt that they were being policed
by the movement, and some radical cells made unpopular public
statements about the tyranny of high fashion, and male standards of
female beauty. Boston's Cell 16, founded by Roxanne Dunbar,
'pioneered the popular movement look of khaki pants, work shirts,
combat boots and short hair' (Echols 1989: 162).[5]

All radical feminists seemed to agree upon the need for separatism, but the scale of separatism varied considerably, ranging from
political separatism (women-only discussion groups, dealing purely
with issues that affect women), to complete separatism (communes,
etc.) – or as complete as was economically or practically viable.
Separatism is one of the most lambasted features of radical feminist
policy. Other feminists, although they also believe in political separatism to some degree, tend to view certain radical 'extremes' as
denying that any successful feminist social transformation should be
directed at changing men's lives too. This form of separatism is
regarded as reaffirming the dominant conflation of biological and
gender difference, which identifies essential and distinct features of
male/female psychology. Despite evidence that radical feminists
concur with other strands that gender difference is a social construct
and therefore subject to change, debates – particularly around issues
of male violence and sexuality – have a tendency to lapse into a
biologism which suggest that men are innately aggressive (see, for
example, Brownmiller 1976). In addition, the commitment to promoting a women's culture can also have a similar effect, since often
this amounted to a celebration of aspects of femininity which had
previously been cast in negative terms – for example, being irrational,
emotional, intuitive, nurturant and passive – rather than a rejection
of the rigidity of such qualities. Communal living was the ideal to
render male assistance redundant, and in some cases (but by no
means all), lesbianism, 'political lesbianism' (the choice of a lesbian
sexual orientation as a political statement, rather than as reflecting
one's primary sexual choice) or celibacy was seen as the preferred
form of sexual orientation. Many factions held penetration during

sexual intercourse to be intrinsically an act of dominance and aggression by the male.

Of course radicals' all embracing notion of patriarchy can lead to a sense of the inevitability of the male will to power. Furthermore, if the female body and its function as vessel for human reproduction is seen as one of the chief reasons for female subordination, the only progress towards a feminist utopia might be seen as a technological revolution, where women are no longer handicapped by their biological processes. This is Shulamith Firestone's position in *The Dialectic of Sex* (1970), in which she asserts that 'the division yin and yang pervades all culture, history, economics, nature itself; modern Western versions of sex discrimination are only the most recent layer' (Firestone 1979: 11). Patriarchy, for Firestone, is therefore a system of power which exploits women's biological incapacity, and it is this fundamental handicap that must be removed to transform our current social order. In some respects, Firestone is in agreement with other radical and socialist feminists – that is, that the construction of the family and the institutionalization of monogamous heterosexuality as the desired norm are crucial factors in women's oppression. Firestone therefore advocates the necessity of removing the biological bond between mother and child, through socializing childcare and domestic arrangements, and thereby rendering the male/female parenting role redundant: 'to free women thus from their biology would be to threaten the social unit that is organized around biological reproduction' (Firestone 1979: 193). Although she demands the use of technology, most of Firestone's accompanying demands – the end of monogamy, incest taboos, childhood sexual restraint, the nuclear family, the reproductive/productive labour binary – are aimed at redefining the meaning and therefore ideological impact of such social 'givens'. One valid objection to her particular feminist utopia is that to deprive women of their 'right to choose' in favour of reproductive technologies is to submit our current attenuated liberty to scientific processes which are at present in the hands of men (see Tong 1989: 78–84; Jaggar 1983: 92–3).

Firestone's work, though it has survived in print to the present, has not been as influential upon radical feminist politics as other texts – perhaps because the crux of her analysis of subordination is that female biology is at fault, rather than the system of male dominance, which interprets reproduction as a reason for social disadvantage. Certainly the most famous early radical feminist work is Kate Millett's *Sexual Politics* (1969), a book that has been comprehensively attacked by literary critics and modern feminists alike, but which is

still compelling in its attempt to create a revolutionary feminist
perspective from a very raw state of bricolage – a heady mixture of
literary criticism, historical survey and political polemic. The fusing
together of the words 'sexual' and 'politics' opened up new theoretical possibilities for feminist debate, enabling the assertion that all
things 'private' and 'personal' in women's lives were affected by the
politics of the state and patriarchy, and that the chief weapon of
resistance for feminism was to politicize those sacred spheres of
liberal individualism:

> The word 'politics' is enlisted here when speaking of the sexes,
> primarily because such a word is eminently useful in outlining
> the real nature of their relative status, historically and at the
> present. It is opportune, perhaps today even mandatory, that we
> develop a more relevant psychology and philosophy of power
> relationships beyond the simple conceptual framework provided
> by our traditional formal politics. Indeed, it may be imperative
> that we give some attention to defining a theory of politics
> which treats of power relationships on grounds less conven-
> tional than those to which we are accustomed. (Millett
> 1977: 24)

Millett's assertion has the ring of a prophetic statement in the light
of contemporary feminist thought, and the way it has moved towards
a more complex examination of the power structures which place
women as subjects in particular oppressive relationships.

In common with Millett, Germaine Greer in *The Female Eunuch*
(1970), concentrates mainly on raising universal feminist consciousness, rather than providing a clear agenda for change, on the basis
that woman 'could begin not by changing the world, but by reassess-
ing herself' (Greer 1971: 14). While Millett embarks on a scathing
critique of the violent and offensively sexualized imagery of women
in novels by male literary lions of the twentieth century, Greer
initiates her enquiry by looking at the construction and fetishized
naturalization of the feminine body. However, both have a similar
end in view: to analyse the way the female body has been situated in
a discourse of normative femininity in order that they may posit a
radical fracturing of such discourse. Greer's view of a positive revolutionary stance is one analogous to the situation of the proletariat
outlined in classic Marxist thought, and her solution is for women
to withdraw their labour. This heralds another important feminist
conviction; that women's work, classically viewed as something they

are naturally equipped to do, is reconstrued as cheap, or often free labour, whose reward is long overdue.

In varying degrees, Greer and Millett see the solution as a revolution in consciousness which can also serve to awaken men to their own internalized position as oppressors. By contrast, Mary Daly's view of patriarchy in *Gyn/Ecology* (1979) is that it is tenacious enough to resist such 'pseudo-feminist' rhetoric:

> However possessed males may be within patriarchy, it is their order; it is they who feed on women's stolen energy. It is a trap to imagine that women should 'save' men from the dynamics of demonic possession; and to attempt this is to fall deeper into the pit of patriarchal possession. It is women ourselves who will have to expel the Father from ourselves, becoming our own exorcists. (Daly 1979: 2)

As well as possessing a clear spiritual and mystical dimension, Daly's work is more far-reaching than that of Millett, Greer or even Firestone, in the sense that she attempts to combat sexism at its very roots in the language one uses to articulate one's oppression, by punning on and expropriating negative gendered words: 'In order to re-member our dis-spelling powers, Hags must move deeper into the Background of language/grammar' (Daly 1979: 328). She aims to create a feminine language which consolidates a separatist vision of a female future. More recently feminist linguists have argued that processes of linguistic signification are more complex than Daly's inference that words and concepts have a fixed one-to-one relationship, and that what is needed is a more wide ranging study of language which links modes of speech as well as writing to women's multifarious and possibly conflicting social identities, in a much broader based interrogation of the means by which meaning is socially and culturally, as well as linguistically embedded.[6]

Radical feminism is potentially more wide ranging than either socialist or liberal feminism – not least because it often explores means by which women can reconceive their relationship to the current social reality, in order to resist it. Rather than putting all its energies into either reform or future resistance, it implicitly argues for constant acts of rebellion within both personal and public lives, to revivify the movement. Alice Echols declares that 'by 1970 there was such enormous interest in radical feminism that some have even argued that it was on the verge of becoming a mass movement' (Echols 1989: 4). But perhaps the emergence of radical feminist

politics as a position which recognizes no preordained parameters
and makes no allies, determined its current fall from grace, in face of
more sophisticated analyses of women's oppression. Nonetheless,
although there is less evidence of organized radical feminist activity
in the '90s – in terms of publications and journals and academic
profiles (the British journal *Trouble and Strife*, and the USA's *Off Our
Backs* are two exceptions) – the continued debates around women's
health, pornography and sexual violence are largely due to radical
feminist studies in these fields.

One of the best known radical feminists still actively militating for
changes in censorship legislation, campaigns against male sexual
violence and prostitution is Andrea Dworkin. For some feminists she
represents an 'extremist' position, which naively attributes a direct
relationship between images of women and sexual violence – for
instance between pornography and rape:

> Pornography is the propaganda of sexual fascism. Pornography
> is the propaganda of sexual terrorism. Images of women bound,
> bruised, and maimed on virtually every street corner, on every
> magazine rack, in every drug store, in movie house after movie
> house, on billboards, on posters pasted on walls, are death
> threats to a female population in rebellion. (Dworkin 1988: 201)

Although Dworkin's stance on pornography, in common with
another US feminist, Catharine Mackinnon,[7] remains uncompromising, many recent feminists are reluctant to cast the debate in such
extreme terms. Some lesbian and socialist feminists, for instance, feel
that a tightening of censorship laws would hit hardest at groups who
already feel the sting of restrictive legislation. In addition, some gays
and lesbians argue that pornography can be empowering; that 'gay
porn offers images of desire which a hostile society would deny and
are therefore real encouragements for a positive sense of self' (Weeks
1985: 235). It has been often noted that a stance against pornography such as Dworkin's and Catharine MacKinnon's creates unholy
alliances with moral majority pressure groups, whose intentions in
stopping the flow of pornographic material are far from sympathetic
to feminism. Dworkin's role on the Meese Commission, which was
set up under President Reagan to determine the impact of pornography on society and to recommend means by which the spread of
pornography could be contained, is one example of such a contradictory alliance.[8]

Radical feminists have often been criticised for re-casting women
in the role of passive victims of their biological impulses – more so

because anti-porn and sexual violence debates often appear to slip into essentialist assumptions about the fixity of aggressive male sexual impulses. Nonetheless, as I shall go on to discuss in Chapter Seven, radicals in particular helped to explode some fairly tenacious myths about femininity, and were at the forefront of theoretical examinations of the construction of female sexuality. Anne Koedt's essay, 'The Myth of the Vaginal Orgasm' (1970; reprinted in Koedt et al., 1973), was a crucial step towards rethinking the means by which heterosexual desire is constructed exclusively around male needs, particularly discussions around the issue of whether all penetrative sex is currently symbolic of patriarchal colonization. Doubtless such debates on the one hand prompted common assumptions that radical feminism is a solely lesbian political stance, even though radical analyses of female sexuality did not always include lesbian perspectives.[9] Nonetheless, they were instrumental in introducing to the feminist agenda a candid and often combustible approach to the subject.

PATRIARCHY, STEREOTYPES AND THE RADICAL FEMINIST CRITIQUE

A position analogous to the Marxist account of the effects of ideological positioning is summoned by early radical feminists to account for the widespread, though chimerical nature of 'sexism'. The extensive use made of the abstract terms 'stereotype' and 'patriarchy' serves to illustrate this point. Both concepts were crucial in the struggle to establish a resistant feminist discourse, yet both tended to be mustered as if they were self-explanatory, rather than a way of facilitating a thorough understanding of the way gender inequality is perpetuated in the current social formation. The early writings of radical feminists – especially in the United States, where the radical tradition had a stronger hold – display a marked reluctance to adopt the analytical frameworks or 'jargon' of established patriarchal academic discourse. This anti-theory tendency, coupled with many feminists' disenchantment with left-wing male-dominated hierarchies, resulted in an almost wholesale rejection of Marxist perspectives. The non-hierarchical organization of early consciousness-raising collectives which attempted to give all women, regardless of educational background, a voice within the movement needed to avoid 'jargon'; but this also indicates a concentration on material instances of women's subordination, mediated through individual experiences recounted by movement women rather than through pre-ordained abstract paradigms. This is not to suggest that non-material aspects of sexism are neglected, but that issue-based discussions (on abortion, contraception, the family and so forth) tend to be conflated with a consideration of the means by which material subordination is sustained at a 'meta' level, designated as 'patriarchy'. The result is that early feminist work often gives the impression that 'sexism' is always conscious, purposeful and can therefore be eradicated by outlawing certain social practices.

There are well-documented problems with this feminist appropriation of the term patriarchy, when it is left crudely analogous to its original definition of 'father-right' – not least that it fails to take account of the social realities of advanced capitalism. These conceptual problems have been addressed in the previous chapter. For the purposes of this discussion, the radical feminist use of 'patriarchy' clearly implies that all men actively subordinate women, but fails to pay more than token regard to the likelihood that men have different degrees of access to mechanisms of oppression (non-white men, for example, find themselves 'outside' dominant patriarchal representations of masculinity). The following passage exemplifies this stance:

> All men are our policemen, and no organized police force is necessary at this time to keep us in our places. All men enjoy male supremacy and take advantage of it to a greater or lesser degree depending on their position in the masculine hierarchy of power. (Dunbar in Morgan 1970: 536)

Such a position evokes the reality of individual male dominance in the private sphere of home and family (acknowledged by most feminists as the crucial site of women's oppression), but does not allow for the possibility that changes in personal power relations will only be effected by intervention at the level of 'public' manifestations of power.

Patriarchy, in common with ideology, is viewed as inscribed within the totality of the social formation; it is implied that an overthrow of patriarchy (enacted primarily at the localized level of the individual's rejection of her 'appropriate' domestic/sexual role) would necessitate a shift in the representation of women, and consequently a renegotiation of current social positioning. Patriarchy, in this context, signifies more than the rule of men; it connotes a ruling body of individual men who directly influence social relations and who could be quite simply dethroned in favour of more egalitarian power structures. Stereotypes and gender socialization are seen, therefore, as contingent effects of patriarchy – and are consequently perceived as the product of conscious intention on the part of the powerful (men) to maintain their position at the expense of the powerless (women).

Admittedly, I am taking common features of radical feminism and to some extent parodying them; but the point of taking the sub-text of such a formulation to its logical conclusion is still ultimately valid. The way patriarchy is used in such work gives the term a material effect which is untenable, given that patriarchy works effectively even when, for example, a woman heads a government. Ultimately stereotypes are seen as transformable into more 'realistic' images of women, as if they can simply take on the 'positive' effects of a 'role-model' given some judicious revision from a feminist perspective. 'Stereotype' and 'patriarchy' become caught somewhere between their implied status as transcendent and elusive or invisible, and as material, visible and transferable. The anti-theory drive of the 1970s has resulted in a theoretical muddle for feminists of the 1980s and 1990s of quite serious proportions. Michele Barrett and others have tried to navigate a way through such a cul-de-sac by talking of a 'patriarchal ideology',[10] which concentrates analysis upon how women and men represent the 'realities' of gender inequality to themselves and act upon it in their material practices, as well being subjected to ideology's gendered central subject. I do not wish to write off radical feminist analysis of the stereotype, or suggest its significance as a representation of power relations embedded in patriarchy is totally redundant. Images and representations of femininity are still central features of contemporary feminist theory, and a revisionary reading of radical texts demonstrates that they shed important insights upon the effects of ideology.

What Greer, Ellmann, Millett, Brownmiller and others share through their explorations into the construction of femininity and the stereotypes used to enforce desired images of the female form, is an awareness of the power of 'gender ideology', in tandem with a sense of its apparent immutability. It has long been accepted that overturning stereotypes – for example using scantily-clad men in advertisements to target women – simply does not work, in that the image may be analogous but possible meanings differ substantially. Men simply do not function as objects of desire; their gendered subject position in society is too deeply entrenched. Germaine Greer perceives the perpetuation of the female stereotype as a function of consumption, mediated through the less tangible process of desire – for men the 'woman' becomes a commodity; and for women she is the unattainable seamless hallmark of perfection:

Because she is the emblem of spending ability and the chief spender, she is also the most effective seller of this world's goods. Every survey ever held has shown that the image of an attractive woman is the most effective advertising gimmick . . . The gynolatry of our civilization is written large upon its face, upon hoardings, cinema screens, television, newspapers, magazines, tins, packets, cartons, bottles, all consecrated to the reigning deity, the female fetish. Her dominion must not be thought to entail the rule of women, for she is not a woman. (Greer 1971: 60)

Greer hints here at a disjunction between the power of the female image and the powerlessness of women. In *Sexual Politics* Kate Millett goes further, and actually situates gendered power relations at the level of ideology – gesturing towards its role in the interpellation of subjects:

Sexual politics obtains consent through the 'socialization' of both sexes to basic patriarchal polities with regard to tempera- ment, role, and status. As to status, a pervasive assent to the prejudice of male superiority guarantees superior status in the male, inferior in the female. The first item, temperament, involves the formation of human personality along stereotyped lines of sex category ('masculine' and 'feminine'), based on the needs and values of the dominant group and dictated by what its members cherish in themselves and find convenient in subordinates: aggression, intelligence, force, and efficacy in the male; passivity, ignorance, docility, 'virtue' and ineffectuality in the female. This is complemented by a second factor, sex role, which decrees a consonant and highly elaborate code of con- duct, gesture and attitude for each sex. In terms of activity, sex role assigns domestic service and attendance upon infants to the female, the rest of human achievement, interest, and ambi- tion to the male. The limited role allotted to the female tends to arrest her at the level of biological experience. (Millett 1977: 26)

Millett's interpretation of the overarching impact of gender sociali- zation analyses the way in which a dominant ideological perspective on gender polarizes the sexes into having two distinct desired roles within the social formation.

This hypothesis, which she terms 'notes toward a theory of patri- archy', implicitly allows for the consideration of class/racial hierarchies in addition to a sexual one,[11] and therefore enables her to speculate that males outside the dominant group are also 'subjected' to gender socialization without it guaranteeing them the same access to power. Yet a paradox confronting all feminists is that all males have access to power over females in the domestic sphere. Another thorny problem outlined by Millett is one which has troubled feminists ever since: that women's socially constructed role has always derived its credibility from the 'fact' of female biology.[12]

Millett, writing in a veritable vacuum at the onset of feminism's second wave, tends to assume the validity of a quasi-Marxist position rather than attempting a 'marriage' between this and her own perspective. Her endeavour to place patriarchy in an historical context effectively points to fundamental flaws in the Marxist historical approach, but she does not pursue the implications of this. She is also not often credited for her awareness of the complexity of constructing a theory of patriarchy which counters the assumption 'that patriarchy is endemic in human social life' (Millett 1977: 27): certainly we find evidence of the prevalence of such assumptions in Friedrich Engels' *The Origins of the Family, Private Property and the State* (1884). Millett, on the whole, gives a very positive account of this text as a contribution to a theory of sexual revolution (Millett 1977: 120–7), especially its descriptions of the patriarchal and bourgeois manifestation of the institutions of marriage and the family. However, she rightly points out that Engels' view of patriarchy – as enacting power over bourgeois women by rendering them chattels to be passed from father to husband in the circulation of wealth and property – disregards the effects of patriarchal power relations at other levels:

> Engels ignores the fact that woman is viewed, emotionally and psychologically, as chattel property by the poor as well as, and often even more than, the rich. Lacking other claims to status, a working class male is still more prone to seek them in his sexual rank, often brutally asserted. (Millett 1977: 122)

Millett, in common with other feminist thinkers, found that Engels might yield possibilities for feminist appropriation, not least because he focuses on the familial institution as integral to women's oppression. Nonetheless, she observes above that the degree of female subordination is regarded as class-specific; yet feminists required a framework which could account for the seemingly universal acceptance of female inferiority.

CRITIQUES OF RADICAL FEMINISM

The most common criticisms of radical feminism are that its view of patriarchy remains uninterrogated; that many of its arguments lapse into biologism of a reductive kind, and that its focus on women's personal experiences renders it politically ineffectual, or at worst prescriptive – if, for example, it is seen to argue that 'lesbian sexuality does serve as a paradigm for female sexuality' (Tong 1989: 123). Although writers such as Millett and Firestone appropriated a Marxist model of historical materialism for their own radical use, the notion of patriarchy as the central system of female subordination is most problematic for socialist feminist thinkers. Its polemical strength has been recognized by writers such as Rosalind Coward, who agree that the use and appropriation of such a term 'has given a theoretical basis for the specificity of women's oppression' (Coward 1983: 271). However, she argues that it is an inadequate formulation from which to discuss the dynamics of sexual relations in their specific, various and changing historic forms:

> For the term 'patriarchal' implies a model of power as interpersonal domination, a model where all men have forms of literal, legal and political power over all women. Yet many of the aspects of women's oppression are constructed diffusely, in representational practices, in forms of speech, in sexual practices. This oppression is not necessarily a result of the literal overpowering of a woman by a man. (Coward 1983: 272)

A universalist concept of patriarchy, then, is regarded as a trap for feminism for it can lead us down avenues of biological essentialism – an avenue pursued by Mary Daly, and other radical feminists who are often dubbed cultural feminists in their primary celebration of women's power as a sub-culture. Equally, it can leave us with a naive and unwieldy notion of power relationships which cannot theorize itself out of the subtle and stubbornly 'naturalized' effects of a patriarchal ideology.

It now seems to present-day feminist commentators that early radical feminism (which rapidly split into several factions itself) over-simplified the causes of female oppression in its assertion that gender difference had arisen as a universal and ahistorical system of male domination. Visions of the end of patriarchy might constitute a utopian image of androgyny or more typically perhaps, a movement towards total separatism. Radical feminists seemed to be the first group to utilize the term 'patriarchy' as shorthand to designate the means by which women are oppressed. It was used relatively unproblematically to signify the subordination of all women by all men; because of its ahistorical, cross-cultural and universalizing tendencies it was held to imply that all men were irredeemably the enemy and that women's subordination was inevitable. In other words, women are perceived as an oppressed class in their own right, regardless of social, cultural or racial distinctions. This argument has been latterly exposed as both contradictory and circular within the terms of radical feminist aims itself, since it returns feminists to the realm of biologically essentialist assertions – precisely those used to strengthen so-called patriarchy in the first place – when the stated goal of most radicals is to expose the social construction of gender roles and definitions.

The term patriarchy can however be used for more positive purposes, one of which is a wilful resistance of all phallocentric categories of knowledge, including notions of historicism and cultural specificity. For radicals, patriarchy is the means for articulating the way in which every aspect of a woman's life appears to be tainted by male domination. It is for this reason that they are accused of failing to recognize that different men have differing degrees of access to power, and of denying the possibility that some men are sympathetic to feminist issues and do not consciously wield their potential power. Radicals largely argue that all men profit from patriarchal systems of oppression and therefore all men are answerable for its continuance – for this reason, the policy of individual acts of resistance by women in their personal lives was seen as an important precursor to collective activism. Although such a position can be deemed weak and a recipe for political fragmentation, it might also be characterized as one of the most potentially far-reaching oppositional strategies devised by feminists – especially when it is accompanied by a call to separatism. As I have already asserted, separatism is to varying degrees a factor of all feminist positions: in the case of radical feminism it is woven into the fabric of their work, even though most writers seem to envisage a time when social sexual divisions are eradicated (see, for example, Kreps in Koedt et al. 1973). Patriarchy is used by radicals as the most forceful evocation of oppression because they maintain that:

> the pathology of oppression can only be fully comprehended in its primary development: the male-female division. Because the male-female system is primary, the freedom of every oppressed individual depends upon the freeing of every individual from every aspect of the male-female system. (Koedt et al. 1973: 370)

Although the use of the terms male/female as opposed to masculine/feminine is potentially misleading because of the biologistic implications of the former, read in context, this particular manifesto addresses the problem of cultural definitions ascribed to sex roles. The notion that sexual difference underpins all other systems of oppression in society is a seductive one for feminists, in that its institutions seems to be among those most resistant to change in contemporary society, and those most neglected by male-oriented oppositional politics.

Radical feminism, although not a strongly visible force in the academic institution, has survived as an aspect of current feminist activism, especially in grassroots work maintaining rape crisis centres, women's aid and other support networks for women – as well, of course, in work around issues of pornography and prostitution. Although the methods and principles of radical feminism render it to some extent incompatible with other feminist theories, this is not because it is resolutely anti-theory, as is often suggested, but rather that theory and practice are viewed as each a product of the other, and therefore mutually strengthening. In recent years, the publication of works which consider the legacy of radical feminism, suggest that radical politics is experiencing a modest renaissance.[13] Radical feminism arguably had a more profound and sustained effect on the development of American second wave feminism than it had in Great Britain where 'socialist and Marxist feminists were the virtual "midwives" of the British women's liberation movement' (Gelb in Dahlerup 1986: 108); however, radical feminist tendencies forced those feminists allied to mainstream political factions to recognize that mere reformism had not proved successful in conquering female oppression.

Much of what was regarded as most extreme about radical feminism has been variously parodied and dismissed by the other voices comprising the women's movement. Perhaps because radical feminists concentrated on cultural awakening rather than theorizing and scholarly debate, its features (often exaggerated beyond all recognition) were regularly pilloried by the mass media as a means of defusing what could have been regarded as quite a significant and concerted onslaught by feminists upon the establishment. Most people if asked to define feminism today would produce a definition which vaguely resembles the radical feminist agenda, and many women writers have described radical feminism as a phase in the women's movement which alienated many of its more 'decorous' members. Lisa Alther's *Kinflicks* (1976) – an important feminist bestseller – itself contains an episode which, in the context of the book as a whole, appears to be intensely parodic.[14]

It is an attractive notion to assert, as radical feminists often do, that every society has two cultures: the dominant male one and the barely visible female one, and thus pinpoint the need to celebrate the features of a female sub-culture both as the source of women's strength and a point of departure from which to organize a sustained threat to male supremacy. Radical feminism, perhaps more than any other strand has tried to define feminist politics as a complete way of life, from sharing experiences in consciousness raising sessions, to living under degrees of separatism in communes and collectives. This seeming refusal to compromise on the part of many of its advocates is seen to be its most intimidating aspect, in that, 'radical feminism reminds women of their own moments of exploitation or abuse, and these memories are not welcome' (Rowland and Klein in Gunew 1990: 299). Separatism can suggest that women's interests will always be in direct opposition to men's, and this is a most unpalatable stance for feminists allied to mainstream politics who do not readily see women as a discrete 'class' of their own. It might also be regarded as racist, in its assumption that black women share the experiences of white women, whereas many may see their alliances divided between all women and men of colour. For black, lesbian and socialist feminists alike, the radical notion of sisterhood – a bond which cuts across all other boundaries – is problematic, in that it blurs the evident fact that women too can function as oppressors of other women. Radical feminists have taken such criticisms seriously and despite clear evidence that some writers do ignore issues of race and sexual orientation in a glib assumption that white bourgeois heterosexual reality is women's reality, their record of attempting to encourage all women to have a voice is better than that of socialists, as the most well-known anthologies of radical feminist writing testify.

Chapter 4

Lesbian Feminism: Exploding 'Heteroreality'

What is a lesbian? A lesbian is the rage of all women condensed to the point of explosion. She is the woman who, often beginning at an extremely early age, acts in accordance with her inner compulsion to be a more complete and freer human being than her society – perhaps then, but certainly later – cares to allow her. These needs and actions, over a period of years, bring her into painful conflict with people, situations, the accepted ways of thinking, feeling and behaving, until she is in a state of continued war with everything around her, and usually her self . . . . To the extent that she cannot expel the heavy socialization that goes with being female, she can never truly find peace with herself. For she is caught somewhere between accepting society's view of her – in which case she cannot accept herself – and coming to understand what this sexist society has done to her and why it is functional and necessary for it to do so.

(Radicalesbians in Koedt et al. 1973: 240–1)

Lesbian women clearly were active in earlier suffrage and reformist campaigns, but it is arguably only in the '60s that there emerged a felt need to identify sexual orientation as a significant factor in their oppression as women.[1] The formation of a specifically lesbian politics itself suggests that lesbians felt themselves to be excluded or their concerns marginalized in the women's movement at large – it also, perhaps, reflects a growing concern with the politics of identity in all militant political movements of the '60s, including the civil rights and gay rights and anti-Vietnam movements. Radical feminism, more than other tendencies, focused upon issues surrounding female sexuality and the female body, and for this reason may seem peculiarly compatible with a lesbian concern to consider how sexual orientation is policed and certain 'appropriate' forms of sexual expression are enforced in society. Matters of women's health, work, and issues of contraception and abortion were overlaid, at a more abstract level, by sustained analyses of the ways women internalize and act upon sexualized representations of femininity.

However, the radical feminist rhetoric of sisterhood emphasized the conviction that the oppression of women as women ran deepest in contemporary society, and consequently demonstrated a failure to recognize that race or class divisions were themselves intrinsically gendered, or that women as a group were divided into constellations of oppressor and oppressed. At the same time as sexual orientation is cast, by implication, as irrelevant to the women's liberation movement, homophobia was a problem, and one which was left largely unscrutinized beneath the myth that an oppressed group could not in turn oppress others. In this sense, developing feminist forms of knowledge themselves created a need for the epithets 'black' or 'lesbian' to supplement the term feminism, since existing positions pursued a methodology more or less based upon the notion of a homogenized 'underclass' of women. The facts of race, sexual orientation or class meant that many women perceived that the nature of their subordination was at least two-pronged; the feminist implication that sisterhood meant pooling one's experience and recognizing our shared oppression by men, was quite simply offensive, not least in its inference that enlightened feminists could never be guilty of perpetuating such power imbalances themselves. Both lesbian and black feminists sought involvement in groups which might prove to be both liberating and affirmative of their identity and specific circumstances. It also creates problems about who the 'women' are in this equation? White heterosexual feminists exhibited a tendency to lay claim to the identity of 'feminist' and by a process of exclusion, simultaneously robbed others.

Just as the birth of women's liberation signalled a new politics centred upon gender identity, so the Stonewall Rebellion in New York in 1969 announced the emergence of the Gay Liberation movement as a political grouping which adopted the militant tactics successfully used by other radical factions in the '60s. The spread of slogans such as 'Gay Is Good', and the beginnings of gay pride parades, was itself a form of consciousness raising which allowed people to derive strength from the knowledge of a shared identity, as an antidote to the previous pathologization of the gay and lesbian. Collective gay action was a call for full visibility and equal human rights, and no longer a meek plea for tolerance. The gay movement aimed to combat all forms of social invisibility, which had previously condemned homosexuals to the margins, deemed as either sick or perverted; they also identified the means by which homosexual identity was perceived to determine one's wider social identity. In common with feminists the crucial factors at stake were effects of both ideological representation and the social and material practices which affirm and perpetuate its influence. Lesbian feminism aimed to fuse the positive aspects of gay and feminist politics, whilst offering critiques of both – particularly sexism endemic in the Gay Liberation Movement, and covert homophobia rife in Women's Liberation. It is interesting to note that the term 'gay' soon began to be seen as applying to men alone, in a similar way that the women's movement was strategically a movement with the interests of heterosexual women at heart. It is not surprising, therefore, that the issue of naming and vocalizing the fact of their sexual orientation as a political move has been a primary aim of lesbian and lesbian feminist activists in both the gay and women's movements.

LESBIAN FEMINIST POLITICS

For lesbian feminists the problems of female sexuality and sexualized images of women were crucial to their analysis of women's oppression. What they objected to about straight feminist political writings was the emphasis upon male–female relationships, at the expense of any sustained focus upon woman-identified concerns plus the assumption among many feminists that potential converts to feminism are all heterosexual and likely to be put off by any association of feminism with lesbian issues. This is not to imply that lesbian feminists are solely, or even primarily concerned with sex and sexual relationships *per se*; but they recognized that lesbian sexual orientation affects all other aspects of one's daily life, because people commonly perceive homosexuality as a sickness which 'incapacitates' people in quite other areas of their lives – their eligibility for jobs, their fitness for parenthood, and so forth. Therefore these perceptions and the ideology of a 'heteroreality' must be a focus for lesbian feminist politics in addition to redressing the balance of focus in feminist politics as a whole.

Heterosexual feminists did not always feel that critiques of feminism's 'mainstream' (for want of a better term to describe the dominant body of feminist thought) were constructive. Instead they felt that such responses were potentially divisive, diluting the power of sisterhood; alternatively, some felt that they were being forced to feel regressive or guilty for still indulging in relationships which placed them in a compromising association with 'the enemy'. In retrospect it is quite clear that lesbian critiques of straight feminist thought did expose the disproportionate amount of attention paid to male–female relationships to the extent that while some heterosexual feminists criticized the way women were only valued in relation to men, their work often suggested that they found it hard themselves to shake this assumption. Lesbian feminists preferred to celebrate woman-to-woman bonds, in all their manifestations, as empowering symbols of female strength and mutual support, and they celebrated the fact that men found the idea of massed bands of women rejecting any reliance upon males profoundly intimidating. Nonetheless these critiques were sometimes interpreted as a deliberate attempt to alienate heterosexual women, by positing a model of women's liberation which questions the political viability of heterosexual relationships; occasionally they are even accused of splitting the women's movement in the '70s, allegedly by their 'proselytizing . . . in the name of feminism itself' (Castro 1990: 106). Although some lesbian feminists undoubtedly felt that to further revolution, all women should become at least 'political lesbians' (which might entail the choice to remain celibate), few seem primarily interested in policing women's sexual preference. In common with gay men, lesbian feminists' initial concern was with transforming the social processes which meant that their sexual choices, and all their personal relationships, were liable to surveillance and control, and to end the association of homosexuality with mental or physical illness. Although gay men and lesbians might well be deeply critical of the way heterosexuality is situated as the central normative and socially endorsed form of 'natural' sexual expression, they do not necessarily conclude that all heterosexual men and women are acting in bad faith by virtue of their sexual relationships.

In the early '70s, statements issued by American lesbian groups such as The Furies or Radicalesbians provoked a profound unease among straight feminists. Both groups, notionally a part of the radical feminist political endeavour, criticized aspects of feminist analysis which focus almost exclusively upon heterosexual relations, and whose assessment of female sexuality blindly pursues an uninterrogated heterosexual model. For lesbian feminists, the term lesbian itself is seen as in need of positive reappropriation: as the epithet so often indiscriminately hurled abusively at women who fail to 'conform', it comes to signify for lesbians the pariah who rejects conventional notions of feminine propriety. Nonetheless, many straight feminists persisted in seeing only its 'negative' connotations, and became defensive in the light of exhortations for all women to become 'lesbians'. Radicalesbians' argument in 'The Woman Identified Woman' (1970 reprinted in Koedt et al., 1973) may well on one hand be interpreted as an example of such a demand; but it is chiefly concerned with the way heterosexual feminists assume a pseudo-patriarchal perspective on lesbianism, conceiving them in purely sexual terms. However the central thrust of the Radicalesbians' argument appears to be that all sexual categories are a symptom of a patriarchal ideology that might well be transformed after a social revolution; but, that in the interim women should make other women the focus of all their political and emotional energies, not least in order fully to appreciate the effects of the dehumanization of male sexual categorization: 'Women resist relating on all levels to other women who will reflect their own oppression, their own secondary status, their own self-hate' (Radicalesbians, in Koedt et al. 1973: 244). Although Radicalesbians are relatively uncompromising on the question of where one's sexual allegiances should lie, it is clear that their primary concern is with homosocial rather than sexual bonding in a society which endeavours to reinforce the view that lesbians and 'normal' women have little in common.[2]

Heterosexual feminists tended to ignore lesbians' implied criticisms of heterosexuality as an institution, and channelled their energies into challenging any notion that lesbian sexual relationships are the only true model for liberated womanhood. This meant that heterosexual feminists of the '70s rarely scrutinized the patriarchal assumptions upon which conventional definitions of heterosexuality rest, nor did they spend much time redefining the terms of their intimate relations in line with the radical restructuring envisaged in other areas of social life. By this lack of attention they risked accepting that being heterosexual was an essential part of their being, and in this way were demonstrably less willing to consider the possibility that sexual orientation is itself a social construct, rendered meaningless if social and ideological punishments and rewards associated with illicit and licit forms of sexual expression were removed. Anne Koedt, in her essay 'Lesbianism and Feminism' (1971 reprinted in Koedt et al., 1973) establishes what she claims are points of disagreement between radical and lesbian feminists – one being lesbian feminists' reputed conviction that they form the vanguard of the women's movement, and that their sexual choices in themselves constitute a revolutionary act. Koedt is clearly antagonistic towards what she regards as a lesbian policing of sexual boundaries, although she seems to have some fairly fixed ideas of what authentic 'feminist' lesbian sexual practice should entail. In this she exemplifies a tendency towards essentialism, and therefore in her article she assumes the 'right' to disallow anything she defines as sex role playing:

> The organized gay movement seeks to protect the freedom of any homosexual, no matter what her or his individual style of homosexuality may be. This means the protection of the transvestite, the queen, the 'butch' lesbian, the couple that wants a marriage license, or the homosexual who may prefer no particular role. (Koedt et al. 1973: 251)

This is reminiscent of a sexologist's check list, complete with inaccuracies (her equation of transvestitism with homosexuality). Her attack on role-playing within homosexual encounters suggests that there is an 'authentic' form of homosexual expression that can transcend the 'patriarchal' stigma attached to such roles. Of course this begs the question as to whether role-play – for example, butch/ femme configurations – necessarily carries the same meanings as it does in heterosexual relationships, and whether the roles correspond to masculine/feminine ones in terms of the degrees of access to material and social privilege they connote. It also reminds us that ironically it is usually only heterosexual sex that is left undefined in the will to categorize 'deviance', so that 'role-playing' in that context would be a contradiction in terms. It is important to note that not all lesbians were prepared to accept the possibility that sexuality might be a fluid and contingent effect of social relations. Many felt that there must be 'correct' forms of lesbian expression, freed from the taint of patriarchy, and within lesbian feminist circles arguments about the desirability of role-playing within gay relationships still rage, informing recent critiques of lesbian sadomasochistic practices.

Koedt seems to have a fairly clear idea of what constitutes a politically correct form of homosexual relationship, by virtue of her list of unacceptable sexual identities; but nowhere does she hint at means to liberate heterosexuality from its present inequities. Neither does she consider whether any relationship can currently be free from the dynamics of power inequality – such as race, class or age – or the possibility that all homosexual 'roles' are ultimately defined and contained by a 'heteroreality' (a world view which assumes the universality of heterosexuality). Radical feminists have been adept at analysing the problems of heterosexuality, but reluctant to translate their findings into a coherent agenda for change, wary of appearing prescriptive or moralistic. Yet Koedt and others failed to perceive how homophobic and moralistic their arguments became when they felt at liberty to determine and categorize the dynamics of lesbian behaviour, just as sexologists had done before them. Koedt particularly objects to women behaving like 'men' or vice versa; although since as a radical she supports the eventual elimination of patriarchally defined gendered sex roles, her argument becomes distressingly circular, caught itself in a mesh of patriarchal logic. Disregarding for a moment questions of the advisability of establishing 'codes' of sexual practice, the inability of such writers to define a positive form of sexual expression, implies that the field of sexuality still required much further and more complex analysis. Koedt's essay is symptomatic of how straight feminists, on the defensive against the 'lavender menace' (to coin Betty Friedan's term, intended to be pejorative, but since appropriated as celebratory), became contradictory in their arguments around sexuality, contenting themselves with often counterproductive attacks upon lesbians – many of whom as feminists, otherwise shared their central political aims.

The Radicalesbians' evocation of the 'woman identified woman', is intended to be more than a depiction of sexual preference; they sought to end the competitiveness that divided women in patriarchy, thence to strengthen political and personal bonds. Their essay certainly implies that heterosexuality is a destructive force in women's lives, but suggests this is the case at present because of the tenacity of the patriarchal sex role system. The urge to categorize identity through sexual orientation would disappear, they argue, in an androgynous utopia where the social meanings attached to such 'roles' had vanished. In her essay 'Compulsory Heterosexuality and Lesbian Existence' (1980), Adrienne Rich extends the notion of the woman-identified-woman, talking instead of a 'lesbian continuum', thus further displacing the focus on sexual love and prioritizing the strength and love to be gained from female friendship and support networks. As Rich says herself, 'I mean the term lesbian continuum to include a range – through each woman's life and throughout history – of women-identified experience, not simply the fact that a woman has had or consciously desired genital sexual experience with another woman' (Rich 1986: 51). This aspect of lesbian feminism, which has become especially prominent in the analysis of literary texts, allows an important focus on something which has never been as central in much heterosexual feminist thought – that is the social and political importance of female bonding, and the means by which a patriarchal ideology attempts to suppress its importance.

In a foreword to this essay, Adrienne Rich states that the piece:

was written in part to challenge the erasure of lesbian existence from so much of scholarly feminist literature, an erasure which I felt (and feel) to be not just anti-lesbian, but anti-feminist in its consequences, and to distort the experience of heterosexual women as well. It was not written to widen divisions but to encourage heterosexual feminists to examine heterosexuality as a political institution which disempowers women – and to change it. (Rich 1986: 23)

Rich offers a point of contact between lesbian and heterosexual feminists upon the issue where the gulf between them was at its most treacherous. Her essay is at pains to indicate that the institution of heterosexuality holds sway over all women regardless of their sexual object choices, having little to do with desire or choice at all: this is heteroreality. Rich emphasizes the point that lesbianism, for many straight feminists, is chiefly a sexual category, and analyses this in relation to what she regards as a serious omission in mainstream feminism. That is, that most feminists have failed critically to evaluate the status of heterosexuality as a sexual preference which cannot be innocent of political or ideological ramifications – not least its privilege to determine the deviant status of all unproductive 'marginal' sexual orientations, and the way the denaturalization of other forms of sexual expression consolidates and strengthens patriarchal ideology. She asserts that the assumption of the normality of a heterosexual existence (lived within the parameters of monogamy and the institutional family form), enables the perpetuation of social and political control over women and sexual 'outgroups'. Rich's (and other's) extensions of the term lesbianism to embrace a lesbian continuum enables analyses of both positive and negative aspects of female bonding – such as mother–daughter relationships – which act as buffers in a patriarchal society, while often reaffirming the patriarchal status quo from generation to generation.

The institution of 'compulsory heterosexuality', Rich argues, facilitates the worldwide sexual exploitation of women from the pimp's 'protection' of the prostitute, to the battered wife's feeling of dependency and guilt towards her husband; and most of all services the supposed uncontrollability of the male sexual drive – a mythification which endorses male sexual aggression:

> Women learn to accept as natural the inevitability of this 'drive' because they receive it as dogma. Hence, marital rape; hence, the Japanese wife resignedly packing her husband's suitcase for a weekend in the kisaeng brothels of Taiwan; hence, the

psychological as well as economic imbalance of power between husband and wife, male employer and female worker, father and daughter, male professor and female student. (Rich 1986: 47)

The above has a striking resemblance to the kind of radical feminist examination of female sexuality pursued by feminists such as Andrea Dworkin and Catharine MacKinnon; except that Rich asserts that there is a 'nascent feminist political content in choosing a woman lover or life partner, in the face of institutionalized heterosexuality' (Rich 1986: 66). This statement, which might be regarded as equating the fact of lesbianism with feminist politics, is of the variety which has heterosexual feminists rushing to their own defence. Yet in her afterword she reinforces the central thrust of her highly polemical essay:

I never have maintained that heterosexual feminists are walking about in a state of 'brainwashed false consciousness' . . . In this paper I was trying to ask heterosexual feminists to examine their experience of heterosexuality critically and antagonistically to critique the institution of which they are a part, to struggle with the norm and its implications for women's freedom. (Rich 1986: 72)

This remains a statement of intent within a piece intended as a work in progress; the problems of resolving the theoretical differences between lesbian and heterosexual feminists are still developing. Whether one sees heterosexual women as colluding with the heterosexual institution and lesbian women as 'outside' of its confines is a moot point. It seems doubtful, given our present social framework, that any woman has the luxury of freedom from 'heterosexual'/patriarchal constraints, or that all heterosexual women actively collude in a hetero/patriarchy, while all lesbians are in the process of sexual revolution.

As Rich's article suggests, the lesbian feminist movement has grown and shown increased theoretical sophistication over the last decade – and it is lesbian feminism that has most categorically asserted that 'heterosexism is the set of values and structures that assumes heterosexuality to be the only natural form of sexual and emotional expression' (Zimmerman, in Greene and Kahn 1985: 179). Certainly writers such as Koedt demonstrate such a prejudice and seem to exemplify the reasons why lesbians found a need to identify themselves increasingly as lesbian instead of radical feminists.

Although the radical movement has always been regarded as predominantly lesbian in its politics, there are many instances of homophobia, which at best ignore lesbian issues, and at worst displace lesbians as the unrepresentative deviant few in the movement. This perhaps exposes fears that many women would find them an unattractive aspect of feminism, so assuming that potential feminist recruits are heterosexual while endorsing conventional views of the 'problem' of lesbianism. Radical feminists seem to have been on the whole reluctant to address instances of their own heterosexism – Anne Koedt's famous article 'The Myth of the Vaginal Orgasm' being a case in point. Presumably many lesbian women had already had their consciousness raised in that respect, and would not be heartened by her throwaway conclusion (in that she fails to consider it a serious possibility) that 'lesbian sexuality could make an excellent case . . . for the extinction of the male organ' (Koedt in Koedt et al. 1973: 206).

Lesbians could not but be aware that their private lives and object choices were susceptible to wider public scrutiny and condemnation. Since feminists were committed to politicizing the personal, they felt that feminist politics should equally address this problem, if it was believed that the private sphere mirrored broader abstract systems of power and subordination. However, feminism's supposed liberalism towards the matter of sexual orientation made homophobia – like racism – within the movement much harder to confront. Hence the problems peculiar to lesbians still tended to be ignored. Lesbians made bad publicity for feminism; they were tolerated but remained theoretically invisible – although of course 'invisibility' outside of the gay scene was already a central problem for lesbians: 'Gay people really are oppressed, although their oppression is a peculiar one since it rests partly on the possibility of always remaining hidden and invisible' (Wilson 1986: 142–3). In perceiving 'out' lesbians as a threat to feminism's coherence, heterosexual feminists colluded with the patriarchal mainstream, and provoked doubts as to whether a feminist revolution would necessarily transform the social status of homosexuals, or redefine the terms of sexuality and its expression at all. Moreover, while 'gender' was vigorously exposed as a social construct ripe for deconstruction, sexuality it seems, was not.

Heterosexual feminists, while busily dissecting stereotypes of the feminine, omitted to analyse the whole representative arena of stereotypical images of the homosexual. Although motherhood was a central issue, the problems confronting lesbian mothers, who face the constant threat of having their children taken away from them, was rarely discussed. Even if childcare was socialized along gender lines, what lesbian or gay man could feel assured that such socialization would also undermine the institutionalized heterosexual norm? Lesbians were left to debate such questions largely amongst themselves, while heterosexual feminists pursued the 'main' objectives of the movement. Their relationship with feminism's 'mainstream' remained volatile: when not seen as aggressively self-righteous, they were heroized as gatekeepers of the model relationship where jealousy, power struggles, violence and oppression had no place. Neither characterization was helpful, and the latter has created some deeprooted silences in lesbian feminism today. The more lesbians debated their political stances, the more differences they seemed to expose within their own ranks – 'on the one side was the "lesbian continuum" and woman bonding, on the other the fetishistic specificity of key codes, leather, and coloured handkerchiefs' (Wilson 1986: 180).

THE 'STIGMA' OF FEMINISM:
CONTEMPORARY LESBIAN DEBATES

In recent years, debates on the politics of role-playing have figured prominently in lesbian circles, where the split is between two main camps – those who see role-playing as empowering and transgressive, and those who maintain that it results in the inevitable return to patriarchally-defined mechanisms of power. The revolutionary lesbian feminist Sheila Jeffreys is fiercely critical of 'role-playing' lesbians, especially those who engage in sadomasochistic practices:

> Once the eroticizing of otherness and power difference is learned, then in a same-sex relationship, where another gender is absent, otherness can be reintroduced through differences of age, race, class, the practice of sadomasochism or role playing. So it is possible to construct heterosexual desire within lesbianism and heterosexual desire is plentifully evident in the practice of gay men. The opposite of heterosexual desire is the eroticising of sameness, a sameness of power, equality and mutuality. It is homosexual desire. (Jeffreys 1990: 301)

Jeffreys, in her book, *Anticlimax* (1990), defines all heterosexual and gay male relationships as sites of the enactment of unequal power relationships – the erotic need for one partner to be subordinate to another. As I think is clear from the above, she tends to characterize role-playing and sadomasochism as part of the same process, and therefore forestalls discussion about concerns around safety and violence in sadomasochism, as well as assuming that role-playing is necessarily violent and exploitative. Sadomasochism, she asserts, is contrary to a feminist agenda for change, since it reinscribes power politics within people's personal lives. She claims that some lesbians have been seduced by libertarian politics, but argues that women, as essentially socially powerless, should have no investment in creating power play in woman-to-woman relationships. Above all she asserts that homosexual desire is the eroticization of sameness; however, it is clear that the 'sameness' in an intimate relationship might have to extend beyond questions of gender to achieve mutuality and equality, when women find themselves occupying differing places on the social strata depending on class, race, age and so forth, and the meaning of these differences cannot be simply willed away through 'de-eroticization'. Although the 'ideal' form of lesbian sexuality is never expressed, it is implied as the opposite to all other forms she lists in her book (heterosexuality, gay male sex, paedophilia, trans-sexualism and so forth), as being the only recourse feminists have to revolution and the only ethical stance any woman can take.

Not surprisingly other lesbians take Jeffreys' arguments to be doctrinaire and analogous, in their perceived narrowness, to women's social purity movements of the last century.[3] Joan Nestle is representative of the opposite pole of lesbian politics, who defends butch/femme roles as giving lesbian sexuality a distinct physical presence, rather than pandering to the heterosexual preference for lesbians to remain discreetly invisible. In common with other lesbians who emphasized the playful, parodic qualities of butch/femme existence, she emphasizes its erotic potential:

> Butch-femme relationships, as I experienced them, were complex erotic statements, not phony heterosexual replicas. None of the butch women I was with, and this included a passing woman, ever presented themselves to me as men; they did announce themselves as tabooed women who were willing to identify their passion for other women by wearing clothes that symbolized the taking of responsibility. (Nestle 1987: 100)

Nestle and others felt that 'vanilla' lesbians (those who eschewed role-playing, and the use of any of the trappings of patriarchal heterosexuality) spent far too much time analysing their political function, and failed to address the fact of a lesbian's sexual desire for other women, which had little means of expression in a heterosexist society. She argues powerfully that butch/femme identities were negotiable and flexible, and that a woman could freely adopt either role according to her desire and that of her partner. Nestle denies that lesbian role-play bears any direct relationship to heterosexual dynamics; rather she insists that it is a playful merging of identities which transforms and radicalizes the originary meanings of masculinity and femininity, releasing an erotic potential that redefines the possibilities of lesbian sexuality, beyond the heterosexual register.

The possible conflicting meanings that could be derived from adopting a role or style, posed problems for those lesbian feminists who struggled to be 'politically correct'. The suspicion shared by lesbians such as Nestle that lesbian feminists attempted to suppress the sexual element of lesbianism altogether, can be paralleled by feelings among non-feminists that feminism meant giving up the fun in intimate relationships. Lillian Faderman interprets political correctness ('p.c.') in a lesbian context as meaning 'that one adhered to the various dogmas regarding dress; money; sexual behaviour; language usage; class, race, food, and ecology consciousness; political activity; and so forth . . .' (Faderman 1991: 230). However, by rejecting certain styles of dress, for example, lesbians still found themselves trapped within dominant meanings of the style they adopted – with the consequence that during the '70s 'everyone looked butch' (Faderman 1991: 231), in their disavowal of things feminine. For some lesbians, it is clear that the dogmatism of so-called lesbian feminist 'lavnecks' (lavender rednecks) was intrusive and oppressive, another symptom of de-emphasizing sex; whereas they determined to produce more sexually explicit material in a celebration of woman-to-woman desire. The '80s saw a new generation of lesbians who, reflecting the diversity of positions feminist and gay politics had spawned, rejected any notion of uniformity in their portrayal of a lesbian identity. They reintroduced a heterogeneous lesbian 'chic' (creating media-hyped phenomena such as the 'lipstick lesbian'), and inciting a return to butch/femme debates (see, for example, Ardill and O'Sullivan, *Feminist Review*, Spring 1990: 79–85), coupled with discussions about the political acceptability of sadomasochistic practices, where 'SM lesbians claim to be putting the sex back into lesbianism' (Blackman and Perry, *Feminist Review*, Spring 1990: 70). In the slow demise of feminist political activity many lesbians struck up new allegiances with gay men, particularly given the growing problem of AIDS and the new militancy it prompted in the form of 'Queer Nation' (committed to direct action around broader lesbian and gay issues – the term 'queer' being chosen, because 'gay' is often taken to just signify male homosexuals).

The '90s has witnessed the emergence of 'Queer Theory' which derives impetus from postmodern debates, and marks a shift away from lesbian feminism, which came to be associated with very narrow definitions of lesbianism that were themselves believed to be oppressive. Sheila Jeffreys' most recent book, *The Lesbian Heresy* (1994), regards the shift in the lesbian community towards a sexual identity which derives meanings from the gay male community, as part of the general backlash against feminism in society. Jeffreys' own lesbian feminist[4] position goes some way to demonstrating why a number of lesbians would find an archetypal lesbian feminist position constricting and ultimately moralistic, although her work on the backlash phenomenon is interesting and provocative. What is of more concern is that in distinguishing between 'lesbian feminism' and 'lesbians who are also feminists', Jeffreys assumes the right to determine what it means to be 'lesbian feminist' in a way that forecloses debate and renders her brand of feminism dogmatic and even dictatorial. The latter, she argues, experience their lesbianism and their feminism separately, whereas 'in lesbian feminist philosophy the theory and practice of lesbianism is constructed through feminism' (Jeffreys 1994: xi). This ignores some of the reasons why lesbians have felt their concerns to be divorced from the 'mainstream' of feminism. Nor does it acknowledge that there might be some practical difficulties for lesbians to coherently merge their lesbian with their feminist identity. It also suggests that lesbian feminism is an orthodoxy that has nothing new to learn from further scrutiny of contemporary social life. This makes her book's title, *The Lesbian Heresy* ironic, in that she regards her own conception of lesbian feminism as the heresy in contemporary lesbian/queer culture, whereas, however ambiguous and controversial the lesbian and gay theory and politics of the '90s might be, it is certainly not orthodox. One compelling aspect of her work is her observation that lesbians have moved backwards in the dominant account of their sexual orientation to essentialism and away from social constructionism. A further explanation, she suggests, of the increasing trend to return to the logic of butch/femme divisions in lesbian sexual life.

During the '90s, the most important theoretical developments in lesbian thought have been the emergence of gay and/or lesbian texts which appropriate aspects of postmodernist thought, in order to rethink the politics of identity. An example are the explorations and critiques of a lesbian 'essentialism'. As 'queer theory' (the very term suggests a postmodern departure from the certainties of fixed sexual/ social identity) has developed in academic circles, and more lesbians seem to collaborate with gay men rather than with feminists in their writings, it is necessary to question the extent to which feminists can

continue to assume a commonality of political and theoretical interests between straight and lesbian women. Second wave feminism's
almost universal belief in social constructionism rather than biological
determinism, has only equivocally (and very recently) extended to
the sexual domain. Meanwhile, gay and lesbian theorists have developed cogent and far-reaching critiques of heterosexuality – aspects of
which I shall return to in Chapter Seven.

Monique Wittig's essay, 'One is Not Born a Woman' (1981)
extends de Beauvoir's famous statement to declare that 'the refusal to
become (or to remain) heterosexual always meant to refuse to
become a man or a woman, consciously or not' (Wittig 1992: 13). In
this statement she posits 'man' and 'woman' as political rather than
essential categories, which achieve meaning through their insertion
into the discourse of heterosexuality. In common with Adrienne
Rich, Wittig sees heterosexuality as a category used to enforce
women's role as producer, simultaneously encouraging her ideologically to reproduce the conditions of existence of the heterosexual
institution. Thus, for Wittig, the category 'woman' is one imposed
upon females in order to enforce their continued exploitation and
subjugation (Wittig 1992: 11). By extension, in 'The Straight Mind'
(1980) she considers that because they refuse to be heterosexual,
'lesbians are not women' (Wittig 1992: 32).

It is interesting to speculate whether in Wittig's own logic, heterosexual feminists might refuse to be 'women' by dismantling the
patriarchal and institutional connotations of their sexual object
choices. Further, one might argue that despite their resistance to
heterosexuality as depicted by Wittig, lesbians are still implicated
within its institutional parameters. Indeed, to some extent the meanings of 'lesbian' generated by the discourses of heterosexuality may
profoundly affect their economic and personal lives, where one might
wish further to question the integrity of such ascriptions as 'lesbian'
free from repressive social formations. Wittig endows lesbians with
an agency which she denies straight women, suggesting an essentialist reading of lesbian in this context, given the polarization of
straight and lesbian identities. Diana Fuss asserts that, 'in general,
lesbian theory is less willing to question or to part with the idea of a
"lesbian essence" and an identity politics based on this shared
essence' (Fuss 1989: 98) than are gay men who have scrutinized sexuality from a social constructionist perspective. She speculates that
lesbians' tendency to adhere to essentialist assumptions around a
discrete lesbian identity may well be a result of the fact that historically and socially lesbians inhabit a more precarious subject position

than gay men. This seems to me a compelling argument, remembering how readily lesbian presence is obliterated or subsumed in the gay and feminist movements. Fuss indicates how invisibility extends into theories of sexuality such as Michel Foucault's *History of Sexuality* which 'effects a complete and total silence on the subject of lesbianism while implicitly coding homosexuality as male' (Fuss 1989: 110). These effects of lesbians' involvement in oppositional discourses, asserts Fuss, are reasons why lesbians may feel at least a need to cling to a 'fictive identity' whilst examining the 'processes of identity formation' (Fuss 1989: 112).

In *The Lesbian Heresy* Jeffreys does extensively chart the growing commercialization of lesbian culture in the '90s, which in line with the demands of advanced capitalism, admits the lesbian into the 'mainstream' as a consumer rather than as a full and equal citizen. While lesbians gain public visibility by their portrayal in popular British soaps (*Emmerdale*, *Brookside* and *Eastenders*) and the first British 'lesbian lifestyle' magazine, *Diva* was published in the Spring of 1994, 'real' lesbians are still demonized in the popular press, in particular the spectre of the 'lesbian mother'. I share some of Jeffreys' concerns that much of this attention serves the interests of the establishment more than it promotes the political concerns of the gay and lesbian community. And in her characterization of role playing lesbian defectors from feminism as in love with the idea of the lesbian outlaw who must free herself from the boring repressive straight society and the boring repressive feminist culture, Jeffreys notes with irony that,

> It is surprising in the end that sadomasochists should choose a form of outlawry which is much more acceptable to the straight world than lesbian separatism could ever be . . . In a sado-society leather and lace are more photogenic than a band of lesbian separatists and the message, that women can abuse other women and love their subordination, altogether more palatable. (Jeffreys 1994: 135)

Biddy Martin also remarks on just how much definitions of 'acceptable' lesbian sexuality have been transformed in recent years – particularly around issues of the acceptability of penetration and the use of sex toys. As she says, 'for self-respecting lesbian sadomasochists, the ante has been upped considerably in terms of what it might take to be a s/m lesbian' (in Barrett and Phillips 1992: 99). At its most extreme this sense of a paradigmatic shift in what it can mean to be a lesbian can result in a homogenization and vilification of the past, particularly the involvement of lesbian feminist politics in the construction of lesbian desire. This has resulted in a resistance to the political implications of a lesbian identity in favour of 'lifestyle' ones. This resistance is set against a currently popular perception of past feminist 'oppression'. Feminism at its most homophobic tended to stereotype the lesbian viewpoint (in the singular), which can then be consigned to a token position on the margins of its philosophy. Lesbians have responded to this over the years by creating their own definitions separate from heterosexual feminists. Jeffreys, despite many both contentious and compelling observations, seems herself to stereotype an ideal-type lesbian feminist viewpoint, which smacks of the archetype which many contemporary queer theorists wish to resist.

Jeffreys' implicit aim to attribute a certain purity to a 'proper' lesbian perspective is becoming increasingly unpopular in academic and wider circles (her work was unfavourably profiled in the first edition of *Diva* in April 1994). In general terms any mention of lesbian *feminism* in this popular context seems to conjure up spectres of tyranny and prudishness to which the new, consumerist face of 'lifestyle' lesbianism is the only antidote:

> A lot of dykes who were around in the '70s, who are very dogmatic about their version of feminism think that younger women do not care about feminism. It's as though we are the 'bad daughters' to their 'good mothers', kind of like a teenage rebellion thing. But we are just as feminist as they are. We just don't want to label ourselves with a word that conjures up such ugly images. Why should we have to be frumpy or bitter and twisted just to be a feminist? ('Generation Gaps', *Diva*, June 1994)

The above speaker replicates the common misconception that the media myths of feminism correspond to the actuality. Rose Collis ironically negotiates between images of the 'old' and 'new' lesbian image, and exposes the means by which they can become homogenized under the idea of a 'post-feminist' lesbian identity:

> They – the media and the heterosoc at large – could only perceive one kind of dyke: a crop haired, cosmetic free, dungaree clad, bollockstomper whose main fashion accessory [sic] were labryses from Lesbos, patriarch-free canvas bags and non leather shoes made in the Welsh valleys by worshippers of the goddess Clenchbuttock Spiritwombyn. Now we're in the

dead-from-the-neck-up Nineties and the rallying cry of the gay community appears to be 'we're here, we're queer, we're going shopping . . . . ' (*Diva*, April 1994)

While an 'old' lesbian identity is being shed in favour of the new, we are constantly reminded that this new 'post-feminist' lesbian version is, in part at least, a revival of a romanticization of lesbian identities of the pre-feminist '50s and '60s, with an increasing reference to the works of older lesbians such as Joan Nestle. As Biddy Martin observes, it is somewhat disheartening 'to see how often a new politics of sexuality has been formulated against feminism, rather than in a more complex relation to it' (Martin in Barrett and Phillips 1992: 117).

Chapter 5

Black Feminism: Reimagining 'Equality'

> No other group in America has so had their identity social-
> ized out of existence as have black women. We are rarely
> recognized as a group separate and distinct from black men,
> or as present part of the large group 'women' in this culture.
> When black people are talked about, sexism militates against
> the acknowledgement of the interests of black women; when
> women are talked about racism militates against a recogni-
> tion of black female interests. When black people are talked
> about the focus tends to be on black *men*; and when women
> are talked about the focus tends to be on *white* women. No
> where is this more evident than in the vast body of feminist
> literature.
>
> (hooks 1982: 7)

The most obvious link between lesbian feminists and black feminists
is their growing conviction during the early years of the second wave
that feminism's 'mainstream' regularly excluded their concerns. Both
groups were therefore fighting for visibility within a movement which
claimed to embrace their interests beneath the umbrella term of
'sisterhood', but which had developed a methodology that used as its
paradigm white, heterosexual and middle-class female experiences.
Just as lesbians encountered sexism in the gay liberation movement,
black women were encouraged to take on a domestic 'servicing' role
in the civil rights movement, which increased their sense of possessing a split identity between both the civil rights and the women's
liberation movement, neither of which took their specific needs into
account. Stokely Carmichael, for instance, became infamous for
declaring that the only position for women on the Student
Nonviolent Co-ordinating Committee is 'prone',[1] suggesting that
black and white women working in civil rights were expected to

carry out the same domestic and sexual service roles as those (white) women who became disaffected with the New Left.

According to Michele Wallace, the black feminist movement began in America in 1973, after a black feminist writer, Doris Wright, called a meeting to discuss the relation of black women to the women's movement, which resulted in the National Black Feminist Organization. She remembers,

> I was fully delighted until, true to Women's Movement form, we got bogged down in an array of ideological disputes, the primary one being lesbianism versus heterosexuality. . . . Dominated by the myths and facts of what white feminists had done and not done before us, it was nearly impossible to come to any agreement about our position on anything; and action was unthinkable. (Wallace in Hull 1982: 11)

Wallace asserts that the National Black Feminist Organization was doomed to failure from the start, because it was consciously set up in relation to white feminist's negation of black women's experience, and therefore its role became primarily that of readjusting feminism's scope. As a result of this perhaps the black women's movement in the United States[2] simultaneously inherited all the divisiveness apparent in white feminist groups. To this day many black writers and critics are uncomfortable with the term 'feminism' as tending to connote a white middle-class world view. Alice Walker, for instance, coined the epithet 'womanist', which signals many black women's concern that feminist politics might potentially create divisions between black women and black men. The 'Black Feminist Statement' from the Combahee River Collective in 1977 (reprinted in Hull 1982) was more optimistic than Wallace, and demonstrated that the National Black Feminist Organization did facilitate progress in the form of consciousness raising specifically directed at black women, and the setting up of clear agendas for intervention in and destabilization of white feminist hegemony. In Britain the Black Women's Group was formed in Brixton in 1974, and by 1980 they had established a black women's centre (Lovenduski and Randall 1993: 102), again emphasizing that black women in the United States and Britain had to organize around their ethnicity as much as their gender in order to appropriate and shape women's liberation to their specific needs. Nonetheless, as the women's movement grew, a 'mainstream' of white, heterosexual and bourgeois thought came to embody the possible meanings and definitions ascribed to feminism, accompanied by a marked reluctance on the part of such dominant feminists to address the degrees of social acceptance and privilege that they enjoyed at the expense of others.

BLACK FEMINIST POLITICS

As the black feminist bell hooks has shown, white feminism was fundamentally racist in two important ways; in 'drawing endless analogies between "women" and "blacks"', and in assuming 'that the word woman is synonymous with white woman, for women of other races are always perceived as Others, as de-humanized beings who do not fall under the heading woman' (hooks 1982: 139; 138). Here hooks raises an issue explored by Monique Wittig and Diana Fuss in relation to lesbian feminism (see Chapter Four), yet beginning from the obverse position. Wittig's view is that lesbians in rejecting heterosexuality reject the oppressive category of 'woman' as a positive oppositional political stance. hooks and other black feminists, on the other hand, aver that one aspect intrinsic to black women's struggle in the United States since slavery has been the fight to be accorded the same status of 'woman' which was, both materially and ideologically, bestowed upon white women. Second wave white feminists, in their continued rhetorical use of the two groupings, 'women' and 'blacks', clearly effaced the specific identity of black women altogether, to the point that they cannot politically lay claim to either identity without first having to engage in a battle for visibility with white women and black men. Kate Millett and Shulamith Firestone are just two examples of white radical feminists who make analogies between the social position of women and the subordinate position of racial and ethnic minorities in Western culture. Firestone states quite categorically that 'racism is sexism extended' (Firestone 1979: 104); Millett observes that 'it was the Abolitionist Movement which gave American women their first opportunity for political action and organization' (Millett 1977: 80). The anti-slavery and emerging women's movements were seen to be mutually strengthening allies in Millett's historical summary, and this had been previously reinforced by pioneer white feminists, with little regard for the crucial participation of black women. Millett goes on to assert that:

> Slavery was probably the only circumstance in American life sufficiently glaring in its injustice and monumental evil to impel women to break that taboo of decorum which stifled and controlled them more efficiently than the coil of their legal, educational and financial disabilities. (Millett 1977: 80)

While it is certainly the case that American feminists were involved in the Abolitionist Movement, Millett's use of the term 'women' in this quote obscures the fact that she is only talking about white women; and that black women active in reformist movements at the end of the nineteenth century were rarely ever allowed a voice at public meetings, and were certainly not held to possess the equal right of suffrage with white women. As hooks points out, 'when it seemed black men might get the vote while they [white women] remained disenfranchised, political solidarity was forgotten and they urged white men to allow racial solidarity to overshadow their plans to support black male suffrage' (hooks 1982: 3). The same passionate Abolitionist women revealed themselves to be uncompromisingly racist in their views; appealing for an end to slavery did not amount to advocating human equality in other areas of social and political life.

Patriarchy and imperialism caught black women in a tenacious double-bind. Whether they chose to opt for racial or sexual solidarity, either allegiance would only address half of the problem. Indeed, experience had shown black women activists that either ally tended to subsume the black female voice, so that feminism seemed to refer only to the needs of white women, and civil rights only addressed the oppression of black males. hooks traces the history of American black women's political and historical invisibility to the inception of slavery – and in terms of the effects of patriarchal/imperialistic oppressive structures, shows that they have consistently remained at the bottom of the social pile just as they have remained at the bottom of all radical political agendas. In a spirited rebuttal of the analogies drawn by white feminists between black experience and female subordination, she argues that such parallels effectively exclude black women as a category in any analysis of gendered or racial oppression:

> Like many people in our racist society white feminists could feel perfectly comfortable writing books or articles on the 'woman question' in which they drew analogies between 'women' and 'blacks'. Since analogies derive their power, their appeal, and their very reason for being from the sense of two disparate phenomena having been brought closer together, for white women to acknowledge the overlap between the terms 'black' and 'women' would render this analogy unnecessary. By continuously making this analogy, they unwittingly suggest that to them the term 'woman' is synonymous with 'white

women' and the term 'blacks' synonymous with 'black men'.
What this indicates is that there exists in the language of the
very movement that is supposedly concerned with eliminating
sexist oppression, a sexist-racist attitude toward black women.
(hooks 1982: 8)

It is this linguistic conflation which hooks upholds as symbolic of the
invisibility of black women in most analyses of social life. What she
alerts us to most strongly is that although white feminists tacitly
'assumed that identifying oneself as oppressed freed one from being
an oppressor' (hooks 1982: 9), such women still retained racist
assumptions which weakened their notion of a universal sisterhood,
since women of colour were always already erased. In common with
lesbians, black women recognized that white heterosexual feminists
conceived of the women's movement as their 'own' – and the consideration of women who experienced oppression not only because of
the fact of their biological sex, was implicitly seen as detracting from
the main 'business' of feminism.

Since the predominantly radical feminist trend in the USA and the
socialist feminist tradition in the UK were advocating nothing less
than a transformation of the entire social fabric of Western life
through a revolution in consciousness, it was clearly a fatal flaw in
1970s' feminist politics not to recognize the dynamic interrelation
between issues of race and gender for black women. Given that their
vision of a transformed society did not explicitly include racial equality, it gave the lie to the assumption that the social status of all
women in American society (for instance) was the same. While it
homogenized female experience, it also alienated those women who
arguably suffered most due to the racist/sexist framework embedded
within Western society. White women involved in radical political
groups during the 1960s and 1970s were forced to come to terms
with the sexist structuring of such organizations and had departed,
concluding that the social revolutions envisaged beneath the rhetoric
were actually entirely male-oriented. But they offered little solace to
their black sisters, in that they denied that the 'mainstream' feminist
analysis of female oppression was flawed and narrow in its focus, or
that being a feminist did not immunize one from being racist. By
seeming to assert that gendered oppression was the most fundamental
form of power relationship in contemporary society, white feminists
implied that other forms of oppression were less crucial or tenacious,
or that advocates of sexual equality were automatically committed to

total social equality in all areas. Feminism's racism became all the more hard to confront by being rendered invisible, a non-issue.

During the '70s, white feminist's commitment to discussions of the effects of sexism only was to a large extent a reaction against the patriarchal structuring of political groups which effectively outlawed discussion of issues relevant to women. For this reason it was commonly felt that, for an interim period at least, analyses of 'related' issues, such as class and race, needed to be shelved to make space for this neglected area of study. Of course such a division denies any investigation of the complex and diverse means by which women are positioned in society as subjects bounded and contained by ascriptions of their class, race, gender and sexual orientation. What black feminists have made abundantly clear is that 'women's issues' considered without a conscious acknowledgement of other oppressive mechanisms at work in society, does not even work productively at a theoretical level, and neither does it accord with most women's lived experiences of oppression. Feminists assuredly need to focus upon social injustices which only affect women, but without a thorough awareness of the differences that divide women into sometime oppressors, as well as part of the oppressed, the political scope of feminism is necessarily curtailed. To some extent modern feminism considered itself an 'organization' which is simply concerned to question all women's basic right to equality. Therefore the specific problems confronting black women and women from other ethnic groups could be satisfactorily accommodated within a gender-specific framework, neglecting the complexities of racist oppression whoever it may affect - in both material and ideological terms. It is clear that there are problems with the maintenance of political boundaries between anti-racist and feminist movements, which preclude any analysis of the complex ways power operates, and the ways the 'powerless' are encouraged to weigh certain interests against those of differently configured groups, despite sharing common ground in the fact of their oppression.

bell hooks locates modern white feminism's central problem as a failure to interrogate the dynamics of power: if feminism at some level wishes to wrest power from men, the meaning of such power relations require transformation:

> Women's liberationists, white and black, will always be at odds
> with one another as long as our idea of liberation is based on
> having the power white men have. For that power denies unity,

denies common connections, and is inherently divisive as a
natural order that has caused black and white women to cling
religiously to the belief that bonding across racial boundaries is
impossible, to passively accept the notion that the distances
that separate women are immutable. (hooks 1982: 156)

Here she implies that divisions between black and white feminists
are sustained because patriarchal notions of racial and class division
are left intact, despite the fact that feminists are largely committed
to radical social change, which might anticipate a dismantling of
imperialist and capitalist social realities. hooks highlights a tension
that I have already hinted at in my examination of lesbian feminist
critiques: that feminists do not consistently deny such social divisions' validity, and that therefore a future feminist utopia might be
one which retains certain aspects of a social hierarchy intact.

Black feminists writing in the 1970s and 1980s have found little
analysis that enables them to theorize about the black female experience, or upon the ways that negative images of black women are
perpetuated throughout cultural history. In a very real sense black
feminists had little option but to work outside the preordained
parameters of the 'mainstream' women's movement, and start from
scratch; exploring the history of black women in the USA, Europe
and the so-called 'Third World', and creating a discourse that incorporates the problems of both race and gender. Because of all these
factors, coupled with the observable fact that there is still a lamentable
shortage of black female academics in the institution (a material reality that is rarely protested against by white women), black feminism
is still in a period of relative infancy. With reference to the specific
problems encountered by black feminist literary critics, Barbara
Smith observes that:

> There is no political presence that demands a minimal level of
> consciousness and respect from those who write and talk about
> our lives . . . there is not a developed body of black feminist
> political theory whose assumptions could be used in the study
> of black women's art. When black women's books are dealt with
> at all, it is usually in the context of black literature which
> largely ignores the implications of sexual politics. When white
> women look at black women's works they are of course ill-
> equipped to deal with the subtleties of racial politics. A black
> feminist approach to literature that embodies the realization
> that the politics of sex as well as the politics of race and class

are crucially interlocking factors in the works of black women writers is an absolute necessity. (Newton and Rosenfelt 1985: 5)

In the field of literary theory, black feminists have devoted their efforts to producing a black positive methodology, which can analyse and contextualize the work of black women writers in particular and which also confronts and comments extensively upon their absence in literary criticism produced by white women.[3] Black voices and experience are at best under-represented and at worst excluded from discussions which produced a feminist theoretical stance that affords a partial and ethnocentric discussion of questions of gender. More recently black feminists have argued that as a consequence, white feminism does not simply ignore the specificity of the black female experience, it also occludes and distorts the nature of those problems peculiar to black female existence in a profoundly ethnocentric fashion.

Even towards the late '70s one of the chief obstacles facing a developing black section of the women's movement which might further interrogate the partial view of existing feminist thought, whilst developing a stronger and more challenging gender/race-oriented perspective, was the inherent racism of white feminists. As I suggested earlier, what made this difficult to confront and overcome was that white feminists almost universally denied its existence. In Britain, Pratibha Parmar reports an incident where she and Kum-Kum Bhavnani submitted an article on 'Racism and the Women's Movement' to *Spare Rib* which argued that the women's movement had never taken seriously the issue of racism within its ranks, and pointing out the anomalous relationship of black women to feminism. The article was rejected by the collective who stated, 'We didn't really feel your article could form a basis for discussion inside the feminist community as it betrays so many misconceptions about the movement's history' (Parmar, *Feminist Review*, No. 31, 1989: 56). According to Parmar's account, the rejection is based on the inference that a select group of (white) women are the keepers of feminism's history, in the powerful elitist position to suppress critiques of their own hegemony which maintains intact unequivocal 'truths' about feminism. The use of the word 'community' belies the inequitable, exclusionary formation of many white feminist groups. Unfortunately it seems to be the case that white feminists have been to some extent responsible for stunting the growth of black feminist theorists in what can only be interpreted as a wish, conscious or internalized, to limit the purview of any feminist perspective to an ethnocentric one. This perspective, in attempting to strengthen the rhetoric of community and universal sisterhood, evades debates which threaten to rupture such fictional unity. Black feminists in the USA and Europe point out that such a specious form of cohesion is bought dear, when it highlights traces of an imperialist power struggle within a movement that purports to deconstruct male-oriented power principles.

FISSURES IN THE WHITE FEMINIST AGENDA:
THE FAMILY, FEMININITY, HEALTH AND POWER

White radical and socialist feminists were committed to an attack on the male-dominated social system – whether they happily termed this patriarchy or not. Consequently they focused upon institutions which shored up patriarchy, such as the family. Conversely, black feminists were faced with the reality that the family forms they experienced were more often than not the only cushion against systematic racism in the public sphere, even if the familial ideology outlined by white feminists also held sway over black communities in different degrees. In addition black feminists set out to combat the tenacious myth that black communities were largely matriarchal in their form, where 'matriarchal' was taken to connote effective material female power which had therefore emasculated black manhood, depriving him of his 'rightful' role as head of the household. Analyses of the matriarchal structure of the black family in the USA circulated during the '60s, and Angela Davis cites Daniel Moynihan's *The Negro Family: The Case for National Action*, published by the US Department of Labor in 1965, as a powerful and influential example of such a thesis. Moynihan had linked contemporary social and economic problems of the black community to their matrilocal structure, and called for the introduction of male authority in the black family system. Such a position ascribes women greater power than they can conceivably have had, and fails to take account of the evidence that black women, like most working-class white women, never had the luxurious position of angel in the house, but always had a clear-cut economic role to perform.[4]

It was pointed out by black feminists that the origins of the matriarchy theory lay in the legacy of women's labour during slavery, where many were required to perform tasks identified as 'masculine' in the white consciousness of men and women's work:

To explain the black females' ability to survive without the direct aid of a male and her ability to perform tasks that were culturally defined as 'male' work, white males argued that black slave women were not 'real' women but were masculinized sub-human creatures. It is not unlikely that white men feared that white women, witnessing the black female slave's ability to cope as effectively in the work force as men, might develop ideas about social equality between the sexes and encourage political solidarity between black and white women. (hooks 1982: 71)

If black women were seen as a potential threat, the real economic situation belies such a vision of strength since, 'at the very time sociologists proclaimed the existence of a matriarchal order in the black family structure, black women represented one of the largest socially and economically deprived groups in America' (hooks 1982: 72). Such a thesis could potentially divide the black community, prompting black men to blame black women for their 'emasculation', and not a sexist and imperialist economic system which exploited black women's labour as the cheapest. Black women might well be their family's 'breadwinner' by default; but perspectives such as Moynihan's demonstrate how black men were encouraged to believe that their 'natural' role as household head had been usurped, and black women's 'femininity' compromised. In Britain within the Afro-Caribbean community, the majority of households are headed by a single (usually female) parent (see Lovenduski and Randall 1993: 82); this fact alone often results in severe financial hardship and its incident educational and social disadvantages (see also Phoenix in Lovell 1990: 117–33).

Feminists were also remiss in assuming that the dynamics within family life would be roughly identical across racial and class divides. A significant distinction which has been called to attention by numerous black feminist writers is the tradition of 'othermothering' in African-American families, a custom thought to be derived from African family forms. 'Othermothers' are defined by Stanlie M. James as:

> those who assist blood mothers in the responsibilities of child care for short- to long-term periods, in informal or formal arrangements. They can be, but are not confined to, such blood relatives as grandmothers, sisters, aunts, cousins or supportive fictive kin. They not only serve to relieve some of the stress that can develop in the intimate daily relationships of mothers and

daughters but they can also provide multiple role models for children. (James and Busia 1993: 45)

As this suggests the role of 'othermothers' is not simply that of providing support to the natural mother in practical and caring matters, but it is often also an important and long-term mentoring role. James, in common with other black feminists, suggests that the legacy of othermothering has led black women to recognize a responsibility for their community without parallel among white women's normal experience, and also to feel that the success of one of its members is a shared victory (see Collins 1990). The relationship of black women to both mothers and othermothers suggests that these bonds have created a long held tradition of mutual support, itself conducive to feminist politics.

An imperialist system had designated black women unfeminine and even sub-human, therefore the representations of womanhood black feminists concentrated upon were those that excluded them as women (positing the white woman as the paradigm of feminine beauty), or which situated them as purely sexual creatures, available to black and white men alike. Mainstream feminist images criticism paid scant attention to representations of black women, and black feminists were accordingly critical of an analytical model which sought to claim the right to redefine what it is to be female, while ignoring black women's endeavours to gain the right to be identified as 'human'. At the very least black feminist analyses of images of black versus white womanhood posed a redefinition of the means by which 'femininity' has been deployed as an ideal type standard of attractiveness and social acceptability. It showed that black women were not so much burdened by the feminine ideal as denied any access to it by the almost wholesale institution of the white female as the paradigm of the feminine. White women were, in addition, regarded as instrumental in the perpetuation of such imagery, derived from the slave era, which tacitly accepted and reinforced the differences between white and black women as if they were immutable. Images criticism was bound up with accounting for the seemingly timeless and universal construction of the feminine as passive, frail, but white. It ignored black women's relationships to such images, and, for American black women one of their incontrovertible sources: 'the controlling images of black women that originated during the slave era attest to the ideological dimension of black women's oppression' (Collins 1990: 7). The black woman was characterized as unfeminine, promiscuous, as a woman who cannot be raped because she herself is indiscriminately sexually voracious; this is set against the view of black men as the rapist incarnate. Feminist 'Reclaim the Night' marches which often passed through predominantly black areas in America angered black women as evidence that the stereotype of the sexualized black man prevailed among white women unscrutinized (see Davis 1982: 172–201). Stereotypes which embrace different ethnic communities in different ways throw up additional issues far removed from the experience of white women, even though the rhetoric of white feminism theoretically broaches them. One example would be the treatment Asian women have received at the hands of British immigration officials, which in the past has included forced intimate examinations. Asian women in Britain have specific needs around issues such as domestic violence, not only because of their experience of racism and stereotypical assumptions made by the police and judiciary, but because they are often under pressure from the wider Asian community to remain silent about such matters. Their sense, often of double betrayal, meant that they did not always feel comfortable in the environment of a women's refuge. At the extreme end some women who felt obliged to endure their husband's violence might resort to killing them in self defence. Southall Black Sisters, formed in 1979, has done much to help such women and to publicize the experiences of women such as Kiranjit Aluwalia who was jailed for the murder of her husband. Southall Black Sisters argued that the plea of provocation should include circumstances involving a lengthy period of physical or mental abuse.

Similarly, debates around reproductive rights in the '70s were greeted with much scepticism by black feminists, who still retained the memory of the rising popularity of the eugenicist movement in the early years of the twentieth century. In the United States the Eugenics Society 'could boast that at least twenty-six states had passed compulsory sterilization laws and that thousands of "unfit" persons had already been surgically prevented from reproducing' (Davis 1982: 214). Although white feminists vigorously campaigned for legal abortions, they failed to acknowledge that the chief source of the problem was among women of colour who comprised 80 per cent of the mortality rate from illegal abortions in the years preceding its decriminalization in the States (Davis 1982: 204). Black women were only likely to seek professional medical aid as a last resort, fearing repercussions as a result of having illegal abortions, which might explain why, 'long after the majority of "granny" midwives in other ethnic groups had been replaced by medical based hospital practices, there were still hundreds of Black lay midwives practising in the deep South, with midwifery lineages extending as far back as slavery' (Ross in James and Busia 1993: 150–1). Black women in both Britain and the USA wanted other measures to be tabled in tandem to abortion legislation – matters such as that of compulsory sterilization, since sterilization abuse, when figures were obtained, was seen to be a widespread problem, as was the use of Depo-Provera, with its incident risks of breast and cervical cancer (OWAAD in Feminist Anthology Collective, 1981: 145–9). In many cases black women seemed to suffer higher incidence of poor physical and mental health than their white and black male counterparts, and in addition are more likely to be the victims of violent crime, especially rape. When it comes to assessing the factors that mean black women are the most vulnerable to illness, violence, poverty and low status, it is clear that they experience 'double jeopardy' (see Barbee and Little in James and Busia 1993: 182–99) in the form of racial and sexual oppression. Further, the problems associated, for example, with ill-health are inextricably linked to the social economic and ideological inequities which disproportionately affect black women.

IDENTITY AND ESSENTIALISM

Feminists such as Pratibha Parmar recognize that just as some issues raised around sexual difference lead us back to the old essentialist arguments utilized to maintain women in a subordinate and quantitively different role, so the notion of 'blackness' can carry essentialist overtones. A black feminist movement established on the grounds of certain seemingly irreconcilable differences with white women, has then to come to terms with its own range and diversity: 'racial identity alone cannot be a basis for collective organizing as the black communities are as beset with divisions around culture, sexuality and class as any other community' (Parmar, *Feminist Review*, No. 31, 1989: 59). The will to categorize differences between women in order to deflect from the sometimes oppressive and offensive notions of 'sisterhood' has resulted in an identity politics within feminism, which though productive in its positive affirmation of heterogeneity, threatens to divert the essence of feminist debate away from the aim of radicalizing a viable political stance, towards the internal politics which almost always seem to assert a hierarchy of authenticity. Many feminists now recognize the need to critique all essentialist notions of 'self' as something absolute and unchanging, in favour of an 'anti-humanist' concept of subjectivity,[5] but as I shall further explore later in this volume, the will to dispense with a high liberal (and deeply entrenched patriarchal) notion of liberalism does not necessarily facilitate the effective disposal of overarching political communities based on identity, since the ability to lay claim to shared experiences of social life is often a vital step in political action.

In the feminist context, bell hooks puts forward the idea of 'solidarity' to replace the overused term 'sisterhood' because, 'the emphasis on Sisterhood was often seen as the emotional appeal masking the opportunism of manipulative bourgeois white women' (hooks in *Feminist Review*, No. 23, 1986: 127), shielding the bald fact that women can and do oppress women. She further argues that the call for sisterhood on the basis of common oppression as women is a call to acknowledge the nature of our victimization and to celebrate as victims rather than push for a rejection of such subject positioning. Ultimately, bonding as 'victims' implies there is no place for strong assertive women (the recurrent stereotypical view of black women in popular Western mythology) in the Women's Movement. She perceives that: 'Ironically, the women who were most eager to be seen as "victims", who overwhelmingly stressed the role of victim, were more privileged and powerful than the vast majority of women in our society' (hooks, *Feminist Review*, No. 23, 1986: 128). The concentration on a shared status as victim, she argues, prevents women from analysing the complexity of their own responses to other women, as well as men; in particular the way sexism, racism, classism and homophobia are perpetuated and naturalized within social groupings to the extent that 'sisterhood became yet another shield against reality, another support system' (hooks, *Feminist Review*, No. 23, 1986: 129). But even today, when there is a recognition on one level that women's social experiences are affected by the processes of racism and imperialism, there is a sense that the movement 'belongs' to the dominant white, heterosexual faction, who are in the privileged hegemonic position of being able to 'invite' other voices, and 'place themselves in the position of "authorities" who must mediate communication between racist white women (naturally they see themselves as having come to terms with their racism) and angry black women whom they believe are incapable of rational discourse' (hooks 1984: 12). Here hooks suggests that white feminists tend to assume a position of superiority over black women whose anger must be quelled as if, in some sense, it is not justified, simply because it is considered to be inappropriate.

Black and lesbian feminist tendencies have been instrumental in constructing a methodology which is able to take account of the effect of other totalizing social factors upon women. If what can be defined as feminist theory remains the prerogative of the white mainstream, black feminists are doubly disadvantaged by an educational system that has historically allowed them limited access to higher education. Many black feminist writers might not 'qualify' as intellectuals in the patriarchal sense in terms of their education; in addition they are always trying to write themselves out of a tradition which has previously successfully absorbed oppositional black perspectives: 'Reclaiming the Black feminist intellectual tradition involves much more than developing Black feminist analyses using standard epistemological criteria. It also involves challenging the very definitions of intellectual discourse' (Collins 1990: 15). The forms of black feminist analysis most likely to find their way into white dominated anthologies appear to be those that most conform to the norms of high theoretical discourse today. And yet there exists, as bell hooks points out, a long informal history of black cultural criticism – 'unfortunately, all that counter-hegemonic cultural criticism that had been honed and developed in black living rooms, kitchens, barber shops, and beauty parlors did not surface in a different form' (hooks 1991: 4). Most feminists intend to transform current epistemological definitions, and both black and lesbian feminism have usefully extended the boundaries of feminist discourse to demonstrate that a patriarchal ideology also supports a racist and heterosexist one. This is something white heterosexual feminists need themselves to counter and actively reject. In classical imperialist universalizing fashion, it is still to some extent the case that black women in academe are assumed to specialize in black women's experience, whereas white feminists, by implication, specialize in all women's lives.

Many radical and socialist white feminists now accept that they were misguided in situating sexism as the 'oldest' form of oppression, since this implies that gendered oppression deserves attention before problems of racism, classism or homophobia – 'suggesting a hierarchy of oppression exists, with sexism in first place, evokes a sense of competing concerns that is unnecessary' (hooks 1984: 35). While many 'mainstream' feminists attempt to incorporate black and lesbian perspectives into their analyses, there is still much theoretical work to be done before the point is reached where the patriarchal meanings of such differences are no longer entrenched in feminist thought. Meanwhile lesbian and black feminists are variously 'accused' of being the maverick groups who fragmented the women's movement; here is, for example, Lynne Segal's statement that the '80s 'has been a decade of increased fragmentation within the women's movement, with the emergence of divisions between women and the growth of Black feminist perspectives' (Segal 1987: ix). Although Segal devotes a few pages of *Is The Future Female?* (1987) to a consideration of black perspectives, her statement might be interpreted as implying that such a fragmentation is necessarily destructive, and a fault of black women. The degree of 'unity' that ever existed within the women's movement is, as I have already suggested, a subject of controversy; but it seems clear that what unity existed, did so at the expense of black, lesbian and working-class women. The addition of prefixes such as 'black' or 'lesbian' to feminism do on one hand very forcefully indicate the extent of exclusionary processes that had become entrenched in feminist politics well before the inception of the second wave. Such prefixes were a vital means to identify points of dispute around feminist politics and methodology, and to contest the sense that a feminism which constructed an agenda around the white heterosexual middle-class 'norm' was an incomplete and often inadequate model of female experience. They also signalled wings of feminism that (unlike mainstream radicals) found it crucial to maintain political and ideological links with organizations or communities that addressed the needs of men as well as women.

Black feminism has grown and flourished and now takes an important part in debates on postcolonialist theory and in questions of difference and ethnicity. The organization and activism of African-American women has helped to encourage other groups of non-white women to scrutinize the ethnocentrism and racism of dominant strands in the women's movement. This creation of space to question notions of difference and racial, sexual and economic identity within the category 'woman', and examinations of the imperialist assumptions which have underpinned Western feminism has enabled feminist research and activity in other countries and cultures to receive further more substantial attention. Black feminists in particular have paid attention to the material lives and work of women in the nations of Africa (see James and Busia 1993). In addition work by feminists from Islamic republics and from the Indian sub-continent is becoming more widely available. Its focus on material and ideological effects of women's subordination in varying contexts both emphasizes the importance of acknowledging the infinite variety of women's experiences of subjugation across continents and cultures, and importantly serves to remind us that the maintenance of an increasingly sophisticated feminist opposition to perpetuation of a post-capitalist patriarchal ideology which is global in its scope and tenacity is crucial.[6]

Latterly, too, black African-American feminists have felt able to begin to scrutinize the cultural images of black people generated by black people more critically; bell hook hypothesises that consumer capitalism and its growing impact on black communities has made them – around the issue of identity – an increasingly passive and depoliticized audience. She is aware that a growing acceptance of tokenistic cultural productions by black men and women can be seen to represent the political stance of the 'black community' even though their offerings may be politically conservative: 'our creative work is shaped by a market that reflects white supremacist values and concerns' (hooks 1991: 18). She suggests that, for example, novels about the black male oppression of black females might be more marketable than a novel which depicts the white racist oppression of black people in general. This certainly seems to be borne out by the popularity of such texts as *The Color Purple* (1982), which in part questions power relationships between men and women and was latterly given a cosmetic overhaul by Stephen Spielberg. In addition hooks asserts that the academic environment of feminism can only undercut gestures towards sisterhood, since in order to get on or simply get by, women are encouraged to supplant and negate each other's work. This competitive environment equally extends to black feminists seeking a platform in a white dominant academic community that gives very few spaces to women of colour: 'Often in white settings we are like siblings fighting for the approval of "white parents" whose attention we now have' (hooks 1991: 92). This also reflects the unavoidable fact that academic black women's main audience (in terms of sheer numbers) will be whites, and that they have to tailor their work to the needs of this audience, possibly over and above the needs of black women, unless they achieve the success of someone like bell hooks. As the black feminist community has expanded, so differences between groups within this umbrella term have been highlighted. The term 'black' itself can be seen as a controversial one in its token embracing of Afro-American, Chicano and Asian women to name a few, not to mention clashes around sexual orientation within communities. In Britain, too, splintering around the identity of 'black' seems to be common where 'black groups in the 1980s brought together women of either Afro-Caribbean or Asian origin; mixed groups are the exception' (Lovenduski and Randall 1993: 83).[7]

Part Two

Crisis in Feminism?

Chapter 6

Crisis in Feminism?: Feminist Debates in the '80s and '90s

> If feminism is to liberate women, it must address virtually all forms of domination because women fill the ranks of every category of oppressed people. Indeed, the ontological status of woman and even of women has shifted for academic feminists in light of influential arguments showing that women, per se, do not exist. There exist upper-caste Indian little girls; older, heterosexual Latinas; and white, working-class lesbians. Each lives at a different node in the web of oppressions. Thus, to refer to a liberatory project as 'feminist' cannot mean that it is only for or about 'women', but that it is informed by or consistent with feminism. It seeks, in current feminist parlance, to unmake the web of oppressions and reweave the web of life.
>
> (Alcoff and Potter 1993: 4)

I hope that the first section of this book has helped to clarify some of the main political divisions that have existed in feminist thought since the late '60s. For my part, it has helped to lay essential ground-work before considering the fate of feminism, as a political wave and as a body of knowledge, in the '80s and '90s. In any case, the useful-ness of dividing feminism into 'strands' is called into question from the latter part of the '80s to the present day; the divisions radical, Marxist and liberal feminism, for instance, 'no longer capture the salient features of the multiple ways in which current feminist theories interact with dominant socio-political theories' (Gatens in Barrett and Phillips 1992: 120). Perhaps the most troubling aspect of feminism is the fact of its own heterogeneity. This makes for a satisfying and enabling cross-fertilization of ideas, but it also results in a sense of imminent crisis in the processes of feminist criticism.

The main purpose of this chapter is to initiate some of the crucial debates in feminism for the '90s. I shall then proceed to chart in detail four major points of disagreement and potential 'crisis' in academic feminism in the following chapters. I hope to suggest that, although these debates are at their most heated in the academy, they have ramifications for political activity beyond scholarly discourse. These four areas – sexuality, men in feminism, postmodernism and 'post-feminism' – are, of course, by no means exhaustive. Yet they are broad sites of intense activity and disagreement which have the force to create more far-reaching reverberations. In addition, this chapter will briefly chart the stages in feminism's 'crisis', suggesting some possible causes and both positive and negative effects of feminism as mature discourse.

THE 'F' WORD: WHAT HAPPENED TO
SECOND WAVE FEMINISM?

In academic circles a 'crisis' in feminism is documented during the mid-'80s, in particular; and this crisis seems initially to be triggered by the recognition that political feminism had gone into such a rapid decline. The danger was that feminism, remaining chiefly as academic discourse, would become politically ineffective; moreover, feminism's place in the institution might defuse its radical thrust altogether. The feminist publications of the mid-'80s seemed to be dominated by summaries, retrospectives and anthologies reprinting pathfinding feminist essays – readers to enable people to 'get by' in feminism. On the face of it this might be seen to reflect a period of renewed interest in feminist thought by a new generation of readers too young, like myself, to experience the birth of feminism's second wave in the late 1960s. Yet one can detect among these writings a note of anxiety, a sense of impending crisis, best illustrated by the publication of Juliet Mitchell's and Ann Oakley's selection of essays entitled *What is Feminism?* (1986). The use of the present tense in the title could not conceal the fact that many of the contributors slipped uneasily into the past tense, and seemed to be asking, 'What was feminism?'.

This trend for nostalgia in contemporary feminist thought was paralleled by a tendency towards amnesia about the achievements of feminist politics in the '70s. Feminism in academe began to consolidate its own position and create its own 'canon' of writings believed to represent a formidable force in contemporary thought. Yet, like other radical political movements, it seemed to lose its edge, not to mention its sense of direction. Both nostalgia and amnesia were produced by the recognition that inner tensions threatened to tear the women's movement apart. Although a dynamic aspect of a developing and challenging body of thought, feminism's heterogeneity was also perceived to be potentially destructive. Certainly many felt that divisions were becoming acrimonious. It was not simply that it became redundant or simply misguided to talk about female experience and feminism in the singular; there seemed to be a tendency to attempt 'ownership' of feminism by the hostile discrediting of another's perspective, particularly through invidious hierarchies of identity politics. A more positive breakthrough of the '80s was the realization that feminism had come of age; feminists could articulate their own position in relation to other forms of academic and political discourse, in spite of the academic mainstream's tendency to render feminist insights of marginal concern. One problem with this new theoretical awareness has been an increased disjunction between feminist theory (as an academic growth industry) and feminist politics – any actual development of the social ramifications of feminism as a body of thought (or 'bodies of thoughts', more properly) which is actively engaged in affirming the need for social change.

Perhaps it is in the nature of academic pursuits to suffer to some degree from a theory/practice dichotomy. In the area of feminist theory attempts have been made to heal this rift by arguing that feminist interventions in the academic sphere are themselves political acts, since they expose other inequities within the institution. Nevertheless, this form of praxis safely occurs within the confines of the classroom: a more pressing concern in face of such a marked cleavage is how to forge a more convincing link between academic and political feminism.[1] Generally speaking it is easy to become complacent in the knowledge that academic debate is of itself a matter of sexual politics. Now, well into the '90s, one needs to realize that second wave feminism has undergone a massive epistemological transformation, and not all the changes in the shape of feminism remain directed at the original goals. A symptom of latter-day feminist theory has been to interrogate internal divisions as a feature of its critique, particularly in a recognition of the importance of theorizing about and reflecting upon the significance of conflicting subject-positions within feminism. This has the positive effect of demonstrating that feminism has the theoretical maturity to reflect upon its own processes. The obverse effect is, of course, that self-reflection begins to take over from reflection upon the original object of study. By the mid-'80s many had commented on the stasis evident

within feminism, coupled with the worrying sense that the time for
feminist protest, outside the academic environment, was at an end.

   In this period of self-reflection and in the sweep of disparate,
complex and challenging theoretical positions from many quarters, it
is easy to forget the 'atheoretical' origins of early Anglo-American
feminism with its uncompromisingly pragmatic location in the politics of experience. However, much of the feminist work that is now
casually ignored on the grounds that it has been superseded and its
lessons learned, holds some vital clues to the development of feminism's 'crisis' in the first place. There has been a tendency among
contemporary commentators to over-simplify the scope of early
second wave work; part of my endeavour has been to identify the
most challenging and complex aspects of these texts, in order to
show how they might be utilized today. Despite all the stumbling
blocks to attempts to pull together the issues raised by various interest groups within feminism, there is a point at which this is the only
way to proceed using feminism's recent past to reflect upon its present rather than the reverse. British feminist politics has always
shown a tendency to operate at one remove from mainstream parliamentary politics and social institutions – perhaps rightly feminists
have regarded the prospect of fully integrating into such a phallocentric stronghold with profound suspicion. Liberal feminists in the
USA have more successfully entered mainstream politics with
reformist zeal, supported by networks such as the National Organization for Women (NOW), founded in 1966. British and American
feminisms share many of the same trends and influences, except
perhaps that British feminism has traditionally favoured a loosely
'socialist' rather than liberal political position. What is exciting about
Anglo-American feminism is the fact of its heterogeneity – that the
political awakenings of groups of feminists are diverse and multiple
– yet this lack of common ground has latterly resulted in numerous
disagreements. Feminism's investment in interrogating contemporary
social life has, to some extent, been compromised by internal divisions which rarely focuses on the one most crucial issue – that of
the 'ownership' of feminism. This question of ownership becomes
more pressing in the '90s in the wake of pro-female, but often anti-
feminist statements, which may be passed off misleadingly as a new
'wave' of feminism, although their content seems set to persuade
women that their fight for equality is misguided, and that this is in
fact the source of much malaise. In latter chapters I shall explicitly
blur boundaries between conflicting feminisms in an attempt to seek
an 'ethics' of heterogeneity, and to argue that even when feminism is

considered to be a veritable battleground, what is common to feminists is far more extensive and enriching than is currently acknowledged. Although it might be true to say that some of the differences in feminist theory and practice are irreconcilable at the present time, it is clear that the common features of contemporary feminisms might be usefully re-examined in order to seek a way out of the critical impasse that best characterizes feminist writings and feminist politics today.[2]

It seems to me that there have been three broad stages in the growth of feminist thought from the '60s to the '90s which might be articulated as a movement from creativity to sophistication to relative stasis.[3] These 'stages' are, of course, purely notional – intended as a useful means of critical shorthand for the reader. As I have previously suggested, although feminists in general agree some basic principles about the factors contributing to women's oppression in society and culture, they have very different ideas about how to resolve these problems, and this remains the case today. Yet from the mid-'80s there has been a tendency to regard inner tensions in the women's movement as a symptom of feminism's coming of age, correlative with the growth of feminism and women's studies into academic disciplines. Juliet Mitchell, for one, harks back with nostalgia to the 'heady days' of '60s protest when sisterhood seemed powerful (Mitchell and Oakley 1986: 34–48). It is more probably the case that tensions were always simmering under the surface of feminist politics, but that the seriousness of some conflicts came to a head when black women, lesbians and working-class women used feminist discourse to articulate their sense of exclusion from its 'mainstream', and in doing so suggested that feminism was quite seriously flawed in its modern conceptualization. Perhaps, therefore, an illusion of solidarity had been created because during the '70s feminism remained, primarily, the province of highly educated, white middle-class heterosexual women. What seems to create the main antagonisms within feminism is the fear that feminism, in common with other radical societal perspectives, will inevitably replicate social hierarchies, thinly veiled by the rhetoric of universal sisterhood. The increased presence of warring female identities necessarily shifted the terms for debate – women could no longer be certain that they meant the same thing when discussing their own experiences of social oppression. To some extent the glorious slogan of radical feminism, 'the personal is political', had backfired. The development of an increasingly complex 'politics of identity' meant women found they had less, not more, in common and a bitterness developed in the will to discover who had the most 'authentic' voice for the women's movement. In other words, who had also been oppressed in terms of her race, class, disability or sexual orientation, by her feminist sisters. Kathryn Harriss observes that by 1983:

> An obsession seized the movement for self-labelling and labelling others, not to elucidate debate but to fix a woman somewhere along a predetermined hierarchy of oppressions in order to justify or contest a political opinion by reference to the speaker's identity. (*Feminist Review* 1989: 37)

It is vital again to exploit all that was innovative and refreshing about radical feminist politics of the '70s – its denial of hierarchy of authority within its ranks, its policy of total support via a concept of a fundamental (if not universal) shared oppression. Later, feminism became a 'dirty' word; something exacerbated by its own fragmentation as it became increasingly at the mercy of the whims of its detractors. In face of the legacy of the dominant New Right politics of the '80s (and its emerging pro-female front in the '90s), it is essential for feminists constantly to re-evaluate their critical positions for flaws and contradictions, to accommodate marked ideological and social shifts. In the current political climate it is clear that feminism has some catching up to do. In common with parliamentary opposition parties, the Women's Movement has as yet been unequal to tackling the subtleties of New Right policies and ideology, which pose a significant threat to the left-wing and arguably an even stronger one to women's rights. It is not altogether surprising that feminists are beginning more frequently to reflect on their past rather than their future, in the wake of a sinister 'new sexism' and 'new racism' which thrive under the rhetoric of cultural and sexual equality. Women and ethnic groups are again encouraged to celebrate (and entrench) their 'differences' and remain a manageable marginalized faction.

In periods of moral terror in any culture, such as the current AIDS trauma, it seems that women, sexual and racial minorities will bear the brunt of social castigation. In order comprehensively to address the problems of ideological and material oppression, it is necessary to approach the subject via a consideration of the wider mechanisms of power and domination. Although conducted to a large extent in a gender-blind context, Foucault's methodological framework usefully provides a point of departure through which to negotiate an exit from the cul-de-sac of oppositional discourse which Foucault, at times, rather pessimistically elucidates. Foucault separates the two elements of power (as an abstract fluid force) and domination (as the concrete privilege of those in power) to construct a model of the process of power that resembles a pyramidal formation. He argues that the state, through ideology and the acquisition of knowledge (about, for example, sexuality, criminality, insanity), is better equipped to police its members, as well as enrolling some at every level of the social hierarchy to act as ideological/moral 'police' (psychoanalysts, gaolers, parents, teachers) at both a 'national' and localized level. If we hold with Foucault that an epistemic discursive formation (historically specific ways of knowing) dictates the conditions of existence of any utterance at any given time and that therefore feminism (like Marxism) is a 'fish in water',[4] the possibility of effective oppositional discourse seems remote. Power is viewed as functioning semi-autonomously from those in the dominant position in a social formation in that it is inscribed in the language we use and knowledge we possess. However, Foucault's analysis of oppositional discourse in *Power/Knowledge* (1980), inconclusive as it is, can be evaluated in relation to radical and later New Right politics in order to attempt to construct an oppositional discourse which refuses to replicate existing power models. Feminism, in its refusal to engage in hierarchical power roles, or to put forward particular spokespeople, seems to be heading in the right direction – though it is doubtful that a 'revolution in consciousness' will ever be realized without limited intervention in either party politics or the mass media.

THE INSTITUTIONALIZATION OF FEMINIST CRITICISM

Unlike the heady days of the '60s and '70s, when women academics seemed to be fighting just to get feminism perceived as a serious object of study at all, feminist theory is now a recognized sphere of academic discourse. As I have suggested above, this might have contributed to the current state of affairs, where the meanings and ownership of feminism are now also being contested by male inquirers. The dangers of institutional acceptance have been discussed since at least 1971, when Lillian S. Robinson wrote 'Dwelling in Decencies' (in Robinson 1978). There remains a recognition that a degree of absorption by the academy is inevitable, even when clear advances in feminist thought and the dissemination of feminist knowledges are in evidence. Nonetheless, as theorists such as Jane Gallop point out, feminist academics are of the institution, and it is less than helpful resignedly to bemoan our role as transmitters of elitist bourgeois values within it. Gallop instead wants, to understand why we are located here, how we got here, what we sacrificed to get here, what we gained: all as preliminaries to the question of how do we do the most good, as feminists, as social and cultural critics, speaking from this location. (Gallop 1992: 5)

Another side-effect of the institutionalization of feminism is the means by which vying feminist positions are accepted or rejected, coupled with the question of who determines this inclusion or exclusion. Early radical feminist fears of an emergent 'star system' of honoured spokespeople, sadly realized in the public recantations of Germaine Greer and Betty Friedan, were also occurring in the academy – especially in the increasingly privileged valuation of feminist 'high' theory. The demarcation between 'high' and 'low' feminism provoked a tendency to characterize earlier second wave feminism as naive, responsible for some of the 'errors' or contradictions in feminist politics today (see Lauretis in Hirsch and Keller 1990: 255–70). While it is perhaps inevitable that 'stars' should emerge in the feminist firmament, the danger is that feminism as a marketable academic enterprise becomes more of a 'career' and less identifiable as oppositional politics. As Marianne Hirsch remarks in conversation with Jane Gallop and Nancy K. Miller, 'there is now a way of building a career on trashing feminist work' (in Hirsch and Keller 1990: 350). Here she signals a danger inherent in intra-feminist debates – that there is a thin line between healthy discussion and diminishing the successes of currently less popular feminisms.

Jane Gallop concludes this conversation by declaring that 'What we need is an ethics of criticism' (in Hirsch and Keller 1990: 368); a sentiment echoed by bell hooks in a discussion on the inclusion of race-specific issues into feminism's 'mainstream' when she says, 'when we write about the experiences of a group to which we do not belong, we should think about the ethics of our action' (hooks 1989: 43). What they both identify are the dangers of feminism as a 'career' in academe, which – in keeping with the demands of scholarly competition – encourages the debunking or destabilizing of alternative feminist positions. Moreover, this is often viewed as a gratifying phenomenon outside feminist circles by theorists who may delight in witnessing what they regard as evidence of splits and factions in feminism, suggesting proof of its inherent weakness. However, few feminists would want to counter the risks involved in intra-feminist critiques by issuing any kind of embargo on the types or scope of criticism 'allowed' – for many since the mid-'80s in particular, the extent of debate within feminism has been taken as a sign of its continued vivacity as discourse.

During the '70s Adrienne Rich was attempting to envisage the shape of a 'woman-centred university'. Some of her critiques of the steadfastly male hierarchical practices of the traditional academic institution remain pertinent today. Rich rightly identifies the means by which women's studies courses within the mainstream are rarely able to transform the epistemological givens in pre-existing disciplines. Whatever victories can be gained in women's studies – for example, by means of making available a new resistant range of knowledges – the overall fabric of the institution remains entrenched in patriarchal ideology:

> Women in colleges where a women's studies program already exists, or where feminist courses are beginning to be taught, still are often made to feel that the 'real' curriculum is the male-centred one; that women's studies are (like Third World studies) a 'fad'; that feminist teachers are 'unscholarly,' 'unprofessional,' or 'dykes'. But the content of courses and programs is only the more concrete form of undermining experienced by the woman student. More invisible, less amenable to change by committee proposal or fiat, is the hierarchical image, the structure of relationships, even the style of discourse, including assumptions about theory and practice, ends and means, process and goal. (Rich 1980: 136)

Here Rich demonstrates the paradox for women working as teachers and students within such an environment – that the framing of women's studies or feminist courses within institutional parameters, means that the definition of the academy or education continues to be resistant to change. The academic institution remains relentlessly male-identified, creating divisions not merely between the successful feminist scholar – who may achieve academic acclaim at the expense of other feminists who cannot get a foothold in the institution – but between women as teachers, students and women who service the institution in other ways. Women workers, such as secretaries, clerks, cleaners and cooks generally receive little support from their feminist 'sisters', although they collectively suffer from the design of an institution created with male needs in mind. This is most evident in the lack of childcare provisions and promotional prospects. All in all, this obviously undermines the scope of feminist intellectual pursuits claiming to be 'political', as well as increasing the threat of absorption by patriarchal ideologies.

Rich and later theorists draw our attention to the fact that there
are numerous factors contributing to the negative features of feminist institutionalization which extend far beyond the subject matter
of feminist thought itself, or indeed any questions of its relation to
knowledges in the 'centre' of the academy.[5] Feminist knowledge,
despite its acceptance within the institution remains marginalized
and 'other', as an optional extra, even though this marginality has at
least allowed feminism to flourish as a critique of the mainstream.
There are, inevitably, problems with feminism remaining a subordinate and co-opted fragment of the mainstream, implying as it does
that feminism suffers from absorption more often than it wins any
victories over the status quo. Yet, there is simply no other option for
feminists; they cannot work 'outside' the patriarchal order, since the
academy is just one example of an institution which perpetuates and
reinforces male-oriented perceptions of social reality. Therefore,
while the problems associated with institutionalization require further scrutiny along the lines of the critique offered above, such
scrutiny has to include an acceptance of feminism's existence 'within'
in order better to construct agendas which resist the demands made
on feminist knowledge to be just one contested scholarly methodology among many. As Gayle Greene observes, 'We need jobs in the
profession in order to have any effect on the profession. As to
whether we can fight the oppressor with the oppressor's weapons, we
have no choice' (Greene in Kauffman 1989b: 82).

The emergence of feminist topics in higher education does not
suggest that these ideas have a widespread circulation, rather, feminist work is commonly regarded by non-feminist teachers and
students alike as an extra subject. This suggests that even the victory
of establishing women's studies as a discipline has its cost and its
paradox, that of enabling the academic mainstream conveniently to
'forget' feminism's political function within the academic institution.
Perhaps feminism as it appears today holds the most ironic and
dualistic of positions. In theory (literally) feminism is becoming a
widespread and respectable academic process (especially in the fields
of English and Cultural Studies). I shall select the publication of
Alice Jardine and Paul Smith's *Men in Feminism* (1987) as a publishing landmark which manifest some of the rumblings in the
Establishment that had been rising to a head, at least since the
publication of Elaine Showalter's article 'Critical Cross-Dressing;
Male Feminists and the Woman of the Year' (Jardine and Smith
1987: 116–32). This article summarizes some of the doubts many
feminists express in *Men in Feminism* about the critical intervention

of 'male feminists' on the scene, sensing perhaps that women, during this period of crisis, need to resolve a few more of their own critical differences before calling in male reinforcements. I share this unease; that despite the well-intentioned, ideologically sound offerings from Paul Smith, Stephen Heath and others in this publication, direct involvement by men in feminist theory can be politically and academically dangerous. As Elaine Showalter observes:

> Feminist criticism has worried too much already, in my opinion, about communicating with the white fathers, even at the price of translating its findings into the warp of their obscure critical languages. If some of them are now learning our language, all the better; but there is more than a hint in some recent critical writing that it's time for men to step in and show the girls how to do it . . . (Jardine and Smith 1987: 119)

In common with Showalter, I remain disturbed by the prospect of a substantial intervention in feminism by men:[6] the authority that a male voice immediately acquires over the female in academic discourse is a problem that I shall return to in Chapter Eight.

ALL THE THEORISTS ARE MEN, ALL THE FEMINISTS ARE WHITE, BUT . . .

A significant shift in feminist thought of the '80s and '90s was heralded by the increasing availability of black feminist work, which demanded that its own agendas be recognized and acted upon by white feminists. It is now a truism that white feminists have until recently either elided the questions that black feminism raises or simply continued to produce theory which operates along a model of white female experience while remaining blind to questions of racial and/or cultural difference. Much of white feminism's reluctance to confront the challenge of black feminist writings, or to discuss them in their own work is couched in terms of not wanting to 'appropriate' the black voice and consequently perpetuate the silencing effect of dominant theoretical discourses. The result is that black feminists tend to take sole responsibility for adding the dimension of 'race' to women's studies; yet unfortunately this implies that racism is black women's problem – or that feminists are by definition anti-racist through the same political process of being anti-sexist.

Adrienne Rich was one of the few white feminists to address the thorny issue of racial difference and its impact on feminist thought during the '70s in 'Disloyal to Civilization: Feminism, Racism, Gynephobia' (1978). In this essay she discusses the difficulties white women obviously felt when attempting to outline issues specific to black female experience. She observes that:

> a great deal of white feminist thinking and writing, where it has attempted to address black women's experience, has done so labouring under a massive burden of guilt feelings and false consciousness, the products of deeply inculcated female self-blame, and of a history we have insufficiently explored. (Rich 1980: 281)

As Rich acknowledges, much of this guilt is a side-effect of white women's ignorance about black women's lives, an ignorance perpetuated by an educational system which fosters white experience as the norm. Nonetheless, it is clearly inadequate to use as one's defence the claim that we white women, duped by the patriarchal ideologies of the dominant white male hegemonic force, share no responsibility for the construction, institutionalization and perpetuation of inequality. It is manifestly obvious that white women can and do contribute to the continuance of such systems of social oppression, and are directly responsible for its reinscription in oppositional discourses such as feminism. Many white feminists feel vulnerable to accusations of being dubbed 'privileged' – in that they have the choice and opportunity to learn about feminism and to identify themselves as feminists, compared to black women's general cultural exclusion from such liberties. Yet hierarchies of privilege among women are a social and historical fact, and it appears futile, not to say dangerous, merely to sidestep such features of women's difference. To do so is to imply acceptance of the power and durability of racism, as well as its influence within feminism.

Rich warns against the feeling of passivity that comes with guilt and becomes an excuse for inadequacy; rather, she recommends a deeper search for common ground, coupled with an investigation of racist fears still residual within white feminism's subtext. Meanwhile she herself is culpable of one cardinal error during the course of her discussion, which is to talk about 'women' and 'black people' as if they were two mutually exclusive interest groups, creating a rhetorical chasm in which black women are absorbed and rendered invisible yet again. Her essay remains, perhaps, too optimistic about the simple measure of sharing experiences and overcoming boundaries, because she is too ready to ascribe all tools of oppression as solely the property of males. In addition she is too willing to attribute critiques of white feminism's racism to male left-wing groups anxious to expose feminism as a distinctly bourgeois and counter-revolutionary phenomenon (Rich 1980: 290). Despite its flaws, Rich's essay had groundbreaking potential by the mere fact that she acknowledged race to be white women's problem too, and suggested that white feminists should begin to examine the reasons for their ethnocentricity rather than simply summon guilt as a viable response. However, black feminist theorists of the '80s and '90s, committed to constructing a discourse which unseated the dominance of the white gaze, still found that their work was often consigned to the 'black perspectives' margins. Even though there are many black feminists such as bell hooks who see a future for feminism in a sharing of experiences, critiques and perspectives, they are also made angry and impatient by the seeming arrogance of some white feminist positions which situate themselves as though they are in a position to bestow the 'honour' of acceptance on to black women. Meanwhile black feminist scholarship has developed and expanded through producing collections devoted to black women's work;[7] whereas within white feminism, black feminist critiques are still regularly marginalized as the token essay or footnote, and 'overviews' of second wave feminism are produced which appear to ignore the existence of black women altogether.[8]

hooks characterizes the emergence of the women's liberation movement as being dependent upon its voices being those of white, middle-class women, and that therefore it is inevitable that their experiences shaped and determined the main agenda for feminism – 'what other group of women in the United States had the same access to universities, publishing houses, mass media, money?' (hooks 1984: 6). Even though white bourgeois women's initial hegemony in the movement might be partly attributed to their greater access to educational and other privileges, this alone cannot explain their retention of the power to police the boundaries of feminism – not by excluding women on the grounds of race or class, but by dictating the range of 'acceptable' issues for discussion, with the result that, 'we could be heard only if our statements echoed the sentiments of the dominant discourse' (hooks 1984: 11–12). This is particularly apparent when race and class are considered, but maintained as subordinate to gender, as if gender oppression operates autonomously from other forms of social and cultural subordination. The tendency to distinguish gender difference as the most crucial issue for all women, denies black women the right to assert that racism plays an equally important role in the shaping of their lives and politics, and perpetuates a corresponding sense of 'them' and 'us'. In this way, hooks's judgement of feminism as primarily founded on privilege (of race, class and education) is a correct one.

The prevailing sense that white feminism 'allows' black feminists to contest or 'correct' designated areas of discussion, inhibits the interrogation of what women can be deemed to share in terms of experiences of oppression, and prevents the revision of other features of feminist thought which currently do not reflect a female consensus across racial and class boundaries.[9] The rhetoric of equality itself is problematic; since if the central thrust of white feminist thought is formal social and economic equality with (white) men, is it assured that women (and men) from less privileged positions will attain the same equality? One might predict that were white women's equality achieved, they might retain an investment in the continued exploitation and oppression of other non-hegemonic groups (hooks 1984: 15; 18). From this perspective, feminism's focus might be better relocated to concentrate on the removal of oppression, rather than a concern with equality. Such a change in emphasis does not appear to me to be incompatible with a sustained focus on the ideological construction of gender and a corresponding analysis of its effects upon women of all groups, as a contribution to the erosion of patriarchal oppression, rather than risking replicating pre-existing power dynamics.

At present – particularly in the United States – black feminist thought flourishes semi-autonomously, developing in academe via women's and black studies courses and furthering the analysis of the nexus between racial and sexual oppression. Although black critiques of white feminism have drawn attention to white feminists' questionable universalizing accounts of women's relation to economics, the law, medicine and the family, a primary focus (in common with earlier second wave white feminists) has been on the area of representation and ideology. As Patricia Hill Collins asserts,

> From the mammies, Jezebels, and breeder women of slavery to the smiling Aunt Jemimas on pancake mix boxes, ubiquitous Black prostitutes, and ever-present welfare mothers of contemporary popular culture, the nexus of stereotypical images applied to African-American women has been fundamental to Black women's oppression. (Collins 1991: 7)

Certainly in the area of cultural criticism and the theorization of female spectatorship, white feminists have been largely blind to the fact that the ideal-type feminine image which bombards all women, at least provides a point of identification with white women in that she is normally white. When white women have turned to black female experience, they show a tendency to admire black women's personal strength; though of course, this image itself is partially a myth, in that it tends to ignore the adversity of a racist society which supplies an interpretation of 'strength' to a situation within which black woman as subject may only be thinking in terms of survival (Collins 1991: 116–18). Black feminists have devoted much of their energies to debunking such myths, while celebrating the endurance of their foremothers for surviving, and educating their 'daughters' – whether biological or affectional – to learn the necessity of resistance to the dominant culture's worldview of black inferiority. Many black writers – of both fiction and theory – emphasize the importance of the mother's de-socializing role in teaching their daughters self-confidence and self-worth.

Perhaps white feminists still tend to see black feminist theory as a threat to an epistemological centrality that they have enjoyed for two decades, instead of observing – as Collins does – that multifarious feminist standpoints all provide important but partial visions. These should explore each other's work not just as a corrective of their own but to enhance the overall growth in an increasingly non-racist, non-homophobic body of feminist thought. hooks argues that broadening and shifting the terms of the commonly accepted central feminist agenda is not in itself enough. She also suggests that feminists might adopt a linguistic shift in the way they identify themselves, on the grounds that the statement, 'I am a feminist', implies that concerns of gender difference exclude all others. hooks argues that a modification of this statement to 'I advocate feminism' implies one's commitment to a feminist viewpoint, but does not exclude the possibility of supporting other political movements (hooks 1984: 29). This distinction appears to be a valid one, in an era where feminism has often come to designate individual lifestyle politics, which tends to prioritize certain exclusive interests: yet, to advocate feminism suggests a certain distance from its processes and politics, as if feminism is a pre-established dogma. This also implies that feminism is irredeemably entrenched in a bourgeois vision of oppression. To identify oneself as a feminist at least indicates an active engagement and commitment to the further development of a feminist theory which can do justice to all groups of women, regardless of present access to social privilege. This is not to advocate complacency with the term feminism, which has till now been tardy in recognizing its potential for the perpetuation of certain forms of dominance. As hooks asserts in a later book, 'It is necessary to remember that it is first the potential oppressor within that we must resist – the potential victim within that we must rescue – otherwise we cannot hope for an end to domination, for liberation' (hooks, 1984: 21).

THE FIGHT FOR OWNERSHIP: GOOD MOTHERS OR BAD DAUGHTERS?

In the '90s there is clear evidence of a generation gap in feminism, which, exploited in the popular media, results in a disproportionate degree of attention being given to the 'new' wave of writers such as Naomi Wolf and Katie Roiphe. The implication is that they have something original to say about feminism, but on closer inspection it is clear that the main thrust of their arguments are very old indeed – an improbable mixture of early second wave positions, coupled with classic anti-feminist sentiments. One new aspect which frames such discussions, however, is the cult of woman-blaming loudly endorsed by proponents such as Wolf, Roiphe and Camille Paglia. One of its chief assertions is that feminism encouraged a greater passivity among women in its supposed affirmation of the role of victim:

> The image that emerges from feminist preoccupations with rape and sexual harassment is that of women as victims, offended by a professor's dirty joke, verbally pressured into sex by peers. This image of a delicate woman bears a striking resemblance to that fifties ideal my mother and the other women of her generation fought so hard to get away from. (Roiphe 1994: 6)

As I shall go on to discuss in Chapter Ten, this kind of position deftly singles out feminists themselves as the progenitors of a backlash against their own political interests. This circular logic in its ellipsis of the role of feminism in changing the social perceptions of women since the '50s, reduces feminism to issues such as whether today's women are strong enough to stomach sexist jokes and harassment. It is as if the only obstacle to social advancement for the woman of the '90s is the need to dispense with the 'luxury' of victimhood.[10] Writers such as Naomi Wolf see their 'new' feminism as dispensing with many of the mistakes of the well-intentioned but hopelessly naive 'old' school of the women's movement. In *Fire With Fire* (1993) she maintains that the most crucial factor in the perpetuation of women's oppression is women themselves and, more precisely, the culture of competition between women. At the same time as being encouraged to blame themselves for feminism's demise, women are being exhorted to throw off their love affair with victimhood in favour of a new (that word again) assertion of strength. The radical feminist notion that all women are potential victims of male power because of the tenacity of patriarchy, is supplanted by a notion of victimhood as a form of unconscious abdication of responsibility.

The 'good mothers' response is encapsulated by somewhat weightier volumes such as Faludi's *Backlash* (1992) and Marilyn French's *The War Against Women* (1992) which examine the enormity and effectiveness of a continued social will to patriarchy, as I shall later discuss. Sheila Jeffreys, however, identifies another 'backlash' which has thrown lesbian feminists into a degree of disarray:

> Within the lesbian community there has been a parallel back-lash. The conservatism of the '80s in the malestream world had a particularly damaging effect on the lives of lesbians and gay men. Conservative groups and governments sought to scapegoat lesbians and gay men to divert attention from the widening social divisions that their economic policies were creating. (Jeffreys 1994: x)

Jeffrey's unyielding response towards libertarianism in lesbian feminism sets her up as the caricatured 'puritan' feminist so often pilloried by contemporary women's magazines. Jeffrey's stance reflects the huge spectrum of disagreement in relation to debates around sexuality, particularly classic flashpoints of debate around pornography and heterosexuality. The Feminist IX conference 'Towards a Politics of Sexuality' held at Barnard College in the USA on 24 April 1982 is a landmark in feminist politics because of the vehement splits it caused around the subject of sex. It is described by Carole S. Vance, in her new preface to the conference papers written ten years later, as 'the moment where the dominance of the anti-pornography analysis from 1977–82 came to an end' (Vance 1992: xxii). She explains the context and purpose of the conference as questioning 'how could feminism at the time reduce the sexual danger women faced and expand their sexual pleasure without sacrificing women's accounts of either one?' (Vance 1992: xx). She discusses how the anti-porno-graphy wing of the women's movement began to be regarded by other feminists as needlessly narrow because

> The fantasy that violence against women is located or originates in objectionable sex magazines or videos rather than being part of the deep cell structure of every institution in our culture

struck some feminists as hopelessly naive and wrong, as did the suggestion that the excision of the sexually explicit would solve the problem. (Vance 1992: xx)

Vance's account includes a description of a fairly fundamental split between anti-pornography and anti-censorship feminists where those who didn't follow the anti-pornography stance were sometimes treated as if they were as culpable as the sex industry which supports such images. Many feminists felt that the assumption that the eradication of porn was the key to the sexual exploitation of women had also closed down discussion – women were encouraged to accept this as a truism in ways that they had never tacitly accepted any other feminist position. Further, those who demurred from the straight forward anti-porn line were labelled anti-feminists, even though anti-porn campaigners seemed prepared to liaise with right wing anti-feminist groups to support their anti-pornography agenda (Vance 1992: xxiv).

Debates such as those encapsulated in the Vance volume stand as testimony to the continued healthy development of a feminist epistemology which never attempts to simplify the complexities of women's lived experience of material and ideological realities. Moreover such debates around sexuality point to the fact that much feminist work has been focused on the 'negative' side of sexuality at the expense of considering ways in which women may explore their own desires in the will for a utopian future for female sexuality. This is in particular the recurring complaint of writers such as Wolf and Roiphe, that of the woolliness of debates primarily around sex, but also around romantic love and the countless emotional and material investments and tradeoffs young women make in their relationships not only with men, but also with other young women (see also Thompson in Vance 1992: 350–84). Feminism is perceived as creating a tough path for women with 'normal' desires (for men, fashion, fun) to follow. There are of course clear reasons why these stances emerged – in radical feminism's resistance to beauty myths, and so forth – but it is an example of an issue that demands a wholesale review, before it is destructively trivialized by detractors to be used as an example of how feminism does not speak to women in general. Naomi Wolf exploits this idea that feminism spoils women's fun and encourages, I would argue, a social and political quietism among young women beguiled by writing which posits a 'new' feminism based on individual liberal and elitist competition by emphasizing that 'old' feminism is 'about' restricting women:

> My friends and I are all self-defined feminists. But ⸗
> that if we were to stand up and honestly describe our liv⸗
> room full of other feminist 'insiders' – an act that should illu-
> minate the route to female liberation – we could count on
> having transgressed at least one dearly held tenet on someone's
> list of feminism's 'do's' and 'don'ts', and being called to account
> for it. 'Don't tell the sisterhood,' we often joke, uncomfortably,
> when we are about to confide some romantic foolishness or
> unsanctioned sexual longing or 'frivolous' concern about clothes
> or vulnerability or men . . . If you can no longer square your
> feminism with your real-life experience, then something has
> gone seriously wrong. (Wolf 1993: 68)

This image of 'the sisterhood' again conjures up images of a select
group antagonistic to the appointment of new members, just as the
'brotherhood' conjures images of a selective professional organization
that one needs the right connections to join. Feminism for Wolf is
always already doctrinaire, and this idea that the women's movement
is rife with rigid proscriptions discourages younger women or sceptical older women to read feminist accounts for themselves. There is
little evidence of proscription in the feminist endeavour as a whole,
although of course certain groups and perspectives may alienate or
antagonize other feminists as well as a broader range of women. This
need not suggest that feminist philosophy is necessarily tyrannical,
but direct us to gaps and shortcomings which should be addressed,
rather than to allow feminist detractors to rehash the old arguments
about tyranny as if it is some given truth and as if all these so-called
proscriptions are actually written down in some feminist bible.[11]

If I have dwelt upon the negative constructions put upon feminism in the '90s, it is to outline the range of challenges that I feel
feminism needs now to address, and perhaps be more candid about
its own processes. These negative features should be here at least
briefly counterpoised by mentioning a marked increase in feminist
contributions to philosophy and political science which emerged
during the '80s. This resulted in works which question the development of a specifically feminist epistemology, and again draw attention
to the problem of creating an effective oppositional discourse which
is not immediately discredited by a dominant world view which
denies the validity of a feminist perspective, because the means by
which arguments are expressed are not recognized as 'reasoned'.
Elizabeth Grosz argues that feminists should be committed to such
a reconsideration of the means by which knowledge is legitimated:

> where feminism remains committed to the project of *knowing*
> *women*, of making women objects of knowledge, *without in*
> *turn submitting the position of knower or subject of knowledge to a*
> *reorganization*, it remains as problematic as the knowledges it
> attempts to supplement or replace. (Alcoff and Potter 1993: 207)

That feminism needs to be aware of its responsibility to investigate
the means by which feminism 'knows' women, in the light of my
comments above, seems a crucial aspect of developed feminist
discourse.

Politically and in the wider public sphere, feminism seems to have
died an untimely death – if media pronouncements of the 'post-
feminist' age are to be accepted. The Old Guard of feminist pioneers
are exhumed to support this view – such as Germaine Greer, latter-
day doyenne of the chat shows – who gracefully do their bit to kill
the cause they once championed. These speakers for womankind are
a striking reminder of the New Right transition of 1980s Europe and
the USA. Feminists in academe need to turn to this confusing and
contradictory blaze of signifiers which pepper the media and constantly remind us that we still have our work cut out if a feminist
revolution in consciousness is not to be diverted into a series of
pyrrhic victories – such as getting women's studies courses on the
critical agenda – no matter how important these individual gains are.
We are seduced by images of career women enjoying their new-found
prosperity; sanitary products may now be advertised on television,
showing women wearing tight fitting clothes with the promise that
it is their 'secret': both these images of women, however, remain
seamlessly 'feminine' – the 'new woman' is almost identical to the
old. What is clearly apparent is that women are constantly being
reassured that neither 'success' nor biological femaleness need
compromise their quintessential femininity – and it is this ever-
shifting ideological construct 'the feminine' that has to be critically
re-evaluated by feminists.

Returning to the academic institutions themselves we find an
attempt at practice – the women's studies courses or options offered
on numerous humanities and social science degrees. Here women of
the second wave generation attempt to raise the consciousness of
younger women who tend to think that feminism is a dirty word.
Moreover, it is becoming increasingly common for women's studies
to be regarded as separate from feminist 'high' theory – a process
which seems to be aligning the well-known feminist theorists with
male counterparts in the sphere of critical theory. This is especially

true of discourses on postmodernism, couched as they are in the language of resistance and transgression, in a celebration of postmodern aesthetics as an effacement of the boundaries between 'high' and 'low' culture. The discourses of postmodernism seem to lend themselves to feminism, since in the past cultural productions by women have proliferated or have at times been relegated to the realms of popular culture; and accordingly a serious approach to forms of popular culture can only (on the face of it) raise the profile of feminist research. Having said this, the forms of analysis and definitions of what constitutes the postmodern moment are as heterogeneous as the variety of feminist positions we witness today.

In the 'feminist' forms of postmodern approaches, postmodernism is defined as the epistemological meeting place of feminism, deconstruction and Lacanian psychoanalysis. E. Ann Kaplan, for one, sees this merger as the point of formation of a 'utopian' manifestation of postmodernism which she describes as involving 'a movement of culture and texts beyond oppressive binary categories and could not be imagined without the work of, among others, Bakhtin, Derrida, Lacan, Cixous, Kristeva and Roland Barthes' (Kaplan 1988: 4). The radical decentring of the subject which a deconstructive reading of a text entails, and the gesture towards an end to the binary oppositions masculinity/femininity is at one level very attractive to modern feminists, just as it seemed to Virginia Woolf in *A Room of One's Own* (1929). But sixty years on, the moment of that dissolution in opposition seems to me still a utopian moment, and though utopian writing is a useful and undervalued aspect of feminist politics, it must be emphasized that this erosion of the dread binary has yet to be witnessed by current feminists in their personal (political) lives.

Many feminists might wonder whether feminism is to be subsumed in this particular brand of 'utopian' postmodernism, or if feminism is in fact the organizing principle. I suspect the former trend more likely, given the fate of feminism to date as a marginalized discourse in academic thought – something to be summoned as an interesting and diverting 'perspective', rather than an impressive mode of autonomous discourse. Interestingly (but not surprisingly), the emergence of postmodern culture has been situated as parallel to the rise of the second wave of feminism. Within these theoretical debates of 'men in feminism' and postmodernism, feminism again appears to be conceived as a largely homogeneous evolutionary process which has at its heart a series of well-directed goals. In reality, the minority of published feminists are totally committed to the form of feminism which takes as its condition of existence post-Lacanian psychoanalytic theory or post-structuralism. If I seem to be negative about the contributions acknowledged by feminism to other radical theories of subjectivity, it is because I remain wary about the potential appropriation of feminist achievement within a wider intellectual tradition of radicalism, into which feminism might be neatly slotted and gradually swamped. Feminist theory – a term I use in its widest sense to embrace earlier feminist writings which were not originally acknowledged as 'theory' because of lack of 'rigour' or unorthodox methodologies – has drawn strength from its marginal position in academe and politics although conversely, it suffers from this ghettoization. Here I locate one of the most infuriating and exciting of contradictions inherent in feminist discourse: on the one hand it needs to emphasize its separateness from the disciplines, as they are traditionally defined, because of its nascent interdisciplinarity; and yet on the other hand there exists a profound desire to be credited for attempts to transform and expand those disciplines from within by highlighting the gaps and silences on the subject of women (as subject) in relation to Western social and political thought. As I have argued throughout, although feminism as an object of study is going forward, feminism as a political methodology engaged in the material and social problems of women's oppression, has remained depressingly static. Feminism needs to re-emerge from the mire of 'identity politics' in order to fully engage with and interrogate the nature of subtle ideological and material shifts which have occurred since the beginnings of its second wave. I would not wish to suggest that a single unifying feminist discourse is either possible or desirable, but rather that feminisms can thrive upon such a diversity of approaches, moving towards a celebration of heterogeneity, and away from the more negative influences of the 'founding fathers' of academic discourse.[12]

Chapter 7

Sites of Fissure:
Putting the Politics of the
Personal to the Test

> What sustains our eagerness to speak of sex in terms of
> repression is doubtless this opportunity to speak out against
> the powers that be, to utter truths and promise bliss, to link
> together enlightenment, liberation, and manifold pleasures;
> to pronounce a discourse that combines the fervour of
> knowledge, the determination to change the laws, and the
> longing for the garden of earthly delights.
>
> (Foucault 1979: 7)

Foucault's statement cogently sums up the dilemma that the so-
called 'Sexual Revolution' posed for feminists in the 1970s. On one
hand, calls for liberation from sexual repression seemed perfectly
compatible with women's liberation and the demand that women
should have control over their own reproductive capacities. However
women soon discovered that participating in the heretofore forbidden fruits of sexual freedom revealed many conceptual problems with
sexuality itself. Female sexual desire had been defined and categorized by men; the terms themselves required redefinition in order to
cleanse them of patriarchal connotations. There is of course a recurring problem with defining feminist terms and being always in the
process of 'borrowing' and extending the conceptual apparatuses of
our forefathers; it is common for oppressed social groups to appropriate negative terms, defining and positioning them to redefine
them positively. However, one is still left with the problem that
previous negative connotations exist in a wider sphere. This is true of
sexuality, where definitions of the female sexual response are construed as the obverse of male sexuality – the passive to complete the
active, the lock to fit the key. Sexuality, then, has a history of its own

in the women's movement, where the question is of a woman's relation to sex and (if sex is destiny) to herself. Early debates about
female sexuality tended to focus on 'proper' forms of sexual practice,
or more commonly upon the means by which female sexuality has
been used as a tool of repression, related to issues of sexual violence
and pornographic images.

There has been a tendency within feminism to portray women as
the guiltless yet guilt-ridden victims of marital sexual relations. The
onset of the 'Permissive Society' of the '60s was supposed to change
all that. Women were to gain the 'right' to choose sex before marriage with more than one partner (this did not extend to being able
to refuse sexual contact within marriage) and the 'right' to enjoy sex.
A volte face had occurred in medical/social thinking in terms of
female sexual response: no longer were women who actively enjoyed
sexual intercourse to be pathologized, and sex was to be perceived as
an important aspect of physical and mental health. Facing a dearth
of writings available on female sexuality, feminists relied upon insights
offered by sexologists such as Kinsey or Masters and Johnson. As
Lynne Segal argues, 'by the mid '70s heterosexual sex was taken out
of the context of personal relationships and put in terms of individual
needs which were being met, or not met' (Segal 1987: 93), creating
an atmosphere where pleasure and satisfaction within relationships
was calculated purely on the basis of a single 'end product' – the
orgasm.

Many feminists remained sceptical that a vision of female sexual
autonomy would actually change the way female sexuality is conceived of as being in the service of male pleasure, since they argued
that women's bodies have always been sexualized as objects for male
desire. They also doubted whether identifying an 'authentic' anatomical site of female pleasure would provide clues to the dynamics of
female desire, which had been distorted and suppressed for centuries.
The female body in Western medical discourse was a volatile mecha-
nism, whose balance could easily be upset. Contemporary theorists
perceive tensions in the way desired forms of sexual behaviour are
enforced by means of identifying and cataloguing forms of deviance.
Although heterosexuality is situated as correlative with the most natural form of sexual expression, the body of sexological and psychoanalytical casework deals with the sexual 'failures' of this world
– people whose responses turn out 'abnormal'. This points to what
Jeffrey Weeks terms an 'enduring paradox' – 'heterosexuality is
natural yet has to be attained, inevitable but constantly threatened,
spontaneous yet in effect to be learnt' (Weeks 1985: 85).

DEFINING SEXUALITY AND THE LEGACY OF SEXOLOGY

One formidable difficulty lies in attempting to limit and determine what 'sexuality' means. The breadth and scope of the term makes it unwieldy to the point of meaninglessness. It is summoned by sexologists, feminists, and libertarian theorists alike, and has passed into common usage to encompass many aspects of human sexual life; it throws up tensions between what might be deemed biological fact and what is overlaid by cultural convention. Analyses of human sexuality tend to assume fundamental distinctions between the sexes on the basis of anatomy, and when we talk about sex it is tacitly accepted that we are talking about coitus between a man and a woman. As Jeffrey Weeks avers, the centrality of definitions of sex as a procreative force has hierarchized sexual practices, with heterosexuality at the centre, the diffuse but defining principle against which deviations from the 'norm' have been identified (Weeks 1986).

The procreative capacity may well be a biological given, but sexual pleasure and desire exist outside such constraints, and are affected by historico-cultural and ideological forces, as well as being subject to social control. The categorization of heterosexuality as a discrete set of sexual practices which announces a complete identity in itself is a relatively new phenomenon, corresponding with the creation of the 'homosexual' as a medical model, which described an individual rather than an act which potentially could be practiced by all humans:

> The nineteenth-century homosexual became a personage, a past, a case history, and a childhood, in addition to being a type of life, a life form, and a morphology, with an indiscreet anatomy and possibly a mysterious physiology. Nothing that went into his total composition was unaffected by his sexuality . . . The sodomite had been a temporary aberration; the homosexual was now a species. (Foucault 1979: 43)

In the face of the multiplication of discourses around sexuality, there grew a quest for the origins of the sexual response in biologistic explanations, linked to the organs requisite for procreation – and in the cases of 'deviance', these organs' malformation. Male orgasm, synonymous with ejaculation, is fundamental to the 'natural' expression of sexuality (coitus); whereas female orgasm has, conversely, had a more chequered history.

In Freudian psychoanalytical theory sexual 'health' became one of the indicators of mental health, and female sexuality is merely considered as an adjunct to male sexuality. The Penguin collection of

Freud's essays on sexuality contains a piece devoted to the problem
of female sexuality, implying simultaneously that its construction is
different and problematic, whilst being subordinate and marginal to
a broader theory of sexuality based on the male model. For Freud the
active sexual urge is itself 'masculine', something which both pre-
pubescent girls and boys experience auto-erotically, but something
which is repressed in the 'normal' pubescent girl, to facilitate her
entry into a passive feminine sexual order (Freud 1977: 141; 340).
Children, in Freud's terms, possess masculine terms of sexual reference, which girls acquire by means of a seemingly universally
acquired penis envy, leading them to regard themselves as castrated,
and necessarily inferior beings. This conceptual framework leads to
a very complex view of the development of female sexuality. While
the possession of a penis allows boys a relatively trouble-free transition from immature auto-eroticism to adult quest for an appropriate
sexual object, the female's path from immature (clitoral) to mature
(vaginal) sexual identification is a treacherous one:

> When erotogenic susceptibility to stimulation has been success-
> fully transferred by a woman from the clitoris to the vaginal
> orifice, it implies that she has adopted a new leading zone for
> the purposes of her later sexual activity. A man, on the other
> hand, retains his leading zone unchanged from childhood.
> (Freud 1977: 143–4)

The implication in Freudian theory that female sexuality constituted
the underside of male sexuality conceptualized as a lack, or absence
of the penis, made concrete notions of female inferiority into psychoanalytical and sexological thinking. Coupled with this is Freud's
suggestion that in order for the transition from clitoral to vaginal
identification to be achieved the girl begins to sense shame and disgust at her previous masturbatory pleasures.[1] It is certainly the case
that Freudian theory is ineluctably entrenched in the discursive formation that enabled its appearance, and the uses to which Freudian
theory have since been put seek to provide a model of sexuality
which hinges on the biological and natural rather than the social and
cultural.

In common with Freud, sexologists such as Havelock Ellis considered a person's sexual history as of vital importance to understanding the development of psycho-sexual problems in adult life.
Sexology, the 'scientific' examination of sex, involves cataloguing and
interpreting of all forms of sexual practice which are then hierarchized as more or less 'deviant'. Again, the assumption is that at the

origins of the human sexual impulse there is a natural form of response, which can be corrupted by biological or cultural means. In a positive light, the sexological tradition is seen to have offered individuals a space to explore their inhibitions, their fetishes, or their 'perversions' in a more tolerant atmosphere of objective scientific exploration: often a person might find that they belong to a category, and that their 'problem' is not unique. More negatively, it can be argued that sexology inscribes in our culture notions of proper and acceptable forms of sexual behaviour, and comprises 'a more or less coherent body of assumptions, beliefs, prejudices, rules, methods of investigation and forms of moral regulation, which still shape the way we live our sexualities' (Weeks 1986: 14). Sexology might well be perceived as a body of research which in its claim to a privileged knowledge of the sexual impulses, has 'the power to adjudicate on normality and abnormality' (Weeks 1985: 80). In addition, it arguably possesses a hidden agenda that is rooted in a biologistic model of sexuality, which necessarily includes a view of female and male sexuality as different and complementary. The passive female responds to the active male, whose sexual urges are only barely held in check by cultural behavioural norms; and women are themselves implicated in containing this explosive male force.

'Sexuality', however, might be more provocatively regarded as a social presence which bears little relation to 'nature' or 'biology', and whose realm incorporates all humans, bringing together the capacity to reproduce, desire and need, fantasy, gender identity and bodily differences. Unlike sexologists, theorists such as Jeffrey Weeks and Michel Foucault do not accept the veracity of 'scientific' claims, and assert to the contrary that there is no inner truth or sexual essence at the heart of every human being. They argue instead that in the wake of the demise of Christianity over the past two centuries, sex became destiny – that is to say, we are what we desire.[2] Accordingly homosexuals were not just men and women with a non-heterosexual orientation, they were defined as a different breed, a third sex – Ellis coined the term 'invert', implying the status of a congenital anomaly. Until recently feminists have seemed reluctant to interrogate the field of sexuality and the theories that inform it, although the problem of the sexualization of women is a central issue in feminist thought. The dominant feminist line tended to be one of defence – to argue that women's sexual authenticity lies elsewhere – rather than taking the form of an attack upon entrenched beliefs around sexual selfhood. Later feminist theorists have followed the lead of thinkers such as Michel Foucault, arguing that sexuality is an historical construct, and is meaningless without its relevant socio-historical context. This facilitates a further and more concerted attack upon the status of the natural in Western epistemology; a move readily compatible with earlier feminist endeavours to deconstruct the naturalization of the social self.

Feminism, meanwhile, still tends to conflate the biological and cultural when it comes to studies of female sexuality, and this seems to be an inevitable effect of drawing upon theories of sexuality constructed with male sexual response as the motivating force. This is true of Freudian theory which 'uses visible anatomical difference as its guarantee of psychic difference and women's inferiority' (Weedon 1987: 49), and focuses discussion around anatomy, whilst decentring questions of cultural and ideological influences upon a person's sexual motivation. In the case of Freudian theory and its legacy, 'anatomical division is seen as equivalent to sexual identity and has been privileged as the fundamental symbolic category in sexuality' (Coward 1983: 280), with the effect that at an ideological level anatomy is regarded as the irrevocable defining principle of sexual response. Foucault has asserted that 'it is possible that where sex is concerned, the most long-winded, the most impatient of societies is our own' (Foucault 1979: 33). Nowhere is this impatience, this eager search for the truth about sex, more evident than in sexological thought. During the early years of the twentieth century, Havelock Ellis was credited with heralding a new era of sexual enlightenment, by establishing sexology as an exact science. He identified the existence of a female sexuality which was not pathological; and in creating 'scientific' explanations for homosexual desire he promoted some degree of tolerance. Nonetheless, his relatively radical views on human sexuality did not lead him to interrogate the qualities assumed to govern discrete forms of masculine or feminine behaviour. Female sexuality was still viewed as determined by the reproductive urge, and the power dynamics invested in heterosexual sex were endorsed as an expression of the natural biological order of things. His most influential volumes – *Studies in the Psychology of Sex* (1913) – whilst libertarian in some respects, continue to view women as the receiver of the male, arguing that some conventional feminine attributes, such as modesty, are essential to trigger the chemistry of sexual attraction: 'the woman who is lacking in this kind of fear is lacking, also, in sexual attractiveness to the normal and average man' (Havelock Ellis, cited by Jackson in Coveney et al. 1984: 54). Women, Ellis maintains, desire to be conquered: this, of course, seems to be a small step towards legitimizing rape as something women 'unconsciously' desire (Jackson in Coveney et al. 1984: 66).

Sexology bases its hypotheses of sexual behaviour primarily upon perceptions of the male, and:

> takes as given the particular form of male sexuality that exists under male supremacy and attempts to universalize it, so that it becomes the model of sexuality in general . . . The model thus reflects and reinforces the male supremacist notion that the (male) sexual urge is either uncontrollable or, if repressed, causes neurosis or finds an outlet in sex crimes. (Jackson 1984: 45–6)

In common with Freudian theories, sexology appeared to accept that the male should provide the paradigm for natural, healthy sexual response defined in terms of a goal-oriented role, beginning with penetration and ending with ejaculation. Normal masculine sexual behaviour was still cast in acquisitive terms, whereas the female sexual response should be passive and receptive. Later sexologists such as Kinsey and Masters and Johnson refuted Freud in his distinction between the clitoral and vaginal orgasm – and therefore the notion of a female transition from immature to mature sexual behaviour – by asserting that all orgasmic sensations emanated from the clitoris. Such findings suggested that sexual intercourse was not necessarily the most effective means by which women could receive sexual pleasure, prompting a degree of moral confusion about the legitimacy and normality of other types of stimulation. It announced the legitimation of sexual pleasure in women as natural for any healthy woman, and constructed a model of fulfilling 'married love' via the simultaneous orgasm, after the woman has been dutifully 'prepared' for intercourse:

> It is not so much denial of the clitoris that is striking as its appearance and disappearance in favour of the mythologized vagina, in defence of the penis as the organizing principle of the sexual act. This displacement allows the idealization of the simultaneous orgasm and a plethora of neurotic symptoms, notably premature ejaculation and frigidity. (Campbell 1980: 6)

Sexuality is still associated with coitus, and though other practices of stimulation are acceptable, they remain subordinate to this as the organizing principle: 'In fact the very term "sexual intercourse", which would in theory mean any form of sexual interaction, is in practice synonymous with coitus in everyday speech as well as in the scientific literature' (Jackson in Coveney et al. 1984: 71). Sexuality has been implicitly accepted by psychoanalysts and sexologists to represent a fusion of culture and nature: the instinct is there from birth, but our transition to healthy adult (hetero)sexuality is a tortuous journey affected by our successful or unsuccessful entry into cultural/social/gendered norms. Foucault, Weeks and many feminist theorists have opposed the biologistic dimensions of sexology, arguing that sexuality is only definable through specific social meanings – that correct practices, choice of partner/object and periods of abstinence and forms of desire have always changed according to the vicissitudes of history and changing social relations. The way we learn appropriate forms of sexual expression seems to be through punitive responses to undesirable forms of childhood sexual behaviour; the 'secret' of sex is one which many moral reformers would like to retain, even though the will to hide sexual realities is embraced by a 'veritable discursive explosion' (Foucault 1979: 17). The association of sex with secrecy and privacy still pervades discourse around sexuality today, and perhaps goes some way to explaining feminists' enduring reticence about the subject. This explosive obsession with sex is primarily exhibited as a concern to catalogue unnatural and 'deviant' forms of sexual expression, whereas the 'natural' that presumably underpinned all this chaos was left largely undocumented: 'the legitimate couple, with its regular sexuality, had a right to more discretion' (Foucault 1979: 38). Foucault's critique of psychoanalytical and sexological discourses has proved an important source for feminists, because he identifies clear links between social control of licit and illicit sexual practices and the operation of power between individuals and institutions. The notion of sexuality as natural instinct is one utilized within society to reaffirm preferred social/gendered hierarchies. It has no currency or meaning outside these modalities of power:

> Sexuality must not be described as a stubborn drive, by nature alien and of necessity disobedient to a power which exhausts itself trying to subdue it and often fails to control it entirely. It appears rather as an especially dense transfer point for relations of power: between men and women, young people and old people, parents and offspring, teachers and students, priests and laity, an administration and a population. (Foucault 1979: 103)

Networks of power and their relation to individual drives and practices is complex, and yet in Foucault's analysis 'power is everywhere; not because it embraces everything, but because it comes from everywhere' (Foucault 1979: 93). One cannot identify a singular oppressive force from whence all definitions of sexuality derive; and the more sex is cast as the root of the self, the harder it is to combat the tenacious association of certain practices with the natural. Yet such practices remain the most ill-defined. For feminists approaching the problem of sexuality in relation to women's material and ideological conditions of existence, it is necessary to reinforce the point that, 'sexuality is as much about words, images, ritual and fantasy as it is about the body: the way we think about sex fashions the way we live it' (Weeks 1985: 3). Many of the images, words, rituals and fantasies utilized in modern representations of sex and sexuality involve the use of women's bodies – often fragmented and idealized – to stimulate male desire. It is these sexualized images of women which early second wave feminists took as their primary object of study maintaining, to varying degrees, that 'what is specific to the oppression of women of all races and classes is that it takes a sexual form' (Jackson in Coveney et al. 1984: 46).

THE EARLY SECOND WAVE:
REVOLUTIONARY OR PRESCRIPTIVE?

However widespread permissiveness is believed to have been, this new wave of sexual 'revolution' spawned an increase in the production and sales of mainstream 'soft' pornography, and also heralded the inception of journals such as *Forum*. *Forum*'s subtitle – 'The International Journal of Human Relations' – effectively announces its major intention of being a serious publication for the dissemination of information around sexual matters. It became specifically associated with the Sexual Revolution and the era of 'swinging' (group sex, and partner swapping) – ostensibly addressing the needs of both men and women, via features designed to increase enlightenment and combat sexual 'hang-ups'. In actuality, most of its regular features, including the problem page, reinforced gender differences in the field of sexuality, where problems were what women suffered from and needed advice about in order to better satisfy their husbands.[3] Although visual pornographic images were secondary to erotic fiction and articles, and despite the fact that – in theory, at least – it demonstrated a liberal attitude to homosexual relations, *Forum* served to reinforce a heteroreality, where 'lesbianism' was acceptable purely as a prelude to heterosexual 'consummation'. In *The*

Sexuality Papers (1984), Coveney et al. surveyed numerous editions of *Forum* issued during the '70s, and argued that these ironically demonstrate that women were actively coerced into 'swinging' and 'free' sexual expression for the greater titillation of their male partners – as well as affirming the male 'right' to promiscuity within marriage. Their overall conclusion is one shared by earlier commentators such as Dana Densmore: the belief that the Sexual Revolution liberated women is a myth and the 'discovery' of women's multiorgasmic potential was co-opted into the service of male-oriented eroticism. In fact they identify women as moving from a period of guilt about demonstrating active sexual feelings (only 'bad' women did) to a New Guilt if they were reluctant to participate in an environment of free sexual expression:

> This is how the New Guilt works. Instead of women feeling guilty because they don't want sex at all, or because they experienced sexual pleasure in the days when women weren't supposed to have any sexuality, they now have to feel guilty because they have these 'unliberated' antisocial attitudes towards their husbands' 'liberated' practices. (Jackson in Coveney et al. 1984: 91)

What is interesting is the coincidence of the 'soft' pornography explosion and media representations of the late '60s and early '70s as the golden age of sex, with the feminist concentration on the need to define personal relationships and redefine female sexuality and desire. The notion of there being any common ground between the two is particularly problematic, since the anti-pornography lobby became a powerful arm of the women's movement. Radical feminists, such as Andrea Dworkin, interpreted the images purveyed by pornography as a kind of patriarchal propaganda which reinforced male notions of women as sexual objects who can be 'taken' if necessary by violent force or rape.

> Pornography is an essential issue because pornography says that women want to be hurt, forced, and abused: pornography says that women want to be raped battered, kidnapped, maimed; pornography says that women want to be humiliated, shamed, defamed; pornography says that women say No but mean Yes – Yes to violence, Yes to pain. (Dworkin 1988: 203)

For radical feminists of the 1970s, pornography quite simply objectified and dehumanized women, and legitimized the perpetuation of male violence against individual women in their everyday lives. Their

definitions of pornography vary, but in the main such representational forms were regarded as fluid enough to encompass all aspects of
culture, including advertisements. Radicals such as Adrienne Rich
had no doubt that sexualized images of women affected their social
experiences and the way men are encouraged to view women: 'The
most pernicious message relayed by pornography is that women are
natural sexual prey to men and love it' (Rich 1986: 40). Early socialist
feminists, especially in Britain, were more lukewarm and tended to
consider pornography in the light of the boundaries of censorship;
that the definitions of 'obscenity' were governed by the moral purity
lobby and censorship might equal denial of free speech for women
too. Nonetheless the feminist pornography debate became inextri-
cable from the sexuality debate, and tended to further occlude the
issue of female desire, since the female body through pornography
had seemingly been subjected to wholesale colonization by the male.
Dworkin exemplifies this conflation of perspectives:

> The sexuality of women has been stolen outright, appropriated
> by men – conquered, possessed, taken, violated; women have
> been systematically and absolutely denied the right to sexual
> self-determination and to sexual integrity; and because the sex-
> uality of women has been stolen, this sexuality itself, it – as
> distinguished from an individual woman as a sentient being – it
> can be sold. (Dworkin 1988: 229)

In the early days of women's liberation, therefore, most discussions
of what could constitute an authentic female sexuality were necessarily tainted by the notion that sexuality had been commodified,
and that female sexuality could only be critically cast in negative
terms – as something women historically lacked. In this context
Shere Hite began her research into how individual women regarded
their sexuality, and their own personal relationships.

The Hite Report (1976) surely emerged as a result of the collision
between an atmosphere of increased explicitness prompted by the
Sexual Revolution and the women's movement itself. The report
collated the responses of 3,000 American women to a questionnaire
addressing issues surrounding sexuality and sexual practices. It con-
sists largely of quotes by these anonymous contributors, categorized
under headings such as 'Masturbation', 'Orgasm', 'Intercourse',
'Lesbianism', etc. The findings and ramifications of these replies
have been seen as of importance for the early women's movement as
a means of sharing experiences and providing statistics about

women's attitude to sex across the ranges of age and sexual orientation (although the sample is still relatively small and ethnic origins
of respondents were not recorded). For the purpose of this discussion, the most interesting part of the book is the section dealing with
the Sexual Revolution, where most of the women's responses are
profoundly negative, and appear largely pessimistic about the possibility of there being a sexual revolution that would benefit women
equally. One woman directly relates sexual revolution to the images
of pornography:

> It's got a long way to go. If the crap in Playboy or Penthouse is
> anybody's idea of a sexual revolution then it's revolting all right.
> As long as women are exploited sexually, viewed as sex objects
> and raised from the cradle to accommodate men, the sexual
> revolution is meaningless. It seems to me that the sexual revo-
> lution has just given the con men the chance to sell douches
> and razors, but that you don't see much in the way of real free
> expression and happiness, or joy in the body and in sex. (Hite
> 1977: 455–6)

Another woman comments:

> What 'sexual revolution'? I am struggling in a feminist revo-
> lution! The so-called sexual revolution, from my point of view,
> did nothing to liberate women or men. Men got a screw for free
> and it was done out in the open and under the liberal-radical
> guise of a revolution against antiquated sex attitudes. Women
> still wanted those men for lifetime companions because they
> gave away their bodies and minds and found identity in the
> man instead of in themselves. Men still maintain the top posi-
> tion in the job market, in women's magazine stories, in bed and
> in the mind of the female psyche. So really the sexual revolu-
> tion advertised something I already knew. Women are treated
> as objects. Only in this 'revolution' the oppressed didn't gain a
> thing. The oppressor began the 'sexual revolution' through rock
> music, the cosmetic market, Hugh Hefner, etc., but we weren't
> liberated from our roles, only more objectified. (Hite 1977:
> 456–7)

From these two examples it is clear that women were beginning to
see more liberal acceptance of expressions of female sexuality as further
means for male exploitation. Both respondents make connections
between sex and its cultural commodification, and this awareness in
itself seems to be a tribute to the power of the radical feminist

message. However, responses quoted in other chapters demonstrated a depressing inability among women to translate this consciousness into their daily lives.

Although Hite amongst others calls for a redefinition of what we see as sex – where reproduction is no longer perceived as the sole reason for sexual contact and intercourse need not be central to heterosexual experience (Hite 1977: 527–8) – heterosexuality remains the assumed norm for women. The respondents of the survey saw penetrative sex as a 'goal' in their relationships (even if it is a goal that left them feeling largely unsatisfied), and the questionnaire itself is inevitably weighted towards heterosexual experience. Although Hite is careful to use the non-gendered term 'partner', she specifically addresses a question to lesbians which reveals their effective exclusion from other questions. In addition she persists in using the term 'intercourse', which is popularly considered to connote penile penetration. Later, women are asked whether they prefer clitoral stimulation to penetration – a distinction which only makes clear sense in heterosexual terms, where foreplay is seen as part of a progression to 'real' sexual congress.

Nevertheless books such as *The Hite Report* clearly aided the consciousness-raising aspects of the movement, including as it does frank descriptions of individual women's experiences of various sexual activities. Perhaps its major success lay in its exposure of the fact that many women felt pressurized to perform in this 'new era' of sexual freedom, just as they had accepted the 'fact' of female sexual repulsion in the 'dark ages' of sexual ignorance:

> Yes, I feel the need to perform orgasmically, competitively with other women at large in the community. I wish I didn't. It really got started when I used to feel pressure from my former partner, because if I didn't come, it proved he wasn't a 'real man'. But I'm not a star of a two-ring circus. (Hite 1977: 130)

The Hite Report reads like a catalogue of restraint, disgust and capitulation. 'Freedom' of sexual expression did not guarantee any increased freedom or change in status for women in other areas of their lives. Many feminists associated this failure with the way female sexuality is used and objectified by the media, where 'permissiveness' appears to sanction permission for men to use women as sex objects.

The Permissive Society meant many things retrospectively – not least the opportunity for people to bemoan the increasing promiscuity of youth and the subsequent threat to 'family values' of monogamy and female chastity. If something 'offended' against public decency, then it all too often became linked with counter-cultures from hippies to feminists, despite feminists' obvious unease with their supposed leading role in the Sexual Revolution. The Permissive Society is also famously the era when the Pill became widely available, coinciding with feminists' struggle for women's right to greater control over their bodies, especially in the sphere of reproduction. The commonplace that the Pill liberated women more than anything else cements the assumed link between reproduction and female sexuality. It is a link which many feminists left unquestioned, with the result that coitus still determined sex, and the association between contraception and 'family planning' implied that the only freedom women should have in this field is the freedom to space their pregnancies once a long-term (marital) partnership is achieved. Female sexual expression was still associated with risks, because it remained centred upon penetrative intercourse: you either risked an unwanted pregnancy or accepted the long term risks of the Pill. Contraception and abortion, not a revolution in sexual practices, remained central to feminist debate and in this sense heterosexual feminists contributed to the commonsense view that penetrative intercourse was the pinnacle of sexual experience.

Feminist discourse was and still is dominated by heterosexual women, and the area of sexual identity itself was often neglected as a potentially divisive subject, which meant that lesbians felt alienated and unrepresented by mainstream feminism. Heterosexual women themselves appeared to be threatened by lesbian dissenting voices in the movement, especially in face of calls for the interrogation of heterosexuality as an institution as well as a sexual choice. Lesbians with a history in gay activism were accustomed to being outspoken about their own right to sexual self-determination, but even today heterosexual feminists remain reluctant to scrutinize the social construction of heterosexuality, and the means by which – as institution – it exerts a powerful influence over women's social/sexual lives. Discourses which inform knowledges of human sexual behaviour contain and categorize homosexuals as subjects bounded and determined by the perceived nature of their desires; heterosexuality evades such simplistic definition – not least because it is synonymous with a 'normal' way of life, and therefore its practices and characteristics are deemed to be self-evident. This abstract slippage between heterosexuality and homosexuality is perhaps a contributory factor in heterosexual feminists' reluctance to analyse their own sexual choice. Until very recently it has been left largely to lesbian and gay male critics to examine the differing social/sexual meanings of heterosexuality, and to investigate its ideological power as an institution which affects everyone's lives regardless of one's orientation, and is, accordingly, much more than a mere 'preference' or choice.

Utopias involving total sexual freedom have endured since the nineteenth century. Radical feminist sexual utopias of the '70s increasingly took on a specifically lesbian identity. Such separatist havens were to be for women whose chosen sexual orientation was lesbianism, and also for those who ended sexual relations with men for 'political' reasons, and who may or may not have sex with other women. This reflected a conviction that heterosexual sex reflected, in microcosm, gendered power politics played out in the wider social sphere so, for the interim, one could only truly liberate women by liberating them from sexual relations with men altogether. Such a view is problematical for feminists who felt that heterosexuality – ill-defined as it is – could be reformed from within. As it is, a call for the rejection of male lovers on political grounds, in favour of female lovers or celibacy, implies that the women's right to choose her sexual orientation (assuming the recognition that heterosexuality is not automatically chosen) might metamorphose into no real choice at all within a radical feminist world view. Feminists who retained their sexual ties to men were afraid of being accused of acting in bad faith and shielding the enemy, instead of exposing him to the consequences of men's past atrocities against women. Although very few feminists explicitly called for all women to reject men, the elision of discussions around politically appropriate forms of sexual desire fostered the common conception that there was a correct form of sexual response – even though feminists had only really got as far as identifying the negative effects of the prevailing patriarchal ideology of heterosexuality. It seems that in the sphere of sexual relations at least, straight women found it difficult to collapse the public and private spheres, and were enraged by what they regarded as the coerciveness of manifestos such as 'The Woman Identified Woman'.[4] Such a conflict is expressed by a respondent in an interview conducted by Anne Koedt in 1971:

> Many feminists are now beginning to at least theoretically consider the fact that there's no reason why one shouldn't love a woman. But I think that a certain kind of experimentation going on now with lesbianism can be really bad. Because even if you do ideologically think that it is perfectly fine – well, that's a political position; but being able to love somebody is a very personal and private thing as well . . . . (Koedt et al. 1973: 91)

Despite a commitment towards politicizing the personal, many women wanted to draw the line at a policing of sexual practices, which was often perceived as an invasion of a sphere of privacy that should be demarcated as beyond even sexual politics. Heterosexual women were often antagonistic to lesbian feminist writings on sexuality, although happier with Adrienne Rich's potentially more moderate conception of the woman-identified-woman, which could suggest a lesbian bonding, but was mainly interpreted as an exhortation for women to give support to each other rather than drain all their energies in total emotional investments in men. Few pursued Rich's interrogation of heterosexuality in the light of constructions of sexual desire and pleasure, preferring rather to analyse its effects outside of this domain – via the institution of marriage, the availability of contraception and so forth.

One slogan – 'Feminism is the theory; lesbianism is the practice', reputedly first coined by Ti-Grace Atkinson[5] – exemplifies a deepening rift between some radicals and the main body of heterosexual feminists through its uncompromising link between a feminist political identity and a lesbian sexual one. And such a position – undoubtedly a minority one – was used to suggest that feminism was necessarily prescriptive in its delineation of appropriate forms of sexual response. The notion of a correct political identity which encompasses women's most private lives caused heated controversy in the movement, and still does. Many feminists might accept that as an institution, heterosexuality warrants deeper scrutiny, while maintaining that this should not affect women's 'right' to retain the sexual 'preference' of heterosexuality. The breadth of disagreement surrounding the issue of sexuality highlighted it as a real theoretical and political problem for feminism. If you could identify 'bad sex' in the form of power plays of dominance and submission and reliance on penetration in heterosexual behaviour, then it is implied that one must set the terms for 'good' non-exploitative sex. Some straight feminists reacted to criticism of their own bad faith by arguing that many lesbians mimicked traditional sex role definitions, particularly in butch/femme roleplay, and were therefore equally inauthentic in their open parody of male/female power axes. Lesbian sexuality itself was gradually rendered vulnerable to extensive criticism.[6]

Sheila Jeffreys, a revolutionary feminist who has had a significant impact upon feminist thinking during the 1980s and 1990s, perhaps exemplifies the most uncompromising position on what constitutes appropriate and inappropriate forms of sexual behaviour. Jeffreys paints a harshly essentialist view of male sexual impulses, where the male is predator, whose penetration of the female necessarily and always connotes colonization and aggression (see Jeffreys 1990). The more common position adopted by lesbian feminists from the '70s to the present is characterized by their struggle to make heterosexual feminists confront elements of homophobia; particularly in some feminists' paranoic fear of a lesbian takeover within the ranks. Straight feminists often rather wilfully ignored the fact of their tendency to 'masculinize' sex; to conduct discussions solely around the arena of sexual violence, pornography and contraception, and to block debates around female desire and sexual pleasure. Meanwhile lesbian feminists pursued a commitment to explore lesbian sexuality and its expression – the resulting debates often causing rifts and conflict, revealing a painful tension between concepts of sex as an expression of one's own personal desires, and sexuality as a political battleground for both feminists and the gay movement. In retrospect, it seems that heterosexual feminists exaggerated the takeover threat of the 'separatist' tendency, perhaps because debates about sex created real, but misguided, fears that each feminist in her private life did not act ethically; misguided in that such demands contributed to the popular consciousness that feminism was an ultimately tyrannical form of orthodoxy. Anne Koedt, in her essay 'Lesbianism and Feminism' (1971) attacks what she sees as prescriptive tendencies among radical lesbian feminists as a perversion of 'the personal is political': 'While it is true that there are political implications in everything a woman qua woman experiences, it is not therefore true that a woman's life is the political property of the woman's movement' (Koedt et al. 1973: 255).

Adrienne Rich's famous essay 'Compulsory Heterosexuality and Lesbian Existence' (1980) was one of the earliest attempts to analyse the effects of heterosexuality as an institution which taints women's lives whatever their sexual orientation, and which constitutes a major aspect of women's experience of social and sexual reality. Since much of the rhetoric of the modern feminist movement is arranged around notions of 'choice' or 'freedom', Rich's analysis of heterosexuality as a compulsory practice is challenging: 'Feminist theory can no longer afford merely to voice a toleration of 'lesbianism' as an 'alternative life style' or make token allusion to lesbians. A feminist critique of compulsory heterosexual orientation for women is long overdue' (Rich 1986: 27). Seeming to concur with the findings of Michel Foucault and Jeffrey Weeks, Rich identifies the problem of male sexuality as not limited to their predilection for penetration, but something that as an expression of male power amounts to 'a pervasive cluster of

forces, ranging from physical brutality to control of consciousness'
(Rich 1986: 39). Rich gestures towards a consideration of the ideological impact of dominant definitions of sexuality and their entrench-
ment within the master discourses of Western patriarchal social
reality; but it is a theme which has only latterly been developed.

Feminists of the 1970s, because of their forthright views on sex,
tended to be perceived by outsiders as either sexually available women
('liberated' from chastity) or prudes (liberated from sex altogether);
but the problem of female sexuality and the means by which to redefine it positively became an increasingly thorny one in the '80s and
'90s, and the prudish image of feminism has held sway. Few feminists dared to suggest a possibility of a future where everyone was
'bisexual', in face of internal debates about sexual identity, even
though most believed in theory that current sexual identities were
socially constructed and therefore ripe for redefinition. Shulamith
Firestone's *The Dialectic of Sex* (1970) does display her deep conviction that humankind is innately bisexual, and her bio-technologized
utopia predicts a period of total sexual freedom (including the aboli-
tion of incest taboos and childhood sexual repression), particularly in
her proposed removal of the link between procreation and sexual
intercourse in the era of the text tube baby. In common with many
early feminists, she believes that sex roles can be transformed by a
transformation of sexual behaviour, although her assurance that 'a
revolutionary in every bedroom cannot fail to shake up the status
quo' (Firestone 1979: 44), had not caused any tremors in the world
order by the time the New Right moral reaction began to be felt in
the 1980s.

DEBATES AROUND SEXUAL IDENTITY: THE 1980s AND '90s

Recently, feminists have viewed the early years of women's liberation
with a colder eye, and sexuality, a subject which always underpinned
the central precepts of feminism, has become subject to more intense
theoretical scrutiny. Questions of pleasure, desire and difference are
examined, and many theorists became dissatisfied with what they
regarded as the simplistic analytical premises of the early second
wave where it was often assumed that there was a one-to-one
relationship between images of women and female oppression. Most
notably this has led to intense rifts around the area of pornography,
where some women would argue that sexualized images of women
can be renegotiated in a way that is empowering and self-determin-
ing. In the past, talking about sex in feminist terms meant talking

about anything but the dread act itself; simply to address the 'problem' of sex might risk reaffirming the status of women in Western society as primarily 'sex objects', defined by lack of a penis/power. Feminists, after all, had campaigned for a women's right to complete access to human relations in personal and social terms; and this had to involve, to some degree, a decentring of the image of woman as sex object.

In fact, by the 1980s, feminists were becoming rapidly more conscious that earlier arguments about 'true' female identity might equate all too closely with the old patriarchal analysis of feminine 'weakness'. It was on the whole easier to emphasize the non-violent, emotional aspects of femininity as positive than it was to address the image of a liberated woman with an even sprinkling of 'masculinity' – including sexual acquisitiveness. To address the problems at the core of definitions of female sexuality, begged an openness about how women really perceived and conducted their sexual relationships, as opposed to the mythologies that surrounded this area, and which feminists seem to have internalized along the way. Changing definitions of female sexuality were sorely required, and were directly related to projections of what a feminist future might hold.

> Often to talk about sexuality was to talk not about sex at all, but about relationships, about life styles, about emotions. The word 'sexuality' went wider, in any case, than sex: 'sex' referred to acts and the engagement in practices; 'sexuality' was about identity and gender, about masculine and feminine, about desire, fantasy, and the whole construction of the self. (Wilson 1986: 173)

Certainly French feminisms and psychoanalytic theory discussed desire and pleasure extensively, but Anglo-American feminists found supreme difficulties in reconciling a political position which aimed to reinvent a social reality, with a stance that engaged with sexuality at more than a high theoretical level, and which often simply alienated women who might be seeking guidance about the politics of their own desires.

The central theoretical position of Jeffrey Weeks and Michel Foucault – that sexuality was bounded and defined by social and cultural meanings – was embraced by many feminist theorists. Such a view appeared to provide a shifting perspective where change might be negotiated, and the fusion of female sexuality within the parameters of reproduction and domestic servicing could be fruitfully exposed as a construction deeply entrenched in Western medico-juridico-political discourse. Only once the interdependencies between these forms of discourse and their utilization are identified, can the seeming fixity and naturalness of the view of female sexuality as simply complementary to a male sexuality, which becomes the central determinant of definitions of human sexual response, be exposed. Such theorists challenge essentialist views of sex, seeing the notion of sexuality as a fluid concept, an historical construct, which to be analysed effectively needs to be broken down into social categories of class/race/gender differentiation, the role of the state, and analysis of discourses (e.g. medical, legal, religious) which have sought to control and therefore determine sexuality. The myth of sexuality in its current usage is that it affords the individual liberation through free expression of her/his desires; it is a myth because these desires are mediated through a powerful ideological image of 'good' and 'bad' (usually non-productive) forms of sexual relations, sanctioned or prohibited in social relations. Viewed as a site of symbolic enactment of unequal power relations, female sexuality can be defined as having nothing to 'add' to that of the male; and the masculinized hegemony of definitions of sexuality is maintained.

In *Anticlimax* (1990) Sheila Jeffreys is resistant to the position held by Weeks et al., and suggests that current feminist adoptions of analogous positions is part of a 'libertarian backlash' against the critiques of pornography and sexual violence initiated by the women's movement. She goes so far as to suggest that 'in the 1980s women's liberation has been hijacked by the sexual libertarians who are devoted to persuading women that the enthusiastic celebration of our oppression in sadomasochism is the same thing as liberation' (Jeffreys 1990: 3). For Jeffreys, heterosexuality embodies and gives meaning to the sadomasochistic role-play of dominance and submission, in whatever context it is conducted – hence it necessarily interfaces with broader social relations of power at more than a symbolic level. She denies that there may currently be any distinction between heterosexuality as an institution which shapes sexological, medical and political discourse, and heterosexuality as a definition of desire between members of the opposite sex – no matter whether in the future this might be determined along more egalitarian lines. Many feminists would agree with her assertion that 'sex as we know it under male supremacy is the eroticized power difference of heterosexuality' (Jeffreys 1990: 3), but few would be currently willing to accept that only an outright rejection of heterosexuality as a form of object choice would pave the way for a feminist revolution. Her analysis of the effects of sexological research and sex therapy can, however, be acute and enlightening; as she points out, if it is accepted that sexuality is socially constructed, then the chief function of sex therapy as a curative process is that of social control. It would not be fair to suggest that sex therapy only performs the function of social control; but it clearly has the capacity to project a model of appropriate sexual appetite and performance against which individual performances and choices can be gauged.

Jeffreys views all forms of discourse around sexual liberation – whether it be sexology, sexual therapy, pornography, or a new wave of sexually explicit literature engendered in the 1960s – as perpetuating a male model of sexual normality and an apologetic for male dominance in all areas of private and public life. In this context she makes the reasonable point that sexual libertarianism can seem to reaffirm the public/private distinction – that anything goes for consenting adults – whereas feminism needs to interrogate such a divide because it fosters other forms of inequality.[7] The gay liberation movement is itself viewed as being appropriated by gay men who, Jeffreys maintains, subsumed and negated lesbian sexuality (and with it feminist egalitarian values) in an eroticization of difference within same-sex relationships: 'As men gays receive the same socialization as do heterosexual men. Dominance and submission are eroticized for them too' (Jeffreys 1990: 145). There is one singular flaw in Jeffreys' argument: having implied that heterosexual socialization taints all male sexual response and therefore that all individuals regardless of sexual orientation, collude or resist, but necessarily act within a 'heteroreality', she appears to deny that lesbians might also be susceptible to the erotic symbolization of power play in their sexual lives.

This is where Jeffreys' work is at its most unsatisfactory; having concurred with other sexual theorists that sexuality is a social construct which enforces a set of norms that have a dubious bearing on biological imperatives, she isolates lesbianism as, in its 'pure' form, untainted by such networks of dominance and power. She highlights what are assumed to be predominant forms of gay male sexual behaviour such as 'cruising', 'cottaging' and habitual promiscuity, setting this against statistics provided by the Kinsey Institute to show that lesbians do not tend to cruise, and prefer instead long-term commitments (Jeffreys 1990: 151). The central problem here is that she uses such information to appear to claim that there are essential differences between the behaviour of gay men and women. Yet it could equally be argued that each group is responding to the socializing tendencies of a heterosexual institution which endorses different attitudes to sex and emotional commitment along gendered lines.

Thus, it must also inform the way homosexuals develop their own specific social environments – where, for example, bar culture is more commonly an entrenched and acceptable outlet for male recreation.

Not only does Jeffreys attack gay men and heterosexuals, but also particular forms of lesbian sexual expression, such as butch/femme role-play, and especially sadomasochism. For her, sadomasochism is a practice embedded in gay male sexuality, something which some lesbians have adopted, despite Jeffreys' personal conviction that 's/m ideology is in contradiction to the most cherished precepts of feminism' (Jeffreys 1990: 210). What Jeffreys' own precepts are and how she envisages a future feminist political stance on appropriate forms of sexuality is difficult to determine, except to say that she perceives all forms of sexual relationships – apart from so-called 'vanilla' lesbian sex – as tainted by powerplay politics. She implies that male heterosexual urges are charged by violent and aggressive feelings towards women, ineluctably informed by their perception of their own ruling class status (here all men regardless of race and class are seen as possessing equal measures of this).

Of course most feminists would agree that women's social experiences of violence and harassment colour their perceptions of sex, but this view can be shaped to quite different ends – other than condemning all heterosexual practices as essentially determined by violence and exploitation. Undoubtedly pornography in its current form is perceived by many as exclusively structured by preconceptions of the nature of the male sex drive, and it informs many men's attitudes to women in a sexual context. Research on the relationship between pornography and acts of sexual violence has never been conclusive, and many have decided that although pornography can 'educate' men in ways to abuse women, to argue that it directly incites acts of violence is probably not the most effective way to redefine pornography. Many contemporary feminists prefer instead to contrast the images of women portrayed in mainstream pornography with other dominant images of women, which also speak volumes about the presumed social/sexual status of women (see, for example, Gamman and Marshment 1988).

The main problem with *Anticlimax* is that Jeffreys' arguments are inconsistent, because she draws upon biological and cultural considerations simultaneously. On many issues she is incisive – for example that libertarian approaches to sexuality effectively block the development of a political interrogation of sexuality: if the premise is that one's private pleasures are sacrosanct, then there is no space to proscribe certain practices, which may well not involve the full consent

of both parties – for example paedophilia. Nonetheless her consequent dismissal of writers such as Foucault and Weeks as libertarians
is debatable, since neither of them appear to have a clear investment
in retaining the public/private divide as it now operates, or to perceive
this as individually liberating. Jeffreys' own position as a revolutionary
feminist becomes clear: she believes that lesbianism is an important
political strategy for women to end their subordination, and any view
of an egalitarian future for heterosexuals and gay men is deferred, on
the grounds that we cannot predict what choices people would make
in such a situation.

Jeffrey Weeks sees the discourses around sexuality as much more
complex and contradictory, and in *Sexuality and its Discontents*
(1985), while acknowledging that sexological thinking has contributed to modern meanings of sexuality, argues that their theoretical
work is far too heterogeneous to be dismissed simply as a vehicle for
greater social control. Sexology remains a vital component of our
existing definitions of the boundaries of desire, and although it may
need to be rejected, its contribution and its terms of reference need
firstly to be re-examined.[8] In fact, in the radical feminist reaction
against the male-oriented rhetoric of the Sexual Revolution, he perceives the risk of a peculiar coalition of interests with feminism's
'ideological enemies in feeding the new puritanism of our time'
(Weeks 1985: 19). This is the kind of accusation that Jeffreys objects
to, but does little to reject by outlining a future agenda for increased
freedom to negotiate one's own sexual choices. Weeks denies Jeffreys'
inference that sexual libertarianism has depoliticized the feminist
agenda, arguing instead that 'the contemporary political agenda on
sexual issues is being written not by the libertarian left but by the
moral right' (Weeks 1985: 32). Jeffreys cites the former as the enemy
and Weeks the latter; and for feminists in general there may well be
a pressing need to seek a new discursive ground divorced from both.

The Right is associated with moral crusading, the Left with libertarianism, and yet both associations are with conventional mainstream
political demarcations, which make little sense for feminist theorists
in the wake of their destabilizing of the agendas of the mainstream
parliamentary system. Libertarianism and moralism are both features
of an old patriarchal order; arguably what most feminists seek is an
ethics of sexuality – a consensus of definitions around this area that
neither leads to prescriptiveness nor to the myths that sex has got
nothing to do with other aspects of our social lives. For women this
has never been the case; and as long as sexuality has bearing on the
processes of reproduction it never will. Weeks himself suggests by

the logic of his own argument that there has to be some form of
social ethics in our consideration of the construction of human sexuality, if we are to avoid a libertarianism that implicitly argues that
we should be freed as individuals to pursue our own sexual choices
on the grounds of natural self expression: 'We need, therefore, to tear
open the assumptions which lock us into conflicting views about
what is natural or unnatural, true or false, right or wrong' (Weeks
1985: 56). Later he states that:

> It clearly cannot be the case that all manifestations of non-
> orthodox sexuality are equally valid; that no real distinctions
> can be made. To argue that 'anything goes' is to fall back into
> an easy libertarianism which ignores questions of power and
> the quality of relationships. (Weeks 1985: 210)

Surely this indicates a need for a more general overview of how a
theory of sexuality – of appropriate and inappropriate forms of sexual behaviour – dominates Western consciousness of sexual difference
in men and women, and extends far beyond the biological – even
beyond observations of what we do in bed. Theories of sexual
response embrace much more than an individual's expression of
desire, or need for gratification; a person's sexuality, whether they are
heterosexual, homosexual, transsexual, auto-erotic and so on, comes
to define their very essence.

CURRENT REFLECTIONS

Feminist theorists have begun to recognize the pitfalls of a position
which tends to cast female sexual responses in purely negative terms,
as shaped and defined by the dominant male imperative. However,
the connections that have been made between sexological and psychoanalytical descriptions of human sexuality, and the enactment of
such notions of difference at the level of social relations have been
crucial to the development of feminist thought, and the value of this
enterprise should not be underestimated. Nonetheless, at present,
Anglo-American feminist explorations into the realms of female
desire are still too dependent on patriarchal representations of sexuality. Even if this dependency only perversely manifests itself as a
rejection of such representations, it blocks attempts to signal a way
forward for feminism, and sometimes – as in the case of Sheila
Jeffreys – marks a retreat into dubious truth claims around an
authentic female nature. Jeffrey Weeks pinpoints such a retreat as a
significant danger within contemporary theories of sexuality: 'Sex
exists today in a moral vacuum. In the resulting confusion and

uncertainty there is a temptation to retreat into the old verities of "Nature" or to search for new truths and certainties, a new absolutism' (Weeks 1985: 3). Weeks suggests that those who do not accept the challenge of a new (politicized) libertarianism which decentres the family form as the purveyor of social norms, are frightened of the possible moral chaos outside its parameters. I would argue that sexuality is such a minefield for feminists that perhaps they recognize a need to construct quite well-defined models of appropriate forms of sexual expression to prevent a perpetuation of male definitions of sexuality outside the existing familial organization.

Once sex is scrutinized in relation to its social meanings we can identify a proliferation of sexualities contained within the consensual reality of heterosexuality, most of which are negated by prevailing structures of power. Michel Foucault argues that 'sex is placed by power in a binary system: licit and illicit, permitted and forbidden' (Foucault 1979: 83). For feminists it seems abundantly clear that in relation to sex, power is additionally organized around the binarist meanings ascribed to gender difference in psychoanalytical and sexological thought. This crucial binary is largely ignored by writers like Foucault and Weeks, and yet just as we act upon our knowledge of the licit and illicit, any sexual utopia is hampered by the affirmation in discourses of power, of the notion that two sexes act upon completely separate sexual and emotional drives in their responses. Foucault's observation that 'in political thought and analysis, we still have not cut off the head of the king' (Foucault 1979: 88–9), has a particular resonance for feminists in their analysis of the perpetuation of gendered power relationships. To extend the analogy, to cut off the king's head finally, there is nothing to be gained by simply replacing it with the head of the queen: we still need to heed his laws and understand the maintenance of his sovereignty in order to subvert them, which engages us in a seemingly incontrovertible double-bind. For example, Freudian discourse, as reassessed by feminists, reveals its own points of fragility, its own radical inconsistencies which have facilitated feminist enquiry in thwarting some of the more tenacious claims to truth around sexual response.

For most mainstream feminists, heterosexuality as a sexual 'choice', as an institution, as an instrument of coercion – in whatever guise it appears in the field of human sexual response – is resolutely avoided as a topic of debate. The attempts by early radical feminists to encourage women to understand their own bodies and to explore their own sensual feelings are not pursued today in any refined form; generally such activities are simply treated to an embarrassed silence,

and the issue of sex is elided – not surprisingly confirming the fears
of sexual radicals that feminism has the potential for a strong puritan streak. As I suggested earlier, lesbian feminists have had a much
more extensive engagement with these areas; and as much as they
have addressed the demonization of lesbianism and homosexuality in
general, they have in addition attempted a critique of heterosexuality
and its part (as institution) in women's oppression. Sheila Jeffreys has
gone as far as to suggest a one-to-one correlation between lesbianism
and feminism, stressing that lesbianism is the only political choice
for women, thereby conflating the issues of desire and sexual choice
with that of an appropriate political/personal stance. Such a position
effectively blocks further discussion by heterosexual feminists, who
might be forgiven for feeling automatically accused of 'inauthenti-
city', and declining to enter into such debates. Such a deadlock risks
a perpetuation of the popular belief that feminists are prescriptive
and tyrannical, and perhaps a little too moralistic about sexuality.
Conversely, Beatrix Campbell argues that:

> Heterosexuality has to feature in our politics as more than a
> guilty secret; indeed, in order that women mobilize any polit-
> ical combativity around it, it must be restored as a legitimate
> part of feminism's concern. It is, after all, the primary sexual
> practice of most women. It also needs to be present to help
> clarify lesbianism's place within feminism. (1980: 1)

As Campbell hints above, lesbian explorations into female sexuality remain the most far-reaching available within feminist discourse
– to the point where lesbian feminists are assumed to have forcibly
occupied a position of moral superiority in relation to their 'guilty'
heterosexual sisters. However, it is evident that essays such as Rich's
'Compulsory Heterosexuality and Lesbian Existence' were sustained
attempts to enable heterosexual feminists to take the opportunity to
relinquish their status as guilty 'bad girls', and seriously engage with
the ramifications of their own sexual 'choice'. In other areas of feminist investigation it is clear that a lesbian or black perspective is still
lamentably regarded as the minority one, suggesting that white heterosexual women have tended to leave the 'problem' of sexual orientation to lesbians, just as there is a tendency to place the 'problem' of
race firmly in the laps of black feminists. This indicates a marked
reluctance on the part of 'mainstream' feminists to focus on issues
which demand further scrutiny of many women's most deeply-held
prejudices.

The 1990s has seen increased reflection upon issues of desire and the reconstruction and redefinition of female sexuality from both heterosexual and lesbian perspectives. For Jeffreys this new slant to feminist debates marks an incursion by dominant patriarchal ideological interests, particularly around the commodification of sex and desire signalled in the lesbian context by a return to butch/femme preoccupations and a growing sex industry focusing on dildoes and porn:

> What is astonishing is the lack of a widespread lesbian revolt against the incursion of the dildo, a symbol of male power and the oppression of women, into lesbian culture. The lesbian pornographers and sex industrialists are telling us that lesbians are disadvantaged by the absence of a penis. (Jeffreys 1994: 35)

As I have suggested above, heterosexuality has until recently been undertheorized; the absence of such discussions around the means by which heterosexual desire might be separated or recuperated from the heterosexual institution has potentially alienated women who are otherwise attracted to feminist politics. Recent publications have however addressed this most inexplicable gap in mainstream feminist thought, pointing out that this almost wholesale silence around heterosexual desire suggests by default that straight women are weak-willed or even treacherous in a feminist context.

Sue Wilkinson and Celia Kitzinger, in gathering papers for a special issue of *Feminism and Psychology* dealing with heterosexuality discovered that '"heterosexual" is not a popular label' (Wilkinson and Kitzinger 1993: 5); many women, although not lesbians or active bisexuals, were unwilling to accept the identity 'heterosexual', and some found it offensive. One distinction between the labels 'lesbian' and 'heterosexual' for women is that they are not exact polar opposites and only the former is adopted as an act of positive resistance and affirmation of a particular sexual orientation. Heterosexuality, by contrast, smacks of oppressive conventionality and the prioritizing of married monogamy, a position which many heterosexual women reject. Heterosexual feminists may want to assert that they have 'chosen' their personal sexual orientation, but that does not mean that they endorse the institutional features of heterosexuality, and this particular contradiction seems to underpin feminist interventions. As Lynne Segal observes, 'If we really cannot offer a response to much of women's sexual experience, other than to condemn it as part of a repressive social order, we can only dishearten rather than inspire the majority of women' (Segal 1994: xii). Segal's book *Straight Sex* (1994) appears at a time when the 'politics of pleasure' is being debated within feminism and signals a perceivable move away from a focus on ways in which women can confront their sexualized image – via anti-porn positions and so on. Segal's position advocates a '"queering" of traditional understandings of gender and sexuality' (Segal 1994: xv); and this notional meeting of lesbian and straight feminists under the aegis of 'queer theory' certainly allows for the deferral or denial of fixed meanings attributed to sexual roles, and desire itself. Yet Segal herself seems ambivalent about who the culprits were in the suppression of heterosexual desire in a feminist context, or what their motives might have been. It is suggested that feminism itself is at fault; but this gives the lie to the massed heterosexual constituency of feminism. She suggests that tendencies to position lesbianism as a political imperative for feminists in the 1970s denied women the right to 'discuss the realities of lesbian desire or the complexities of lesbian relationships' (Segal 1994: 53). She goes on to assert that the hijacking of arguments around sexuality into the 1980s around pornography and sexual violence further repressed the possibility for straight feminists to be honest about their own sexual lives and experiences in print. Segal's conclusions however do not appear to take us any further in the destabilization of the most tenacious aspects of the heterosexual institution. Her book ends on this note:

> There is feminism and there is fucking. As I see it, they can fit together quite as smoothly (or as painfully) as feminism and any other human activity. Straight feminists, like gay men and lesbians, have everything to gain from asserting our non-coercive desire to fuck if, when, how and as we choose. (Segal 1994: 318)

Although her work provides a useful contextualization for straight feminism and its links with sexual radicalism in the '60s and '70s, her dissociation of 'sex' as simply the act of 'fucking' from other social and cultural elements of a woman's life may well take us back to the circular binarism of earlier feminist positions on sex.

To continue to ignore the problem of female sexuality implies that heterosexual women retain an investment in heterosexuality as the norm, as well as indicating a wish to avoid areas of debate where differences between groups of women are at their most obvious. As Jana Sawicki argues, for white radical feminists, 'sexual freedom is construed negatively as freedom from male dominated institutions whose elements are crystallized in pornography, particularly in its sadomasochistic varieties' (Sawicki 1991: 35): and the problem with this model of female sexuality is that it is resistant but does not transform existing meanings of female sexuality. Lesbian sexuality is held, at best, as the 'moral conscience' of feminism and at worst its scourge – either way such ascriptions are only intelligible when it is assumed that both lesbianism and heterosexuality comprise two distinct but single forms of sexual expression. The recent theoretical splinterings of lesbian feminism into a multitude of sexual identities – not all of which are held to be conducive to the mythology of a homogeneous 'feminist community' – has further divided feminist accounts of female sexual response. Lesbian advocates of butch/femme and sadomasochistic eroticism have questioned the relevance of the old binary of vaginal versus clitoral pleasure, arguing that the notion of pleasure as lying within anatomical or sexological definitions is a specious one. It is contended that sexual 'identities' can themselves be parodied and freely interchanged in a new assertion of transgressive oppositional sexual behaviour. Although debates about the veracity of the adoption of such subject positions has resulted in much acrimony, the resulting critiques signal a new departure for feminist approaches to sexuality and subjectivity, which perhaps owes much of its dynamism to feminism's relatively recent engagement with discourses of postmodernism (see, for example, Butler 1990).

Feminist theorists are beginning to review dearly-held beliefs about the path of female sexual revolution, and are no longer confident in the binaries they themselves produced – for example that either sex equalled sexism, or lesbian sex *per se* equalled a radical or revolutionary political stance. Now that heterosexual feminists are also beginning to investigate the areas of desire and pleasure within and outside a psychoanalytical model, it is probable that a whole constellation of warring (hetero)sexual identities will be born. Perhaps it will not be long before the butch or sadomasochistic heterosexual women will emerge from her guilty closet. This is not to suggest that existing critiques of sexual violence, sexual objectification and patriarchal heteroreality should be subordinated to the utopian search for a language and representation of desire. Rather that such critiques be interpreted as an effort to locate another missing piece of the jigsaw in feminism's current political agenda. Carole Vance has recently charted the dangers of feminist perspectives on sex lapsing into dogma or pursing the same tired old discursive paths initially rejected by feminism's second wave:

The dangers of political analysis transmuted from illuminating vision to stale dogma loom especially large in regard to sexuality. Our vast ignorance, our reliance on overgeneralization, and the invisibility of so many groups suggest that we are in a particularly resourceless position to determine which sexual paths will lead to heaven. Although declaring opposition to patriarchal culture, some recent feminist pronouncements about politically desirable and undesirable forms of sexuality bear a striking resemblance to those of the dominant culture, with one possible exception: the repositioning of certain varieties of lesbianism. Within feminism, lesbianism has been rehabilitated, undergoing a transition from the realm of bad sex to the realm of good sex, and within some sectors of the movement, given a privileged position as the most egalitarian and feminist sexual identity. With this exception, new feminist punishments are still meted out to the denizens of the same old sexual lower orders. (Vance 1992: 22)

Chapter 8

Men in Feminism

As men, we've responded to the woman's movement in different ways. Some of us ignored it, thinking that it would
disappear. Some of us felt that it was a dangerous distraction
from the central issues of class politics. Some of us were
simply excited by it, but we were all, in one way or another,
threatened and confused by it, as soon as it touched the
everyday reality of our relationships.

(Seidler 1991: 64)

One of the earliest and most significant debates for Women's
Liberation was whether men should feature in the ranks. At early
conferences and protests in both the USA and Britain men attended
and were allowed a voice, but many women felt that the presence of
men altered the nature and quality of debates, and that they often
dominated discussion. Initial discussions necessarily centred upon
the question of whether men could be ousted if one accepted that
'the creation of a new woman of necessity demands the creation of a
new man' (Rowbotham, in Wandor 1972: 3). Most second wave
feminism focused on social constructionist, rather than essentialist,
arguments and therefore casting men as the 'enemy' was tacitly
accepted as a temporary socio-historical subject positioning which
would be open to transformation. Although perhaps the majority of
feminists did not foresee total separatism as a workable long-term
solution, they craved the autonomy to construct a movement for
women: 'They wanted their movement not to reject men so much as
to be independent from them' (Coote and Campbell 1987: 27). It is
clear, therefore, that in the formative period of the second wave
movement, feminists were determined to create a political forum
that addressed only women as its subjects. This meant, necessarily,
that the term 'feminist' was held to apply to women exclusively: that
feminist politics created a single sex space to redress the tenaciously
exclusionary practices of mainstream parliamentary politics. But

separatism has since become one of the most misunderstood of feminist tactics – regarded as a naive attempt to ignore the problem of men and to construct a utopia that would only function in their absence.

Radical feminists had characterized patriarchy rather loosely as an expression of male power over all women. Socialist and liberals alike turned their gaze to women's private lives and personal experiences, which seemed to affirm that women's problem was, generally speaking, men – not just those who held the reins of power in government, but also fathers, partners and contemporaries. The observation that the hold of patriarchy seemed to be maintained across history and culture with little disruption emphasized the point that this form of power operates most effectively in the private sphere. The idea that the 'personal is political' gained impetus among feminists, and the scrutiny of their own life histories was seen as enabling and potentially liberating, accompanied, as it was, by endeavours to change the dynamics of male/female relationships. 'Sexual politics' must at one level relate to sex and an awareness that power relationships both exist and are perpetuated in the most private domains of a woman's life:

> 'Sexual politics' held together the idea of women as a social group dominated by men as a social group (male domination/ female oppression), at the same time as turning back to the issue of women as sex outside of the bounds of reproduction. It threw political focus onto the most intimate transactions of the bedroom: this became one of the meanings of the 'personal is political'. (Delmar in Mitchell and Oakley 1986: 26–7)

Although heterosexual women could not conceive of total separatism as a viable feminist alternative to their current social arrangements, critiques of the means by which prevailing norms within heterosexual practices reaffirm female subordination demanded that heterosexual relations be scrutinized and revised. No matter how well-meaning pro-feminist men appeared to be, at the level of sexuality and relationships they were all implicated as having a vested interest in the status quo. One of the single most important pamphlets in circulation during the late '60s was Anne Koedt's 'The Myth of the Vaginal Orgasm' (1968), which cited the findings of Kinsey and Masters and Johnson that the clitoris and not the vagina was the site of orgasmic pleasure in women. If penetrative intercourse was viewed as the central determining feature of heterosexual union, it was now conceived as a sexual practice defined only in terms of male desire – a focus which had not appeared to shift despite the emergence of the so-called 'permissive' era. The logical conclusion of Koedt's observation that penetration was of secondary importance to women was that men were, theoretically at least, sexually expendable; but more than this, that definitions of heterosexuality were open for renegotiation:

> Many have described the impact of Koedt's paper as 'revolutionary'. It didn't tally with every woman's experience, nor did it lead to wholesale abandonment of heterosexuality. But it did enable women to talk about their sexuality in their own terms, to escape from male definitions of 'normality' and 'frigidity', to feel they had a right to make demands, and to perceive what had previously seemed to be their own individual 'problems' as part of a pattern which was essentially political. (Coote and Campbell 1987: 11)

Radical feminists emphasized the repercussions of sexism in women's domestic and sexual lives, and therefore forced individual men to confront the means by which they directly benefited from the assumption of their sexual/social hegemony. Since the institution of the family was targeted as the primary site of women's oppression, a familial ideology which naturalized many of the features of family life held to be oppressive came under close scrutiny. Radicals unquestionably perceived the work of redefining the limits of biologist defences of male power, and mapping out the effects of culture and ideology upon the individual woman, as women's work. Separatism in the sphere of political debate was, then, a fundamental requirement.

MEN'S MOVEMENTS: SEXUAL POLITICS AND THE REDEFINITION OF MASCULINITY

There is no notional singular 'men's movement' or even movements that correspond in any direct way to the women's movement, in that some were established in order to question or undermine certain feminist precepts. However, during the early '70s men's movements, in the form of consciousness raising and discussion groups, did develop as a direct response to second wave feminism. In particular they served as a useful compromise for feminists who believed that feminism should transform men's lives, but who needed to maintain separatism at the level of consciousness raising, future planning and political action. It also meant that women could continue to investigate the lives and experiences of women and their relations with patriarchy, while groups of men could analyse the way a patriarchal ideology shaped their lives and how masculinity in particular could be especially stifling. Such groups and organizations did not always meet with the unqualified support of the women's movement, since feminists felt that such investigations could degenerate into a form of 'me-tooism'. Such suspicions are not without grounds when one sees how this 'me-tooism' is imported into the popular consciousness, evident in recent books such as Neil Lyndon's *No More Sex War* (1992) and David Thomas's *Not Guilty* (1993). When the mass media report cases of male rape, or domestic violence by women against male partners, they do so not to highlight the problem of violence and abuse in general, but to attempt to diminish the clear fact that the majority of rapes, and incidences of domestic violence are perpetrated by men against women.

Some British men who formed consciousness-raising groups decided to produce a journal, and *Achilles Heel* was first circulated in 1978. In common with much British feminist thought, its links with socialism are emphasized and its critique of patriarchy and sexual divisions is also a critique of capitalism and class/racial divisions. This journal, produced by a collective and still available to this day, is concerned at heart with the social construction of masculinity, and the way this construct is perpetuated in daily public and private lives. The contributors seem to be keenly aware that their attempts to deconstruct the means by which they enact their own masculine dramas is likely to be met with derision by both women and 'unreconstructed' men: it can seem churlish to balk at the means by which one gains access to power and social superiority. As feminists might feel tempted to point out, acknowledging one's own collusion as an oppressor does not stop society at large from perpetuating the means by which women are oppressed, nor from seeing individual men as privileged and having the right to shape the lives of their female partners and children. This is the classic double-bind for men involved in pro-feminist men's groups. As Victor Seidler remarks, 'It seems as if men alone cannot escape an essentialism that for generations had been used to legitimate the oppression of women, gay men and lesbians. Masculinity could not be deconstructed, it could only be disowned' (Seidler 1991: xi). The men's movement reaches this impasse with depressing regularity, where masculinity appears to be the most tenacious of givens, perhaps because it is largely defined by its 'deviant' obverse femininity, whereas masculinity is associated with a transparent wholeness. The problem with disowning masculinity, with disavowing one's own investment in the networks of power it is a part of, is that one creates an analytical vacuum. Ultimately a men's movement realizes the need to engage with masculinity in order to interrogate its various culturally inherited forms, and to distinguish the lived experience of individual men set against the seemingly monolithic patriarchal construct. Here consciousness raising becomes crucial as a site where individual men can attempt a greater degree of honesty about their personal experiences and their ambivalence to the pulls of masculinity. *Achilles Heel* specializes in such consciousness-raising accounts relating to topics as diverse as parenting to dealing with other men's sexism in the workplace.

The work of the Gay Liberation Movement is acknowledged as beginning the challenges against patriarchal and heterosexist constructs of masculinity. This reminds us that to this day the biggest problem for a men's movement separate from gay politics is to find a means by which to define its own terms without seeming to be parasitic upon gay politics or feminism, and thereby to find a role that is peculiar to itself:

> We in this collective [*Achilles Heel*] do not agree with men who say that the men's movement as such has no right to exist, except perhaps in a service role in relation to the women's movement. We see this attitude partly as another aspect of the guilt and self-denial we have been brought up with since birth. It also reflects contempt for other men. And in its extreme form it becomes another form of being dependent on women, allowing them to do all the work in making the changes that we need. Men can put feminism up on a pedestal just as they do to women in general. (Seidler 1991: 31)

This statement importantly signals how men can see sexism as 'women's problem' if they see it as a problem at all. Moreover, it addresses head on the problem of men's main response to feminism being that of guilt, a position that connotes political inertia rather than potential transformation. But the question of where men's groups fit in with feminism remains a thorny problem, and even those men who attempt to write frankly about masculinity and its discontents too often exhibit a crippling sense of guilt and self-denial as identified by Seidler above, to the degree that some analysis of personal relationships and sexual response is almost always missing.[1]

In *Recreating Sexual Politics* (1991), Victor Seidler acknowledges that mainstream socialist politics has never adequately addressed the problem of how men can respond to the oppression of women and their own implication in it, and 'no systematic critique of the traditions that dominate the Left has emerged' (Seidler 1991b: 16). As he suggests, consciousness raising for men became a response to developing feminist positions: feminism both facilitated this form of experientially-based discussion through the lessons learnt by its own personal politics, and necessitated a response. By contrast, the socialist tradition remained silent, tending to assent to a continued personal/ public divide by evading the whole issue of women's oppression within the web of oppressions around class. But the difficulties around male consciousness raising exposed that, in a sense, consciousness raising as a political response came 'naturally' to women because they were accustomed to making informal collective arrangements as part of an indistinct underclass or sub-culture of kinds – women were used to cooperating, whereas men were brought up to compete with each other on all fronts. So, 'in the early days of consciousness raising, men would often admit that they did not really like men and that their closest relationships were with women' (Seidler 1991b: 15): of course their closest affective female relationships tended to be with lovers who often provided an emotional crutch which was not reciprocated. Seidler in fact argues forcefully that consciousness raising is vital in the male dominated Left, and a recognition of its political validity would help destabilize the firmly held conviction on the Left that it only amounts to talking about one's own personal experiences, and that these can have no resonance on wider public political life.

Seidler also argues that feminism's tendency to associate men and male behaviour with the dominant construction and meanings of masculinity makes it 'almost impossible to explore the tension between the power men have within the larger society and the ways they might individually experience themselves as powerless' (Seidler 1991b: 18). He shows that the Left itself has unquestioningly built upon bourgeois notions of guilt and self-denial, emphasizing duty and the obligation to sacrifice ourselves in the name of our career, state or so on. This necessarily perpetuates the common wisdom that the man faces an imperative to be breadwinner and family protector; and not only does this perpetuate a patriarchy that functions in the interests of capitalism, it is also an unquestioningly heterosexist model. Gay men in the gay liberation movement have also become accustomed to consciousness-raising practices, and to developing networks of mutual male support. Their support of feminism and feminist political strategies tends to emerge, therefore, from a closer understanding of the necessity of such practices in a society deeply entrenched in denying the personal whilst positing a model of personal life which is far from the realities of most individuals' lives. Something Seidler evokes very clearly is the double-bind that anti-sexist men can find themselves in:

> I think this experience of shrinking away from defining our wants or needs happened to many men in the early years of the women's movement. We were left feeling guilty, almost because we existed as men. We did not want to be thought of as sexist, so we watched ourselves very carefully. (Seidler 1991b: 36)

It is clear that pro-feminist men should not simply accept their guilt as oppressors and perform a purely 'servicing' role in relation to the women's movement. Not only would this suggest an indulgent, patronising and deeply apolitical role for men, it also serves to deny the possibility of a future social formation where the changes envisaged by feminists might be realized. In particular, the acceptance of men's current social/economic position as being generally more privileged than women should not be allowed to inform feminist views of the future redefinition of masculinity and femininity. To allow masculinity to take on a quasi-essentialist stasis, while interrogating the social construction of femininity at every level is to lock men into 'a state of non-existence, a kind of silence as regards our masculinity' (Seidler 1991b: 40). One could argue that consciousness raising gives men the opportunity to situate themselves as private beings against the public face of 'man' – an experience which may make many seek to withdraw their investment in mainstream patriarchal capitalism.

Where women were able to find a focus for their anger and a direction in their determination to transform the status quo, the men's movement as yet appears to lack any clear location, and the links between anti-sexism and socialism remain partial. Vic Seidler rightly points out the counterproductiveness of guilt as a response to the knowledge that men possess the means to oppress women. Clearly to disown masculinity is simply a way of deferring responsibility, and denying one's choice to participate in the will to change. One of the clear strengths of the establishment of men's groups has been their consciousness-raising function, allowing a space for men to explore feelings and emotions they have been socialized to deny. Such groups also develop a platform from whence men might determine their own responses to feminism so that the men's movement has a more significant role than that of servicing the women's movement, but a role which facilitates the development of feminist ideas, in contrast to the competitive atmosphere that has developed among 'men in feminism' in academe.

MEN IN FEMINISM: CONFLICTS IN ACADEME

The mid-'80s signalled a return to an argument that was fiercely debated in the late '60s about the place of men in feminist debate. As I have already outlined, most feminists agreed that women needed space and time to develop their own arguments and theoretical perspectives, because men – regardless of the benignity of their intentions – represented the means by which female discourse could be/ had been absorbed and defused by a patriarchal sleight of hand. But in the academic institution in the face of feminism's rapid expansion and perhaps by virtue of feminism's increasing engagement with critical theory, men felt that they had a contribution to offer, as if feminism's involvement in new theoretical departures signified a commitment to male alliances. Just as feminists had previously exposed the male exclusivity of radical discourses such as Marxism, so male theorists felt justified in questioning feminism's right to female exclusivity. Some men were content to use feminism as a point of departure further to explore the social construction of masculinity; others wanted to engage more directly in the heated and lively debates that had come to characterize '80s and '90s feminism. The latter primarily wanted to demonstrate that they, too, had been profoundly affected by the way feminism undercut the epistemological foundations of contemporary socio-philosophical thought. From a more cynical standpoint, it is important to observe that – in academic terms – feminism had come of age, and women's studies as a discipline, and as an interventionary project within existing disciplines, was a force to be contended with. One might suspect that male theorists, looking for new theoretical pathways in an increasingly competitive area, alighted upon feminism as another mode of abstract thought which might yield new possibilities.

The anthology *Men in Feminism*, published in 1987, is an example of such a male intervention: in it an almost equal number of male and female contributors challenge, posture, agree and vilify. The formula was evidently successful, and the dialogue aspects of the volume were extended in Linda Kauffman's two later volumes, *Gender and Theory* (1989) and *Feminism and Institutions* (1989). As the 'dialogue' format suggests, the male contributors were to some extent framed and moderated by female respondents; later 'male feminists' felt able to go it alone, as illustrated by the all-male collection, *Engendering*

Men (1990). Joseph A. Boone, one of the editors of the latter, reprints his essay, which first appeared in *Gender and Theory*, accompanied by a response by Toril Moi. However, he does not refer to her in his preamble to the republished piece, relegating all mention of Moi to a footnote, which itself carries more than a taint of retaliation. The footnote ends parenthetically:

> (True confessions: for a long time I fantasized publishing a response to Moi's response titled – to pun my own title – 'Of Moi and Feminism: the Terrifying Toril' – a response in which I would analyse the series of rather aggressive attacks that Moi has levelled against a number of American feminists, particularly those whose work disproves the American/Continental opposition she constructs in *Sexual/Textual Politics* . . . .) (Boone and Cadden 1990: 292)

It is as if Boone can only reconcile himself to Moi's response, by characterizing it as a feature of her inability to broach disagreement; moreover, by suggesting that Moi is 'unsisterly' in her scholarly practice, he attempts to undermine her broader feminist intentions. By secreting these comments in a footnote to the text, Boone disingenuously evades 'confrontation'; in addition the feminist critic is displaced as 'supplement' to the main text of the 'male feminist', which itself becomes dramatized as a gesture of appropriation.

Overall the male contributors to the above-mentioned volumes share certain tendencies within their writings which are worthy of note. There are two main textual strategies commonly utilized by such writers to shore up a rhetorical defence that they clearly feel is needed. The first is to focus upon feminism's heterogeneity as a site of conflict, better to situate the 'right' of their own work to exist within such diversity; the second is to suggest that any exclusionism on feminists' part exhibits the increasing tyranny of feminist discourse, whose 'leaders' reserve the right to prohibit disagreement – even amongst their own 'kind'. The problem with many of these essays is that, such defences aside, their relationship to feminist debate is often strictly peripheral; one might be forgiven for assuming that one of the main objectives for such work is to lay claim to the identity of 'feminist'. Joseph Boone is one such writer who sees himself as a feminist, a claim which engenders the awkward conjunction 'female feminist' (in addition to 'male feminist') throughout the course of his essay. It is interesting to speculate why such men are not content to be 'pro-feminist', or 'anti-patriarchal'; and why therefore, the question of the 'right' to a feminist identity itself seems to be at stake. During the course of this discussion I shall assume, as I have done throughout this book, that feminists are women, and will indicate 'male feminism' in quotation marks to indicate its problematic nature. Many 'male feminists' thus use the tenets of early feminism against current theorists: they often adopt the 'confessional' mode of expression so favoured by radicals, summoning personal identities which signal the inadequacies of the homogenizing signifier 'man'. For example, Terry Eagleton, in response to an article by Elaine Showalter in *Men in Feminism*, foregrounds his youthful social status as maverick working class Marxist at Cambridge: in describing his working class arrogance in face of 'bungling, well-intentioned Alisdairs', he all too earnestly reminds us of his own cultural 'otherness' (Eagleton in Jardine and Smith 1987: 133–5). It might seem churlish to object to a style so vigorously embraced by earlier second wave women, and most feminists would agree that masculinity/maleness as cultural/biological ascriptions are ripe for reinterpretation; but it is worth remembering that this technique proved contentious for feminists themselves, where an identity can be established in order to guarantee authority, and preclude dissent. It needs to be reiterated that the category 'man' is not the simple obverse of 'woman': 'man' the homogenizing identity for half the human population at least guaranteed cultural/social/economic visibility for white heterosexual men; whereas generic 'man' – the subject of Western epistemological being – denied material and ideological privileges to all women for centuries. The central question must be – if feminism is to remain a politics as well as a polemic, an oppositional strategy as well as an academic 'success story' in terms of its academic discursive explosion – what are the political consequences of 'male feminism'? This question is an ethical one ranging from the issue of whether the woman's voice will again be suppressed in favour of the male authoritative one, to whether in the academic institution (the last bastion of feminism's growth) women's tenure – even in the 'ghetto' of women's studies – will face renewed threat.

Tania Modleski sees the threat not only in co-option, but in the trivializing of feminist agendas: 'these books are bringing men back to centre stage and diverting feminists from tasks more pressing than deciding about the appropriateness of the label "feminist" for men' (Modleski 1991: 6). In addition she remarks on the heterosexism underpinning the notion of a dialogue between men and women, accompanied by the tacit assumption that 'dialogue' can herald a sense of formal equality between men and women (including the even balance of contributors in terms of gender), which clearly does not often exist in either the academic scene or the world at large. Modleski indicates that Lee Edelman, a contributor to *Gender and Theory* develops this point. Of the title of this volume, Edelman comments:

> the 'and' identifies the dialogue itself as a type of union or wedding, thus inscribing within the very framework of the discussion, the essential heterosexuality of the project – a project that must always supplement the idealized pairings of 'and' with a reproduction of the confrontational sublime that operates 'between'.[2] (Kauffman 1989a: 215)

The problem with the writings of 'male feminists' might, after all, be more pragmatic. What can cast them as such an irritant to feminist theorists is precisely the sheer degree of textual space and effort they devote to questioning the terms upon which they may enter feminism, whilst effectively blocking any response by identifying ways in which feminists denying them free access to feminist theory would be tyrannical. Thus they construct artificial boundaries around feminism which are counter-productive.

Most feminist academic enquiry has been more in the business of breaking down the boundaries of male discourse, the better to create a mode of speech which is, for political and academic purposes, female-specific. I cannot help but suspect that some current 'male feminists' are attempting to do the reverse – although of course a reversal of roles presupposes at least that those positions are of different but equal value. For many men it seems to be a question of who 'owns' feminism – an issue subliminally contested among vying groups of feminists themselves – although the chief outcome has been to move away from the rhetoric of ownership altogether, into a position of celebration and acceptance of heterogeneity. Such heterogeneity seems to be the hardest issue for men in feminism to accept – as it is a position which involves an acknowledgement of the dispersal of feminisms far beyond poststructuralist theorizing. According to Paul Smith, 'the intellectual task of understanding feminist theory is not a problem since feminist theory is situated within the array of poststructuralist discourses with which many of us are now perhaps over-familiar' (Smith in Smith and Jardine 1987: 35). For many feminists this remark poses two immediate points of contention: (a) that feminist theory resides within poststructuralism, a tendency dominated by male 'greats'; (b) that, this being the case, and male theorists being 'over-familiar' with its methodology, the problem of men in feminist theory is assuredly not one of lack of understanding. Indeed, Smith's construction places feminist theory 'in men', and, further, outlaws or disavows other wings of feminism, so that we might be forgiven for wondering whether this fairly recent male theoretical interest in feminism is not spawned primarily by its seeming 'marriage' with poststructuralism.

Nonetheless, 'men have a necessary relation to feminism' (Heath in Jardine and Smith 1987: 1), if men are supposed to be equally changed by its precepts. As Judith Mayne observes, '"men in feminism" is hardly a new formulation' (Jardine and Smith 1987: 62); feminists have largely assumed as part of their task the necessity of raising the consciousness of both men and women. What distinguishes this 'dialogue', then, is its theoretical dimension; and its male proponents might well be repeating one of the early errors of second wave pioneers in assuming that they can speak for all men. This implies that feminism's major problem is other feminists – not women, and certainly not 'men' (as they represent themselves in these debates as only too willing to learn and admire). Joseph Boone takes up the point of the identity of the 'men' that speak in *Men in Feminism* in his contribution to *Gender and Theory*: 'Of seven added contributors, Jacques Derrida, Robert Scholes, Denis Donoghue (in small print), and Terry Eagleton (in a reply to Showalter) – critics whose relation to feminism has never been, to risk understatement, unproblematic' (Boone in Kauffman 1989a: 168). He suggests that the importation of the 'big' names in theory militates against the serious consideration of 'male feminists' such as himself whose intentions/interventions are entirely honourable. Unusually he pinpoints the heterosexism which has accompanied such projects, asserting that, 'a recognition of the presence and influence of gay men working in and around feminism has the potential of rewriting feminist fears about "men in feminism" as a strictly heterosexual gesture of appropriation' (Boone in Kauffman 1989a: 174). Laudable as this observation may be, in identifying gay men as holding a possible key to solving the problem of men's possibly unwelcome attentions to feminism, Boone implicitly identifies the problem as lying in feminists' fears of symbolic penetration of their discourse. By another sleight of hand he ignores the reality that lesbians have long been exposing feminist's mainstream heterosexism in woman-to-woman debates quite effectively. In his essay Boone has with a bold flourish relegated the term 'feminist' to a gender-neutral status, therefore removing its investment in a meaning which designates it as a descriptive term for women whose political energy flows partly from their experiences of social/economic/ideological oppression. Toril

Moi, in her response to his piece, does not so much take issue with his desire to use 'feminist' as an ascription for his own work, but suggests compellingly that feminists need from men a clear conviction that they are working against the interests of patriarchy, not each other – a sense which pervades Boone's entire essay (see Moi in Kauffman 1989a: 181–90).

Many feminists' antagonism to certain aspects of the 'men in feminism' debate results from the content of the essays, and the wish to appropriate the term 'feminist', rather than from the very idea of men in feminism – which is not after all particularly shocking. In their introduction to *Engendering Men* Boone and Cadden make the obvious but important point that 'there now exists an entire generation of male critics, many of whom, having been educated by "first generation" feminist scholars, have in turn been "engendered" by feminism' (Boone and Cadden 1990:2). Few feminists would wish to hamper the progress of their work, or deny their 'right' of 'access' to feminist thought; but their insistence on the 'right' to be dubbed 'feminist', rather than 'pro-feminist', or some other term which might indicate their interests in gender remains troubling. This would acknowledge that women should retain the most important impact of the term feminism – that it has come to signify a female presence, after centuries of invisibility in very real material as well as ideological terms. Feminism is after all constructed as a work in progress, a debate intended to empower women, and indeed is the only non-patriarchal identity that women can lay claim to. In deconstructing Western binarism, such men appear to believe that men can write the 'feminine', as claimed by French feminists: while it is true that writing is not 'gendered' in any direct sense, feminists have found it politically expedient to take into account the identity of the author, as have gay, lesbian and black theorists. While men perceive the focus of the debate to be around relations of authority/subalternity, women will resist their interventions: these terms themselves are ripe for deconstruction.

NEW MEN, WILD MEN AND ANTI-FEMINIST MEN

Although, as I have previously discussed, there are incidences of men's groups who directly identify their interests as anti-sexist and who often construct their subsequent political position from within the Left, there is no single meaning attached to the term 'men's group'. An example of 'men's groups' which adopt quite a different perspective from that of feminism would be the Iron John groups created by Robert Bly in the United States, but also in evidence in

Britain. Robert Bly's conception of the need for modern man to regain touch with his 'wild' underside reflects a growing unease in popular responses to the phenomenon of the 'new man' in the mass media. Feminism, directly or indirectly, is held responsible for the threatened emasculation of contemporary man. Man, stripped of his macho exterior, is seen to be suffering an identity crisis, in that in the popular imagination, the questioning of the forms of the behaviour associated with masculinity amounts to a repudiation of maleness *per se*.

In June 1990 *The Guardian* newspaper devoted two days of its 'Women' section to the 'new man' phenomena, doing much to substantiate the view that being a new man was to eschew any claim to autonomy. Kimberley Leston, writing in *The Guardian* also pointed out the 'new man' image has been utilized in mainstream advertising to suggest that if men take on 'female duties' they will inevitably perform them better:

> One such television commercial features a compassionate and patient father rushing home during office hours in the high-performance family saloon, to dissuade his four-year-old son from leaving home. The situation passes as believable, if unlikely, but the essential message lies camouflaged in the subtext provided by the minor character of the child's mother. 'He won't listen to me,' she admits with bovine resignation, implying that shared parenting – the key issue of New Mandom – brings something even more desirable than emotional fulfilment, it brings an increase in the male power base. (*The Guardian*, Thursday, 21 June 1990)

As Leston points out, the representation of a 'new man' is used primarily as a new way to castigate women, to create an illusion of changing cultural trends not borne out in a wider political sphere. It appears that the 'new man' largely exists in the creative portfolios of advertising companies and it is another way of reaffirming male power (see also Christian 1994: 3[3]); it is more often a parody of feminist demands than a response to them. As Harry Christian points out men's approach to feminism has to be active if it is to be forward-looking, and there needs to be a distinction made between the anti-sexist and non-sexist reaction: 'To be "anti-sexist" means having an active stance opposed to sexism, whereas the term "non-sexist" indicates an ideal way of relating to women, to which anti-sexist men aspire, not necessarily fully achieved' (Christian 1994: 3). As I think Christian implies, the term 'non-sexist' can also infer an absence of pro-feminist consciousness, or at least a political inertia, where one's personal behaviour is the only indice.

Robert Bly's Iron John movement represents a wing of men's groups which have little or no connection with women's liberation. Although cautious not to attack feminism directly, Bly infers that '70s feminism 'softened' modern man at the expense of male 'wholeness' – 'they are life-preserving but not exactly life-giving' (Bly 1991: 3). Bly's mythopoetic men's movement is derived from the folktale of Iron John collected by the brothers Grimm. It is the story of a 'wild man' captured and imprisoned by a king, later released by the king's son. Bly uses this story as a metaphor for suggesting that contemporary men have a 'wild man' locked within them which needs to be released in order that men experience an authentic sense of their own masculinity. It clearly borrows an essentialist model of masculine impulses suggesting a return to a patriarchal 'prehistory' rather than a future where maleness and masculinity are renegotiated. As Christian observes:

> While Bly disclaims hostility to feminism his movement places no emphasis on helping the struggle against women's oppression, and seems to be part of a series of inward-looking 'men's liberation' activities which may perhaps be of benefit to some men but are hardly likely to benefit women, and may even be part of the anti-feminist backlash. (Christian 1994: 11)

Feminists tend to view the prospect of a men's movement with mixed feelings, in the light of tendencies such as those demonstrated by Bly and his adherents. Just as with the women's movement, there can be no guarantee that all individuals and groups under such a term agree with each other's political perspective, so the term 'men's movement' might embrace anything from an overtly pro-feminist consciousness-raising group, to Robert Bly's 'Wild Man' workshops which, in their identification with the warrior figure, might be seen to celebrate the masculine in an unreconstructed form (see Eisler; Adair in Hagan 1992: 43–53; 55–66). It is not surprising that endeavours such as Bly's are viewed sceptically by many feminists as a cultural 'me-tooism' which does not necessarily engage in any critical debates about gender polarities in society or men's continuing benefit from masculine privilege. As bell hooks asserts,

> we need a men's movement that is part of revolutionary feminist movement. If the masses of men in our society have not unlearned their sexism, have not abdicated male privilege, then

it should be obvious that a men's movement led only by men with only males participating runs the risk of mirroring in a different form much that is already oppressive in patriarchal culture. (Hagan 1992: 117)

Not only do some men's groups work directly against the philosophical bases of feminism, certain male journalists have established reputations as published detractors of feminism. Neil Lyndon is one such figure, but David Thomas's more substantial volume *Not Guilty* (1993) provides an even more recent example of the backlash against feminism which relies on spurious 'statistical' indicators to 'prove' that the lot of man is harder than that of woman[4] and that 'Western society is obsessed with women to the point of mass neurosis' (Thomas 1994: 2). Thomas's book is on the defensive, conceived to assert that men are the victims in our current social order. Predictably he cites cases where men are subjected to physical or sexual violence as if this fact alone counterbalances the horrifying figures amassed by feminists which suggest that women have suffered violence and death at the hands of men for centuries to the point of genocide.[5] Thomas conceives of a world where women and men are in direct competition for healthcare provision and counselling, and where men are oppressed by the burden of their will to power (Thomas asks the reader 'would you really want to be George Bush?' (Thomas 1993: 8) – a prime example of the non sequiturs utilized to give his argument a sense of direction). Thomas identifies what he perceives as crucial differences between men and women, and in common with latter-day patriarchs, seeks their justification in 'evolution':

> Men are able to analyse three-dimensional objects moving in space because that is what a huntsman has to do with his target. Women are able to recall the arrangement of objects because that is what a gatherer, searching the ground for edible plants, needs to be able to remember from one harvesting trip to another. Modern men find it easier than women to drive a car through a narrow opening; but, unlike women, they can never remember where anything in the house is kept. (Thomas 1993: 48)

Thomas pretends to review the facts in a progressive and objective light, but his conclusions reflect the deep conservatism of men who feel threatened by the women's movement rather than challenged by it, and can only respond to it as if presented with a personal indictment.

Many feminists feel disturbed that while a separate men's movement might be justified as fair play – the time is ripe for men to have their space in order to come to terms with changing conceptions of gender roles offered by feminists – continuing male supremacy, whether eschewed by members of men's movements or not, display a deeply entrenched lack of fair play in all the most influential social and economic systems in our world. The continued presence of *Achilles Heel* in Britain and NOMAS (the National Organization of Men Against Sexism) in the USA, suggests that there are numbers of men prepared to translate their anti-sexism into political activism and the interrogation of the assumptions and behaviours associated with masculinity. Still, we need to bear in mind that the political/ media mainstream see it as in their interests to portray feminism as a threat to male livelihood and the cherished rights of man. Thomas, among others, regresses to the rhetoric of high liberalism in order to cast sexual politics as war zone, where 'nature' is under siege. Vic Seidler provides one reason why men like Thomas might be rushing to their own defence:

> I think one of the reasons that many men have felt both deeply jealous and drawn to the women's movement and personal politics, has been a sense that the instrumentalism of life had been cracked by women and, somehow, a sense of what is important in human life has been rediscovered in the questions the women's movement was asking. (Seidler 1991b: 46–7)

It is compelling to speculate that writers such as Bly, Lyndon and Thomas are in fact railing against the crushing alienation experienced by men in a system of advanced capitalism created in their image and conceived to act solely in their interests.

Chapter 9

Feminism, Postmodernism and Theoretical Developments

> Our language, intellectual history, and social forms are 'gendered'; there is no escape from this fact and from its consequences on our lives. Some of those consequences may be unintended, may even be fiercely resisted; our deepest desire may be to 'transcend gender dualities'; to not have our behaviour categorized as 'male' or 'female'. But, like it or not, in our present culture, our activities are coded as 'male' or 'female' and will function as such within the prevailing system of gender-power relations. The adoption of the 'professional' standards of academia is no more an activity devoid of gender politics than the current fashion in women's tailored suits and largely shouldered jackets is devoid of gender meaning. One cannot be 'gender neutral' in this culture.
>
> (Bordo in Nicholson 1990: 152)

I have already indicated that around the mid-'80s in academic circles a 'crisis' in feminism seemed to have been consensually acknowledged: the subject of feminism's differences of opinion was beginning to seem the most crucial in an era of critical retrospectives and summaries. Dominant 'strands' in feminist thought were marking their territory and consolidating their own methodological boundaries, and the impact of French psychoanalytic theory was changing the terms of feminist theoretical debate in the Anglo-American sphere. Radical feminism was increasingly vilified in British socialist feminist circles, and in the United States of America feminist radicalism had become associated with a narrower 'cultural feminist' position, which signalled a return to the celebration of the 'feminine', albeit from a woman-centred perspective. Socialist feminists were themselves more regularly defining their own political stance in terms of a departure from Marxist orthodoxy. Black and lesbian feminists were identifying themselves as organized groupings on the basis of race or sexual orientation, using much of their energies to signal the most grievous sins of white, bourgeois heterosexual feminists. Perhaps their combined critiques – more than any others – exposed the partial and exclusionary nature of the category of 'gender' as it had been used in other elements of feminist thought. Each grouping or 'strand', having been called upon to define its terms and its place within the matrix of feminism as a whole, seemed to settle into degrees of theoretical autonomy that eschewed any comprehensive attachment to male-oriented thought. However, by the latter half of the '80s, the question of male alliances – whether it be the entry of men into feminist thought as contributors and teachers, or the forging of liaisons with an increasingly sophisticated post-structuralist and postmodernist lobby – returned as perhaps the single most pressing debate of recent years.

FEMINISM AND IDENTITY

Many theorists were at pains to demonstrate feminism's compatibility with postmodernist theory in signalling the end of modernity and its humanist account of individuality; they also offered a very significant critique of feminism – namely, its tenacious reliance upon gender difference as the single most important analytical category. This, it was suggested, demonstrated a reliance on totalizing and unifying categories – a revivification of the binarism that typified Western thought within modernity, and a consequently naive, or even regressive investment in notions of progress and continuity. While the radical potential of feminist contributions to postmodern thought were acknowledged because of their recognized contribution to reconceiving Western binarism, feminism was simultaneously regarded as one of 'the flawed grand narratives of modernity' (Featherstone, *Theory, Culture & Society*, Vol. 5, Nos 2–3, June 1988). Grand narratives were perceived from a postmodern perspective as potentially tyrannical and unhelpfully universalizing, and feminism's own meta-narrative of gender was regarded as having trapped feminists in ethno/heterocentric truth claims, which no longer had any currency in a postmodern world view. Nonetheless, it is significant that poststructuralism and postmodernism continue to be determined as something other than feminism, so that feminism remains contemporary theory's significant Other – a predictable and recurring relationship for feminism to academic thought. From the outset, it must therefore be emphasized that those figures acknowledged as having made a significant contribution to the development of post-modern perspectives in theory, art and literature are male. Feminists are perhaps justified in their suspicion that a dispersal of the meanings of gender in such a context fairly swiftly amounts to gender-blindness. In this light, a real danger lies in the possibility that in place of feminism's analysis of gender, originary meanings of gender difference are reinforced.

Within feminist ranks two points of conflict are currently receiving a significant degree of attention: (a) the escalation of 'identity politics' within the movement which threatens to turn feminist theory into a highly individualized, introverted and necessarily fragmented political stance; (b) a recognition that 'many feminist ideas become part of the common sense of our culture; yet those ideas may be expressed in forms we barely recognize as feminist' (Editorial, *Feminist Review*, No. 31, Spring 1989: 3). The two points intersect, of course; whether we recognize a particular stance as 'feminist' depends upon our sense of identity within a particular faction. Nonetheless, most feminists recognize and are antipathetic to a specific distortion of feminist ideas which is sustained within mainstream New Right ideology, identified as simultaneously pro-female and pro-family, and which offers itself primarily as a stance that recognizes and endorses women's current familial location as a position of strength:

> First, it promotes a 'pro-family' stance that views sexual politics, and particularly the politicization of personal relationships, as threatening to 'the family'. Second, it affirms gender differentiation and celebrates traditionally feminine qualities, particularly those associated with mothering. Finally, the new conservatives believe that struggle against male domination detracts from political agendas they consider more important. (Stacey in Mitchell and Oakley 1986: 222)

This view of feminism as detracting from the more important business of 'real' political enquiry is a familiar one for feminists: think of the reasons why many disaffected Left Wing women established feminist cadres in the late '60s and early '70s. Proponents of such a stance often allude to the dawnings of a 'post-feminist' age in which the worst excesses of second wave feminism can be discarded in favour of a political healing process in which the family can be once again made whole – freed from the indecent assaults of a sexual politics which has been held to deny the sanctity of personal privacy.

Perhaps the escalation of 'identity politics' was a contributing

factor in feminists' general inability to produce a concerted response
to such attacks, or at least to deny them any place in feminist thought.
To deny them any currency would after all be to enact a tyrannous
response to other 'pro-woman' forms of thought – to exacerbate both
the problem of vying feminist identities and the question of who is
'allowed' to construct 'authentic' feminist responses to such challenges. Feminism's political roots are, after all, multifarious, and any
such resistance might be seen to mark a precedent, where a feminist
'mainstream' could be construed as holding an unpalatable amount
of authority over the utterances of more 'minority' groups. Identity
politics, of course, need not be interpreted as a challenge against
tyranny and exclusionism; they might be viewed as a positive sign
that feminism remains a fluid site of healthy debate into the '90s.
Nonetheless identity politics, taken to its logical extreme, facilitates
a cacophony of warring feminist voices which can only announce
their authority as speakers 'for' feminism by referring to the complex
nature of their own subject positioning, of which being female is the
lowest of common denominators. The result of such a tendency can
be 'not to elucidate debate but to fix a woman somewhere along a
predetermined hierarchy of oppressions in order to justify or contest
a political opinion by reference to a speaker's identity' (Harriss,
Feminist Review, No. 31, Spring 1989: 37).

There are clearly risks in deriving authority as a feminist speaker
from one's own constellation of personal identities (as white, lesbian,
working class, etc.), and a chief danger is to emphasize the boundaries between major strands of feminism as if they were fixed and
immutable, rather than part of a debate which has as its shared goal
the maintenance of a viable feminist contribution at both a localized
and wider political context. Critiques offered by black and lesbian
feminists have, for example, been salutory in changing and expanding
the terms of reference of what was by default a white, heterosexual
feminism; and the general thrust of this thesis has been to show how
the acceptance of heterogeneity within the term 'feminism' can be
beneficial to all women. It is possibly the case that identity politics
has been construed as fragmentary by white feminists because it is
their definitions of oppression that have been under attack.

Whether or not this is the case, identity politics were prefigured
by the notion that 'the personal is political'. The primary effects of
consciousness raising were arguably to suggest that achieving a feminist consciousness is largely a matter of finding a position which suits
one's own public and personal context. This may well give rise 'to a
self-righteous assertion that if one inhabits a certain identity this

gives one the legitimate and moral right to guilt trip others into particular ways of behaving' (Parmar, *Feminist Review*, No. 31, Spring
1989: 58). Of course consciousness raising was intended to be a preamble to collective action; but in the absence of a transformation of
the social meanings of gender difference, the task of consciousness
raising has to be repeated with every new generation, and in an era
of proliferating academic discourses on feminism, consciousness
raising of sorts can be a useful part of pedagogical practice. This can
itself be rejuvenating for feminism, and might be practiced in order
to forestall the truth claims of anti-feminists who would otherwise
consign feminism unchallenged to the annals of recent history.

FEMINISM/POSTMODERNISM: THEORETICAL REFLECTIONS

It is not only the phenomenon of the 'male feminist' that has caused
feminists to rethink the dominant framework of their theories; since
the mid-'80s feminist postmodern theorists such as Linda Nicholson
have identified the continued existence of universalizing tendencies
within feminist thought, observing that, 'it was the failure, common
to many forms of academic scholarship, to recognize the embeddedness of its own assumptions within a specific historical context'
(Nicholson 1990: 20). A particular trait in Western scholarship is the
quest for objectivity, the notion that a critique can transcend the
perspective of one individual or group, to carry truth claims that
could be recognized as such by other individuals or groups. Although
feminist groups among others have questioned the notion of neutrality and the means by which certain knowledges can be legitimated as
truth, there do remain traces of dominant Western forms of thought
within feminist methodology. Clearly the concept of patriarchy
would be one example of a tendency towards ahistorical universalism,
particularly when summoned by feminists in examining the 'cause' of
women's oppression. Nonetheless I have previously outlined why an
'ahistorical' model of patriarchal power can be politically expedient
in the face of totalizing exclusionary practices of existing historical
ways of knowing. Postmodernist theorists locate the mode of objectivity as a symptom of modernity, a range of epistemic conditions
which they would argue are waning. Postmodern relations of power
therefore render claims of truth or falsehood illegitimate, and displace the unified category of 'woman' as subject – something perhaps
that feminists are reluctant to part with on a political level. In
addition postmodern positioning does not always help the feminist
theorist negotiate a pathway through current materially and economically powerful political 'truth claims'.

The category of gender itself, and the way gender distinctions are culturally manifested, informs a feminist perspective on social realities which many would seem loath to relinquish. Fraser and Nicholson, however, suggest that interfaces between feminism and postmodernism would be mutually beneficial since, 'a postmodernist reflection on feminist theory reveals disabling vestiges of essentialism while a feminist reflection on postmodernism reveals androcentrism and political naivete' (Fraser and Nicholson in Nicholson 1990: 20). Here the relations between feminism and postmodernism are still seen to be tense; particularly, as the above quotation implies, because postmodernism emerges from a very male-identified reaction to modernity. Postmodernist critiques might be used by feminists to cleanse their own reflections of the worst kind of essentialism, but feminism's stake in modernity – or any perspective on male systems of power – can only be partial. Postmodernism has as one of its primary goals the aim of freeing itself from overarching philosophical givens, to ground social criticism within specific contexts and locales.[1] Gone is the dependency upon notions of historical progression, the transcendence of reason and freedom – the meta-discourse (such as Marxism) is reduced to the status of just another discourse with no prior claim to particular privilege. Feminism, in the Lyotardian terms utilized by Fraser and Nicholson, would be just such another totalizing discourse, dependent as it is on the generalising categories of gender (or even race and class), which are regarded as too unitary and too homogenizing to be accommodated or utilized within a postmodern notion of subjectivity. However, there are grounds to suppose that even the displacement of the meta-narrative demands a social criticism that can embrace the local and contextual – and this would clearly be the case for a credible feminist response.

During the past decade many feminists have found previous accounts of female subjectivity to be too reductive – since at the very least they provide grounds for the exclusion of race, class and sexual orientation. But even the inclusion of such categories can be seen to totalize group identity in ways that preclude more cogent and 'localized' analyses of the constellation and mediation of power relationships. In any case, it could be argued that woman remains a totalizing theoretical category, within which other categories of 'otherness' are effaced. Politically, feminists have a strong investment in retaining the masculine/feminine binary in their discourse in order to uncover the multifarious means by which this binary still remains powerful; whereas utopian tendencies in postmodernist thought might envisage an end to the significance of such a binary.

However, it might be advisable to consider Jameson's definition of postmodernism as 'not just another word for the description of a particular style', but:

> also, at least in my use, a periodizing concept whose function is to correlate the emergence of new formal features in culture with the emergence of a new type of social life and a new economic order – what is often euphemistically called modernization, postindustrial or consumer society, the society of the media or the spectacle, or multinational capitalism. (Kaplan 1988: 15)

Such a definition might prove useful to feminism since it offers the moment of postmodernism a historical location, whereby the material and ideological conditions that pertain within such a period can be investigated in relation to women in particular. Moreover, some feminists may be tempted to argue that a patriarchal ideology retains a rigid stronghold within a post-industrial capitalist society, just as it has been argued that the institutionalization of sexual difference can be perceived to predate capitalism.

Most feminists would accept, however, that the meanings and positioning of gender relations do change when there is a changing cluster of power networks, and the identification of a postmodern moment allows feminists to consider the condition of women as a distinct feature of postmodern social reality. If one of the significant aspects of the postmodern condition is the final dissolution of the myth of autonomous subjectivity, this may have a bearing on dominant feminist articulations of subjectivity, which often do depend upon notions of liberation which suggest a quest for a pre-existing putative autonomy available to masculine subjects. Jameson does not wish to suggest that the postmodern moment indicates a radical break with the period of modernity; rather it involves 'the restructuring of a certain number of elements already given: features that in an earlier period or system were subordinate now become dominant, and features that had been dominant again become secondary' (Kaplan 1988: 15). Jameson's assertion is made within the context of cultural productions; nonetheless in both the field of cultural production, and production in a wider sphere, feminism's chief problem is to ascertain whether one feature – the representation/positioning of women as subordinate/other – remains the same. In addition, despite the embeddedness of feminist discourse in identifying a 'reality' of gender difference which finds its intelligibility in essentialism or biology, the cultural logic of sexual difference has gained momentum from its historical longevity, resulting in the 'fact' of difference being entrenched in experience – not an easy category to theorize, or indeed to generalize about. Cynthia Cockburn looks back on the emergence of second wave politics and reflects upon the nebulous sense of difference which pervades feminism still:

> There was a material reason for the growth of difference-politics. It was a response to women's lived experience in the 1970s of struggling with men's response to feminism. We felt different. Not some essential or biological difference but an empowering difference born of our centuries-long experience as the subordinated half of the heterosexual couple. Our history had given us different values. (Chapman and Rutherford 1988: 326)

There may be much that a feminist can invest in the postmodern explosion of the binaries of classic Western thought. But might it not be the case that postmodernism itself derives impetus from a certain binarism in its demarcation of postmodernism and feminist postmodernism? Is it readily apparent that most postmodern reflections are any more gender conscious than other theoretical offerings by radical male academics have been? If dispensing with the binaries means that gender as category has no theoretical currency, then it would be difficult to interrogate postmodernism for instances of gender-blindness. Yet feminist interventions in postmodernism must do precisely that, and find that although large-scale power relationships can be rendered problematic in the delegitimation of the grand narrative, hierarchies of gendered power may exist in the spaces of postmodernist theory itself. Perhaps an analogy can be drawn here with Jonathan Rutherford's comments on the organization of political agendas: 'Men's power is not simply a sovereign, repressive force. It can be that, but it is a more complex phenomenon, and also operates through the ways in which politics and problems are defined, and in determining what are the real issues and priorities' (Chapman and Rutherford 1988: 43). Perhaps the priorities of postmodern theorists are by and large still too entrenched in announcing our epistemological and cultural break with modernity to wonder what women's place in modernity could possibly be defined as.

Modernism in art has often been described as a moment of high elitism and male exclusionary practices; the historical mode of process and objectivity yielded little insights from a feminist point of view. Women are necessarily embedded within these historical moments as material factors, but in terms of their relation to them as grand narratives, they have usually been quietly absent. Christine Di

Stefano seems to be suspicious of the postmodern project itself as having an investment – if mainly in its sense of reaction and destabilizing of the models of modernist thought – in the basis of a gendered social organization which is still left intact by its neglect in mainstream postmodernism:

> The feminist case against postmodernism would seem to consist of several related claims. First, that postmodernism expresses the claims and needs of a constituency (white, privileged men of the industrialized West) that has already had an Enlightenment for itself and that is now ready and willing to subject that legacy to critical scrutiny. Secondly, that objects of postmodernism's various critical and deconstructive efforts have been the creations of a similarly specific and partial constituency (beginning with Socrates, Plato, and Aristotle). Third, that mainstream postmodernist theory (Derrida, Lyotard, Rorty, Foucault) has been remarkably blind and insensitive to questions of gender in its own purportedly politicized rereadings of history, politics, and culture. Finally, that the postmodernist project if seriously adopted by feminists, would make any semblance of a feminist politics impossible. (Nicholson 1990: 75–6)

Stefano's concluding point – that postmodern theory renders feminist politics untenable – offers the bleakest outlook on feminism's engagement with postmodernism. The call to explode gender binaries, might well be perceived as an exhortation to 'gender neutrality', which all too easily slips us back into the bad old days of academic rigour and rationalism. Such a stance denies feminist academics the opportunity to analyse the impact of their own female identity in a social context, that in so many other ideological and material ways reminds us of our own femaleness as otherness. Susan Bordo perceives that this tendency displays further evidence of a backlash against second wave feminism – analogous to debates among some first wave American feminists, who called for an end to discussion focused on gender difference (Nicholson 1990: 152). Then as now, perspectives on the heterogeneity of female experience and aspirations led to an extension of the notion of human differences, a pull to accept differences of identity and their social impact as a fact of 'human' life.

It needs to be stated that other cultural 'outgroups' might also feel unprepared to dispense with their own totalizing and unitary categories, such as being black or gay or lesbian. Again these voices appear on the margins of postmodernism's mainstream, so that bell hooks' sense of being on 'the outside of the discourse looking in' (hooks 1991: 24) might sum up how many non-white/non-male/non-heterosexuals feel; that they are a priori excluded, while at the same time being urged to dispense with their old-fashioned 'modern' ways of thinking. bell hooks points out that when race is discussed in a postmodern context, black women rarely merit a mention, and she convincingly identifies the aims of postmodern thought as themselves paradoxical:

> It is sadly ironic that the contemporary discourse which talks the most about heterogeneity, the decentred subject, declaring breakthroughs that allow recognition of Otherness, still directs its critical voice primarily to a specialized audience that shares a common language rooted in the very master narratives it claims to challenge. (hooks 1991: 25)

Nonetheless, she accepts that postmodern critiques of notions of identity and subjectivity are potentially effective tools for black people, who have after all collected politically under an identity – narrow and constrictive – foisted upon them by an imperialist ideology. For example, critiques of racism have not heretofore been concerned with the way that class mobility has fractured notions of collective identity; and it may well be in black theorists' interest to focus more upon the diverse and multiple experiences and meanings of racial difference. Yet hooks' exposure of the fact that postmodernist thought remains directed at the most privileged, appears to justify the caution with which feminists have in general received postmodern explorations into the sphere of gender, race and sexual identity.

In the face of the collapse of gender identity as a viable concept in a postmodernist worldview, a postmodernist feminist has to negotiate a pathway through the idea of a discourse which can be gender neutral. As Barrett and Phillips observe, 'feminists have become deeply suspicious of theoretical discourses that claim neutrality while speaking from a masculinist perspective, and have at times despaired of the possibility of "gender-neutral" thought' (Barrett and Phillips 1992: 1). This awareness that seeming gender neutrality has always connoted a patriarchal perspective in the past goes some way to explaining the degree of feminist scepticism around the postmodernist dispersal of explanatory categories of identity. Feminist concepts of identity and collectivity had gradually become more complex anyway; in particular because of increasing moves to theorize the triple oppressions of gender, race and class. They emphasize that 'we should certainly reject the simplistic teleology that later theory is therefore better theory, and that the best theory of all is the position from which we happen at the moment to be speaking' (Barrett and Phillips 1992: 7). There may well be concern about what happens to identity in the postmodern project since as Sylvia Walby points out, 'the fragmentation of macro-analytic concepts in the theorization of "race", gender and class is a typical part of the post-modernist project' (Barrett and Phillips 1992: 31). Walby further suggests that the postmodern project denouncing the categories of 'man' and 'woman' because there is no essentialist meaning to each category and that they therefore contain so many contradictory identities, may be a little precipitate. In common with other feminist critics who have explored postmodernist viewpoints she argues that,

> While gender relations could potentially take an infinite number of forms, in actuality there are some widely repeated features and considerable historical continuity. The signifiers of 'woman' and 'man' have sufficient and historical and cross-cultural continuity, despite some variations, to warrant such terms. (Barrett and Phillips 1992: 36)

There is no reason why feminists should not engage with developments in postmodern thought to the full; in fact one could reasonably argue that feminists and the progress of feminist discourse itself have been instrumental, if not essential, to poststructuralist/postmodernist developments. However, one has to retain an awareness that major movements in postmodern thought are seen as being located in 'male' theory; and the 'ownership' of high postmodern theory rests largely in male hands. This does not always allow sufficient space to scrutinize the relationship of discourse to materiality in this context, where discourse invests relations of power. Sylvia Walby suggests that 'rather than abandoning the modernist project of explaining the world, we should be developing the concepts and theories to explain gender, ethnicity and class' (Barrett and Phillips 1992: 48). Michele Barrett has identified how feminist and other oppositional groups can have a kneejerk negative response and 'who see what they call "discourse theory" as an ideologically suspect attempt to deny material reality' (Barrett and Phillips 1992: 209).

PLAYING WITH DIFFERENCE:
ESSENTIALISM, GENDER AND THE CYBORG

The term 'essentialism' has often been used with negative connotations by many feminists; I have used it myself earlier in this work as shorthand description of a feminist stance which makes appeal to a discrete female 'nature'. Most feminists do of course see themselves as social constructionist, believing that gender is an effect of culture rather than a condition for its current configuration. Thus, essentialism and social constructionism take on the appearance of binary opposites; the former celebrating the fixity of female difference, and a revaluation of its social meanings; and the latter expressing a concrete denial of the innateness of sexual difference, arguing that difference is an effect of social and historical relations of power. Yet, as Diana Fuss has pointed out in *Essentially Speaking* (1989), the two terms are not mutually exclusive, and the use by social constructionists of the category 'gender' constitutes an appeal to a community of women as a group with a single identity, which inevitably assumes a broad shared essence. In other words, all political movements that focus on a particular identity (femaleness, gayness) as the basis for political action, effectively presuppose that particular properties define such groups, implying that there is an essence within identity which is fixed and can be unearthed through the discussion of an oppressed group's experiences of subjectivity.

All branches of feminist thought have valued experience, and the garnering of multifarious female experiences – in consciousness raising and in writing – has been a crucial feminist activity. As Diana Fuss has observed:

> The category of 'female experience' holds a particularly sacrosanct position on women's studies programs, programs which often draw on the very notion of hitherto repressed and devalued female experience to form the basis of a new feminist epistemology. (Fuss 1989: 113)

From the outset of the second wave, the explosion of experiential writing demonstrated that experiences are never unified or universal, but reflect differing relationships to class, race and sexual orientation – not to mention more localized variables. Yet the centrality of experience to feminist thought indicates a belief in the authenticity of experience, as if the woman who writes her own life as woman, reveals some previously suppressed truth about the state of being female. It is as if a woman can miraculously distance herself from the cultural and historical processes that make gender difference matter;

yet as Fuss remarks, 'belief in the truth of Experience is as much an ideological production as belief in the experience of Truth' (Fuss 1989: 114). Narratives of experience do regularly yield common elements, which enhance feminist theoretical activities, and in this way the politics of identity is a useful tactic to initiate collective resistance to the patriarchal status quo. But it must be recognized that appeals to experience as authentic reconstructions of the nascent self risk reinstating difference as essence, and have resulted in the dissemination of identities within feminism that are often perceived as counter-productive.

There has been a tendency in feminist thought to recognize the constructedness of gendered identities, but at the same time see female appropriations of 'masculine' qualities in purely negative terms. Judith Butler prefaces her book *Gender Trouble* (1990) with the proposition that the binary framework which informs notions of gender only has real currency within a heterosexual world view, and asks, 'what happens to the subject and to the stability of gender categories when the epistemic regime of presumptive heterosexuality is unmasked as that which produces and reifies these ostensible categories of ontology?' (Butler 1990: viii). The meanings of gender, generally ascribed by feminists to the broad effect of patriarchal social organizations, is thus further recognized as being the product of a heteroreality, where heterosexuality has a clear investment in such delineations of difference. Gender, in Butler's view, is less stable than its 'official' meanings suggest, and she uses the example of female impersonator/film 'hero(ine)', Divine, to argue that his 'impersonation of women implicitly suggests that gender is a kind of persistent impersonation that passes as the real' (Butler 1990: viii). Drag, it is argued, can dramatize the fluidity of gender signifiers and can subvert and parody conventional meanings ascribed to gender difference in a pantomimic performance of their artificiality and arbitrariness. Butler, then, denies gender any originary credence, and considers how the parodic 'quoting' of gender binaries can decentre defining discourses within phallogocentrism for feminist purposes. This position develops the stance of Joan Nestle, who recognizes the resistance possibilities in the adoption of butch/femme roles, where meanings of gender are exposed as innately unstable and therefore ripe for reinterpretation. Other lesbian critics are, however, more sceptical; the most notable dissenter being Sheila Jeffreys:

> When a woman is being beaten by the brutal man she lives with is this because she has adopted the feminine gender in her

appearance? Would it be a solution for her to adopt the masculine gender for the day and strut about in a work shirt or leather
chaps? When gender is seen as an idea, or a form of appearance,
then the oppression of women does disappear. (Jeffreys
1994: 100)

Jeffreys' main concern is that any tendency to reduce the most effective meanings of gender differentiation to the level of play or parody
depoliticizes the fact and effects of women's oppression. A common
concern with poststructuralist/ postmodern articulations of power is
of course the fear that the political status of debates around the
meanings and locations of gender are rendered ineffective; but
Jeffreys' dogged essentialism around the issue of male sexuality being
continually and ineluctably exploitative carries its own epistemological dangers.

The discussions throughout this book stand as testament to the
fact that all feminists confront the problem that 'woman' as category
cannot connote a common identity, and that it is debatable to what
extent all women share a common form of oppression that outweighs
other identities. If we accept that gender distinctions are an effect of
culture, and that their meanings are constantly shifting within different historical and cultural formations, we necessarily accept that
gender is always an ambiguous and contradictory category, which is
independent of sex, 'with the consequence that man and masculine
might just as easily signify a female body as a male one, and woman
and feminine a male body as easily as a female one' (Butler 1990: 6).
Within this context Butler argues that gay and lesbian citations of
heterosexual conventions of gender organization (such as butch/
femme) are not simply representations of heterosexual identities
within a homosexual framework. Rather, such citation throws the
constructedness of such categories into sharp relief, referring not to
an original but a 'parody of the idea of the natural and original'
(Butler 1990: 31).

Feminism's recourse to the representational category of 'woman' is
also viewed by Butler as construct, in that feminism's appeal to the
'we' of womankind is always exclusionary. Butler asserts that gender's
instability 'sets into question the foundational restrictions on feminist political theorizing and opens up other configurations, not only
of genders and bodies, but of politics itself' (Butler 1990: 142). In
other words, if politics did not appeal to categories of subjects
deemed to own pre-existing originary identities, the binarism of
gender relations as they are now understood might be exploded in

favour of a polymorphous range of identities, that would facilitate a better understanding of how gender identity, and all entries into subjecthood are negotiated. Compelling as Butler's argument is, the notion of parody suggests an imitation of something that already exists; and even if, in the case of gender difference, this is the imitation of the idea of gender binarism, that idea itself, rather than any sense of its naturalness, has been and remains the focus of feminism's contestation of dominant patriarchal meanings of gender. The idea of appropriate gender socialization does have a material effect on the lives of women of whatever race or sexual orientation, although it is not the single determinant. Although the idea of parody as a tool in feminist politics is a seductive one, as I've suggested earlier on in this chapter, it is difficult to imagine a situation where denying the impact current meanings of gender difference have on women's lives would not result in a gender-neutral stance.

This is manifestly not the case in Butler's writing, and her thesis indicates the increasing tensions within lesbian feminism as to the range of sexual identities lesbians can or should have. These tensions have instigated new theoretical explorations into the appropriation and manipulation of gender difference – such as the meanings attributed to butch/femme roles. Susan Ardill and Sue O'Sullivan are concerned that in this we lose a feminist challenge to continued gender divisions and inequalities – particularly in the roles adopted by butch/femmes:

> Because lesbian experience is so untheorized and unsupported, even within radical or alternative cultures, any lesbian language of self-description and self-analysis has tended to remain underdeveloped. So these two words [butch/femme] have become dreadfully overburdened. (Ardill and O'Sullivan, *Feminist Review*, No. 34, Spring 1990: 80)

Butler would of course recognize in this a semantic richness, reflecting the continual dispersal of meaning around gender and the playful possibilities of ever-fluid butch/femme identification. Joan Nestle, in *A Restricted Country* (1987), demonstrates how important such identities were for lesbians in the 1950s in making lesbianism visible on the streets as a sexual style of its own, in enraging the heterosexual spectator, and in signalling the eroticism of lesbian differences, despite the threat of violence and censure:

> My understanding of why we angered straight spectators so is not that they saw us modeling ourselves after them, but just the

opposite: we were a symbol of women's erotic autonomy, a sexual accomplishment that did not include them. The physical attacks were a direct attempt to break into this self-sufficient erotic partnership. (Nestle 1987: 102)

In an article on lesbian fashion in the 1990s, Inge Blackman and Kathryn Perry look at the increasing diversity of lesbian style signifiers that suggest and play with roles of butch/femme and S/M 'bottom' and 'top'. They add a cautionary note that, 'style may be subversive, but it can never become a substitute for direct political campaigning. If identity is a constantly shifting and changing phenomenon, it can no longer be a useful rallying cry for mobilizing people into action' (*Feminist Review*, No. 34, Spring 1990: 78). Whether lesbian roleplay is subversive but not political continues to be debated, along with the question of whether the performance of difference necessarily reaffirms the power politics of heterosexual relationships.

Whether such a stance can be rendered politically useful in a broader feminist context remains to be seen; but such debates evidently enrich feminist discourse around the subject of compulsory heterosexuality and the politics of desire. Lesbian theorists remain the leaders in this field, since the political status of desire is as yet a much contested area, commonly avoided by straight feminists, and the notion of gender as parody of a non-existent 'natural' origin offers some challenging possibilities. Butler accurately identifies a paradox in feminism's location of gender as at once constructed and originary, and perhaps her situating parody as part of the politics of gay identity could be extended to heterosexual feminists' work on sexuality and subjectivity – to show the ways in which a sense of the parodic status of gender is already implicitly a part of the codification of heterosexual feminist discourse. Whether or not this extension of theories of otherness occurs, the value of such a position has clearly energized gay/lesbian theories, where the '90s has witnessed the modest beginnings of a new 'separatist' theoretical enterprise, with gay and lesbian theorists collaborating to produce such volumes as *Inside/Out* (1991); and new lesbian insights into feminist cultural criticism, such as *New Lesbian Criticism* (1992). In her introduction to *Inside/Out*, Diana Fuss asserts that 'what we need most urgently in gay and lesbian theory right now is a theory of marginality, subversion, dissidence, and othering' (Fuss 1991: 5). Perhaps this would also make an accurate assessment of feminism's current needs, which in its institutional embeddedness in the mainstream, loses its purchase on the fact of its marginality and otherness.

Perhaps one of the most sustained critiques of gendered binarism, and one of the most compelling images to emerge from feminism's cross fertilization with postmodernist thinking, is Donna Haraway's 'cyborg'. Neither organism nor machine, the cyborg marks a post-industrial, post-humanist fission between nature and culture, which transforms or deflects any originary meanings attributed to either term. The bio-technological contribution to social control remains, however, decidedly patriarchal, and 'the main trouble with cyborgs . . . is that they are the illegitimate offspring of militarism and patriarchal capitalism, not to mention state socialism'; but, as she continues, 'illegitimate offspring are often exceedingly unfaithful to their origins' (Haraway in Weed 1989: 176). The cyborg, then, is not summoned by Haraway as a paradigm of the victim, caught up in the networks of what Foucault would term 'bio-power'; she is more interested in how cybernetics breaks down the humanist divisions between animal and human, mind and body, in a symbolic breach between nature and culture. For Haraway such an 'ironic' political stance as the one outlined in this essay, is an attempt to contribute to feminist debates around the politics of identity, by blocking the feminist tendency to retreat to pseudo-essentialist origins, extending the ground of 'new essentialist' discussions such as Butler's and Fuss's:

> Consciousness of exclusion through naming is acute. Identities seem contradictory, partial and strategic. With the hard-won recognition of their social and historical constitution, gender, race and class cannot provide the basis for belief in 'essential' unity. There is nothing about being 'female' that naturally binds women. There is not even such a state as 'being' female, itself a highly complex category constructed in contested sexual scientific discourses and other social entities. (Weed 1989: 179)

Haraway identifies consequent risks in contemporary feminists constantly summoning the quality of 'being' female (particularly through experiential narratives) in its tendency to mark feminism as a totalizing discourse. Her intention here is to make female identity itself ironic – something some lesbian theorists are also attempting to perform in their belief that gender parody such as butch/femme role-play disassembles dominant meanings of gender identity, rather than simply replicating relations of dominance and submission. Haraway is signalling a position that might also facilitate a renewed rhetoric of resistance and opposition which does not simply rely on an acceptance of the 'realities' of oppressive mechanisms. In a curious fashion her work carries resonances of that of Shulamith Firestone's *Dialectic of Sex*, although feminist critiques of this text have of course focused upon its underlying biologism. Haraway's account, however, denies biologism any privileged epistemological status; and in her portrayal of the cyborg she grounds biology and its possible connotations within shifting conditions of scientific discourse. Her ascription of the cyborgian subject does not deny the patriarchal rootedness of such a construction, but rather sees in the deflection of originary gender binarism, the possibilities of a new ironic form of resistance to existing relations of power.

PROBLEMS AND UTOPIAN POSSIBILITIES

No matter how enchanted one might be by the postmodernist redefinition of the categories masculine/feminine, and even male/female, feminists need to be able 'crudely' to assert that woman as category, encompassing the action and reaction of 'difference' in its many semantic layers, remains the subject and Subject of its political discourse. As Modleski avers, 'in the final analysis, it seems more important to struggle over what it means to be a woman than over whether or not to be one' (Modleski 1991: 20). The luxury of female anti-essentialism is still one only accorded to the privileged; non-white, non-heterosexual, non-bourgeois women are still finding political impetus in summoning up womanhood as identity, and femininity as a construct which excludes and punishes them most painfully of all – as bell hooks' summoning of Sojourner Truth's question, 'Ain't I a Woman?' as title for her 1982 text testifies.

One significant crisis in feminism is, I believe, the overwhelming consciousness that differing internal movements tend to create their own unwritten dos and don'ts; and women gaining access to feminist thought for the first time might be forgiven for feeling that they don't want to label themselves feminist because of the pejorative tone this term has culturally acquired. More importantly, they may feel that they cannot call themselves feminists, if they lack the 'qualifications' that certainly the more arcane branches of modern feminist thought seem to designate, a consideration strengthened by popular denunciations of feminism as prescriptive or even 'puritan'.[2] Alison Light perceives the danger of a tone of piety creeping into feminism, perpetuating the complacency among (white) feminists that they are one of the 'chosen few', and she contests that 'Being a feminist, as I understand it, should not be like being in church: there are no blasphemies, no ritual incantations, no heretics and no saints' (Carr

1989: 28). I would agree with these sentiments, which perhaps deserve restating – despite their 'obviousness' – because recent debates among feminists give the lie to the notion that there are some fairly tenacious 'heresies' which need weeding out. Yet, paradoxically, we are in a position where there are some 'heretics' who use feminism to annihilate it, prompting a need for greater explicitness around the question of what feminism as discourse and action intends to achieve, and whether demarcated 'boundaries' are feasible. Whether or not such boundaries are desirable, they seem to be urgently needed.

Writing in 1971, Juliet Mitchell prophesied that the biggest single theoretical battle would be between radical and socialist feminists (Mitchell 1971: 91); here, Mitchell assumes that radical feminists will overcome their disaffection with the Left to combine their insights into women's experience and consciousness with a socialist feminist theory of women's oppression. Although the rift between these two positions has been demarcated many times since, in retrospect the major battle has been in the field of 'theory' itself and its possible disjunctions with a feminist political practice. Feminism has matured, and the potential sites for conflict – both within and outside feminist parameters – have multiplied. From largely eschewing political/theoretical coalitions with men during the '70s, in the '90s many feminists are forging new connections with men – at least at the level of postmodern critiques. The new battle for feminism, assuming that it survives the most recent crises of confidence/meaning outlined in this chapter, will be to find epistemological measures to defend its autonomy while enacting bridges between the politics of race, class, and sexual orientation. Many women who previously felt that their concerns were not addressed by the dominant forms of feminism might then recognize a newly strengthened location for their own resistance within a politics of heterogeneity. We live in an era which offers academic feminism some confusing messages. The shape and scope of women's studies in face of critical 'acceptance', has been transformed, yet the ideological pressures exerted by a patriarchal social reality still hold sway, and arguably are reinforced in a climate of recession and economic shrinkage.

Speaking of the interfaces between black male and female experiences of oppression and those experiences of white females, Kate Millett comments on how in the case of women and the perpetuation of the ideology of femininity, 'a certain handful of women are accorded higher status that they may perform a species of cultural policing over the rest' (Millett 1977: 57). It is tempting to see this tokenism filtering into increasing incidents of feminist interventions into 'high theory', particularly that of postmodernism. One of my chief concerns about the degree of acceptance, and even popularity, of feminist theoretical positions in academe is that such theorists are accorded by their male counterparts the 'honour' of being the cultural police force for feminism as a whole. Postmodern or poststructuralist feminism is viewed in this light as a sign of feminist thought at its most sophisticated, a methodology which renders other forms of feminist expression redundant. It suggests that feminists are being encouraged to forget the tribulations of their recent past, and throw in their hard-won resources with the anti-humanist men, whose investment in exploding humanist binarism might still represent a somewhat different agenda from that normally associated with feminism.

Feminism has always devoted time and energy to the anticipation of utopian possibilities of social transformation, as do all radical political positions to a greater or lesser extent. Perhaps the value of utopian preoccupations is undermined by postmodern critiques. When I attempt to identify the desirability or otherwise of the continuing production of feminist utopias as a viable political tactic, I recall Foucault's distinction between utopias and heterotopias in his Preface to *The Order of Things*:

> Utopias afford consolation: although they have no real locality there is nevertheless a fantastic, untroubled region in which they are able to unfold: they open up cities with vast avenues, superbly planted gardens, countries where life is easy, even though the road to them is chimerical. Heterotopias are disturbing, probably because they secretly undermine language, because they make it impossible to name this and that, because they shatter or tangle common names, because they destroy 'syntax' in advance, and not only the syntax with which we construct sentences but also that less apparent syntax which causes words and things . . . to 'hold together'. (Foucault 1970: xviii)

Foucault (citing Borges as an example of a writer of heterotopias) is here mocking conventional systems of coherence and classification, which comprise the formation of knowledges from which we seek access to the truth of being. Such ordering instances, it is asserted, provide the conditions of possibility of uttering 'truths', and of founding disciplines of empirical knowledge. Similarly, feminists have long been in the business of mocking, inverting or disrupting the existing 'order of things', particularly in observing that Western epistemology assumes orders which on closer scrutiny conform to and support the conditions of possibility of a distinctly masculine body of knowledge and truth claims. At the centre of this order is language which inscribes gendered and other identities in opposition to one another in the indefatigable tension of the 'either/or' logic of modern thought. In a sense feminists are out to destroy the syntax of phallogocentrism, to get to the cement that binds the logic of such thought together in such arbitrary terms, not in order to rebuild the structure of such syntax in a slightly different configuration, but in order to demonstrate that such a structure has no natural foundations whatever.

Utopias are the 'no-places' of a future where society has transformed into something other than our present realities. In order to construct utopias, writers of fiction or political theory have recourse to the dominant systems of the present to enact a critique of its inequities, or its mistakes. Feminist utopias also seek to enter that no-place where the meanings of gender and oppression are exploded as ever arbitrary relations of power with a chimerical link to the 'natural', which only proves to be an essence constructed from the meanings of social life in its ever changing social and cultural contexts. In offering such utopias feminists remind us of the 'no place' for women in current dominant ideological representations – and as they seek to gesture a future 'no place' for women as well as men, they might also be viewed as venturing a heterotopia of their own. Feminists do not, after all, envisage a future which is simply the obverse of the present; often the aim is to dispense with classic binarist thinking in favour of a multiplicity, which denies all essence, including what are thought of as biological imperatives, in order to think what is, in current discursive formations, radically 'unthinkable'. If we regard utopian texts such as Shulamith Firestone's *Dialectic of Sex* in this light, it is clearly inadequate simply to view her work as racked with essentialist truth claims about female biology. One might usefully review the intentions of Firestone's work, in common with other feminist writings, as an exhortation to women to think outside their current social reality, in order to articulate what has currently no 'language' of its own.[3]

As Angelika Bammer suggests, utopian visions remain partial 'in both senses of the word: partisan and limited' (Bammer 1991: 155). As she indicates, this invites both negative and positive interpretations of the term: the negative side lies in the threat of exclusionism (particularly of the needs of less privileged groups of women), although the threat of the exclusion of men remains a powerful rhetorical challenge. Utopias are positive in the sense that feminists' multifarious and sometimes conflicting views of the desired shape of its utopias remind us that feminist thought is constantly reshaping and re-envisaging gender difference, and still has to focus upon reclaiming women's part in historical and cultural processes as a political necessity. The term heterotopia reminds us that not only are possible visions of the future multiple and ever changing, but that our critiques of the present draw upon multifarious perspectives on present social realities, specific to class, ethnic and sexual locations within patriarchy. Finally, the term heterotopia seems happily compatible with my exploration and affirmation of feminism's hete-rogeneity, where diversity and conflict might better ensure that our future is not a covert repetition of the shape of the past.

Chapter 10

Identity Crisis?: 'Post-feminism', the Media and 'Feminist Superstars'

> The backlash is at once sophisticated and banal, deceptively 'progressive' and proudly backward. It deploys both the 'new' findings of 'scientific research' and the sentimental moralizing of yesteryear; it turns into media sound bites both the glib pronouncements of pop-psych trend-watchers and the frenzied rhetoric of New Right preachers. The backlash has succeeded in framing virtually the whole issue of women's rights in its own language. Just as Reaganism and Thatcherism shifted political discourse far to the right and demonized liberalism, so the backlash convinced the public that women's 'liberation' was the true contemporary scourge – the source of an endless laundry list of personal, social and economic problems.
>
> (Faludi 1992: 12)

REINVENTING THE WHEEL:
FEMINISM'S NEW/OLD FACE – NAOMI WOLF

In 1990 Naomi Wolf's *The Beauty Myth* was published and received more critical attention from the mainstream than was usual for a text that espouses a broadly feminist position, initially because of the publicity that surrounded this book but secondarily because Wolf appeared to promise a new perspective on some old problems for feminism – in particular, the constraints that the ideology of femininity physically as well as mentally impose upon all women. Wolf picked up on rumblings within feminist writings since the mid-'80s that a concerted backlash against feminism is being waged on a number of fronts. Her perception is that:

We are in the midst of a violent backlash to feminism that uses images of female beauty as a political weapon against women's advancement: the beauty myth . . . As women released themselves from the feminine mystique of domesticity, it waned and the beauty myth took over its lost ground, expanding to carry on its work of social control. (Wolf 1990: 2)

She argues that today's successful woman is still tyrannized by Western standards of female beauty – particularly in the age of cosmetic surgery where 'perfection' is seen to be achievable and indeed the ultimate quest for the wealthy female consumer. She adroitly demonstrates how cosmetic surgery is tied into the consumerist culture of advanced capitalism, and sees the beauty industry as a new form of patriarchal control where the woman-made female body is regarded as unfinished, so that one feels compelled to nip and tuck and inject silicone to achieve perfectibility. More than this, she argues that many women's employment is conditional upon them retaining the correct feminine image. Wolf points out that a certain level of attractiveness can be cited as a requirement of certain jobs – in the USA this might be included as a Bona Fide Occupational Qualification (or BFOQ: a Genuine Occupational Qualification in the UK – GOQ) in sex discrimination law as the exceptional circumstance in which sex discrimination for a particular job might be fair. Wolf asserts that this basic exclusion clause has become parodied beyond recognition to what she colloquially terms the PBQ or Professional Beauty Qualification. She shows how the PBQ is militated to different ends according to gender – for example in the case of television news presentation where men are valued for the experienced journalism skills and can look merely 'distinguished', but women have to be young, slim and attractive; where ageing without the aid of cosmetic surgery might be considered a sackable offence.

The major part of the book catalogues the way in which beauty has become a fundamental, almost 'religious' given, in the lives of women in the late twentieth century. She outlines its material effects (how women's livelihood, even in professions where display isn't part of the job, might be profoundly affected by it), and its cultural reinforcement. She focuses in particular upon images of women in magazines and television; on how parts of the female body are fetishized objects for male desire in the sex industry – often grossly distorted, dismembered, or receiving acts of violence – and the way the slimming and beauty industry have caused women to do acts of violence to their own bodies. Incidences of women's violence against

themselves are many, including either starving or binge eating resulting in anorexia or bulimia; or by submitting to cosmetic surgery such
as liposuction and breast implants even though the dangers of these
processes are not fully known and failures are suppressed. Wolf
argues that beauty becomes correlative with fundamental meanings
of what it is to be a 'woman' in women's contemporary existence, and
that the 'beauty myth' has been sustained and updated even in the
wake of the demise of other archaic belief systems:

> In this century, most fields of thought have been transformed
> by the understanding that truths are relative and perceptions
> subjective. But the rightness and permanence of 'beauty's' caste
> system is taken for granted by people who study quantum
> physics, ethnology, civil rights law; who are atheists, who are
> sceptical of TV news, who don't believe that the Earth was
> created in seven days. It's believed uncritically, as an article of
> faith. (Wolf 1990: 65)

Certainly, as Wolf points out, aspects of the beauty industry – particularly the slimming industry – have appropriated the language of
religion, with its guilt, innumerable sins and submission to a greater,
higher being. She takes this analogy much further, comparing the
operation of dieting and slimming regimes to the operation of cult
religions, which attempt to alter people's states of mind in a very
short space of time, to the point where individuals are unable to
make autonomous decisions outside the framework of the cult.

This language of violence and tyranny is reminiscent of the
uncompromising tone of radical feminist writings of the '70s. This
might well lead us to suspect that while the beauty myth has become
a highly technologically sophisticated industry along with other
industries in the past three decades, the dynamism of the beauty
industry has already been extensively catalogued by earlier feminists.
One might be tempted to wonder whether Wolf's new insights are
not really just rehashed versions of the old standards of feminist
thought.[1] But whereas patriarchy was seen to perpetuate such myths
in the interests and to the advantage of all men by radicals, the
'enemy' for Wolf is the beauty industry as an amorphous and powerful
body in its own right. The media and the employment system which
perpetuates the Professional Beauty Qualification system, in addition to the beauty industry are all metamorphosed into a dispassion-
ate degendered power group at war with women, and brainwashing
them despite the best attempts of individual men:

This sexual mutilation is not about relations between real men and women. It is about women's sexuality trapped in the beauty backlash, in spite of men who may love them. Soon, not even a loving partner will be able to save many women's sexuality from the knife. (Wolf 1990: 206)

When Wolf mentions men she characterizes then as desperate individuals trying to convince their female partners and friends that they like them the way they are. Of course there are men who most assuredly do this, and feel equally baffled by the dynamism of the beauty myth. But since as Wolf herself points out, such beliefs are more deeply entrenched than even the most pervasive political or scientific ideas, it seems naive to argue that if men don't invest in this myth directly, they may not 'profit' from it indirectly. Many women don't personally set any store by the value attributed to physical forms of attractiveness, but we all have a sense of the value placed upon women's appearance and have problems avoiding making judgements based on it from time to time. However, it is clear that a group of individuals are profiting from women's hyper-awareness of their body shapes, and the heads of such companies are usually men – as are all leading cosmetic surgeons. Wolf recognizes that one of the most unpopular aspects of contemporary second wave feminism is that it makes men culpable for existing power relations; yet in avoiding blaming men at all, she casts those who wield power merely as 'an inhumane social order' (Wolf 1990: 171), to which we all passively make our obeisance. Feminists have consistently confronted a classic double-bind: that is, how a particular ideology of gender difference replicates itself in numerous distinct social orders over time and across cultures with or without the total collusion of individuals. This obviously cannot be seen to be the dastardly working of a highly organized group of individual men, yet men as an entire group profit from women's oppression; they profit from the sense that women's mental capacities have no value if they are not accompanied by the correct physical attributes; they profit from being masculine and 'whole' as opposed to feminine and 'partial' or pathological.

To exonerate men from blame is to blame women totally for their current material and ideological position – in fact, it is to make them responsible for the historical conditions of possibility of their subjection. Such a construction casts woman as too weak to resist the blandishments and shallow prizes of the beauty myth; yet as Wolf herself demonstrates in her survey of the means by which the myth is perpetuated, resistance might mean the loss of employment, and in many cases it certainly means enduring the antagonism of one's peers, partners and family. What is most significant in Wolf's response to the 'beauty myth' is that she again places the responsibility of resistance in the hands of individual women, just as Betty Friedan exhorted the middle-class housewife to take responsibility for her own destiny in *The Feminine Mystique*. Quite simply, individual resistance will not change this system, which is why feminists have insisted that a collective, concerted response by women is the only way to destabilize and transform this particular mindset. To accept that only women are likely to change this state of affairs – as feminists pragmatically do – is an altogether different matter from implying that the perpetuation of this system is somehow their fault: 'The toughest but most necessary change will come not from men or from the media, but from women, in the way in which they see and behave towards other women' (Wolf 1990: 233). She reminds us that men are becoming sucked in to the 'beauty myth' as a small proportion become victims of anorexia and other eating disorders; certainly this appears to be 'equality' at its most warped, but do women have to save men too?

The 'new feminism' of the '90s, exemplified by writers such as Wolf, is firstly not altogether 'new' in its insights, but displays a tendency to blame women because the revolution promised by the second wave has not yet happened. Wolf's reluctance to talk about collective activism, and indeed radical change, makes her stance entirely compatible with liberal individualist politics. This seems particularly apparent in Wolf's case, where possible male readers are nudgingly reminded that their existence is acknowledged, as if men are some politically overlooked group who deserve a little space marked out for them in an exclusionary mainstream.

FIGHTING THE BACKLASH: SUSAN FALUDI

Since the late '80s the backlash has been acknowledged in feminist circles, but at the time of writing this has still not been consistently publicly challenged or widely responded to in feminist discourse. Perhaps the most interesting accounts of the backlash have come from two accomplished journalists, the American Susan Faludi and the British Yvonne Roberts, and from the American writer Marilyn French (more widely known for her best-selling novel, *The Women's Room* (1977)). All of these accounts first appeared in print in Britain in 1992. Faludi's *Backlash* and French's *The War Against Women*, are the most far-reaching and extensive in their critique of contemporary manoeuvres to discredit feminism. *Backlash* focuses initially on the mass media's capitalizing on the myths of 'post-feminism', and in the development of her argument, Faludi powerfully indicates in whose interests these myths of feminism's ills are utilized.

The most satisfying aspect of the book is that she ultimately returns to consider the material effects of the backlash upon actual women's lives, in terms of work, sexuality and personal relationships. Her 'case studies' of backlash proponents in Part three of the book reveal the complexity of the backlash 'conspiracy',[2] in that figures with divergent political and personal agendas have an investment in it – from latter day feminist pioneers (Betty Friedan) to recanting 'new men' (Robert Bly). What this cogently suggests is that the second wave's earlier conviction that patriarchal ideology – the force which naturalizes our current conditions of existence so that many believe that a sexual revolution would represent a war with nature – is a formidable adversary; it further suggests that material conditions are governed effectively by peoples' investment in notions of correct and viable identities accorded differing access to privilege and financial reward.

As is clear from the epigraph to this chapter that the media at once pronounce the official equality of women, and then go on to catalogue the ills that this brings – the stresses and strains that 'prove' women are biologically incapable of fully entering a man's world. The obviousness of this ploy appears simplistic, but it strikes a chord in the hearts of many women, precisely because women have not achieved full equality in material, social or ideological terms and individual women's attempts to succeed in the workplace are a daily uphill struggle. They are still required to prove themselves to be more than the equal of their colleagues, and if parents, they still shoulder the chief burden of childcare arrangements, often suffering social censure of their 'selfishness' in wanting anything for themselves at all. Women's magazines and newspapers alike are encouraging women to blame feminism for their exhaustion and disillusionment rather than a political structure which profits, quite literally, from the inequalities it perpetuates. It is argued that feminism spoiled women's fun, their right to be sexually attractive and dress up, to flirt and enjoy domestic bliss. It has even been the case that feminism has directly and indirectly been blamed for violence against women and women killing.[3] As Faludi points out, in both Britain and the US women are still only earning just over two-thirds of men's wage for the same work, and are still more likely than men to exist on the poverty line. It is also still true that women are under-represented in state politics and in trade unions, while Britain has the lowest provision of paid maternity leave in Europe. All these issues have consistently been central to the feminist agenda, so it is patently absurd to imply that feminism could possibly have achieved its ends when this state of affairs persists.

Faludi declares that the notion of a backlash against women is not a new concept; that 'such flare-ups are hardly random; they have always been triggered by the perception – accurate or not – that women are making great strides' (Faludi 1992: 13). Their success can be in convincing individual women that their pursuit of the right to exercise life choices is fallacious and ultimately personally destructive – it directly subverts the feminist notion of the personal being political, suggesting that feminist aims are achieved only at the expense of a happy, fulfilled personal life. But as Faludi points out, instead of seeing feminism as having pushed women too far too fast, it is more likely that 'the feminist revolution has petered out, leaving so many women discouraged and paralysed by the knowledge that, once again, the possibility for real progress has been foreclosed' (Faludi 1992: 79), and the blame cannot be simply laid at the door of feminist politics.

In the current of a swing against anything associated with 'political correctness'[4] in the '90s the 'freedom' to express feminist ideas as legitimate contestations of dominant mainstream political views becomes increasingly problematic. The most destructive element of the wave of dominant political and academic opinion against so-called 'p.c.' is that a form of words and appropriate behaviour towards under-represented groups and minorities is now being cast as an obstacle to the 'freedom' of expression of 'others' (generally those whose interests are largely represented by the dominant discourse. In this light, feminism is portrayed as tyrannical, unrepresentative of the demands of women, or just plain boring. It is regarded as *passé* for someone to express a feminist idea or objection in normal circumstances – 'to make a fuss about sexual injustice is more than unfeminine; it is now uncool' (Faludi 1992: 95). This boredom with something compellingly presented by the media as old hat is supported by the technique of 'trend journalism' – the art of creating a 'new' trend through the act of repeating the supposed trend enough times and prefacing it with the word 'new'. Faludi identifies, to name a few, the 'new' abstinence, the 'new femininity', 'New Traditionalist cocooning', the 'new monogamy'. Things to be viewed negatively, as a symptom of the bad old days have terms and phrases attached to them which denote plague, illness or malfunction, such as

'Superwoman burn-out', 'the infertility epidemic', and 'the terminally single woman'.[5]

THE BACKLASH AND RIGHT-WING POLITICS: MARILYN FRENCH

As Faludi observes 'if the contemporary backlash has a birthplace, it was here within the ranks of the New Right' (Faludi 1992: 260). And this political attack on the rights of women is the most obvious backhanded tribute to the perceived power of second wave feminism, where the 'natural' way of life is clearly perceived as being under threat. One of the most emotive issues raised as a challenge to the women's movement was the claim that feminism was an anti-family organization, that it sought to destroy what most people see as the essential base unit of society, without indicating why or what feminists wished to see in its place.

Academics too were to take up arms against feminism imagining an invasion of their territory, and a loss of all that is 'great' about the development of knowledge in a democractic environment. Writers such as Allan Bloom in his *The Closing of the American Mind* (1987) attacked the 'epidemic' of political correctness that he suggested was sweeping American universities, and in particular what he sees as the tyranny of feminist ideas, which threaten to unseat old canons of learning (which are assumed to be self-evidently worth cherishing). It seems that generally when the decline in standards – whether moral, educational or otherwise – is summoned as a reason for political or economic crisis, feminism is seen to be responsible. As an antidote to Bloom's visions of female-dominated campuses, Faludi, rejecting the long-held cherished 'truths' about learning, provides the facts:

> Women, feminist or otherwise, account for a mere 10 per cent of the tenured staff at all four-year American institutions . . . a rise of only 6 per cent since the 1960s. Five times more women with PhDs are unemployed than men. Nor are feminist professorships overrunning campuses; only twelve women's studies chairs exist in the USA. (Faludi 1992: 326)

Bloom's and others' overinflated claims about the dominance of women in academe and the professions represent a lament for the idea of the loss of male authority, both in the home and in the public sphere – a loss which is rather prematurely being mourned given that feminism has assuredly not yet succeeded in eroding these major seats of power.

Marilyn French's book, *The War Against Women* (1992), takes a different tack from Faludi's: to a large extent, they do complement each other impressively. Faludi provides up-to-date statistics about women's pay, reproductive rights and political representation at the same time as exposing the underlying motives of right wingers, religious fundamentalists and feminist recanters in true investigative journalist fashion. French chisels away at the notions of a 'healthy' culture and heritage built ineluctably upon patriarchal precepts. French also identifies the means by which exhaustive information about women's experiences is obfuscated within statistics which pretend to be de-gendered, but actually operate along a masculine paradigm. *The War against Women* is divided into four parts: 1) systemic discrimination against women; 2) institutional wars against women; 3) the cultural war against women; and 4) men's personal war against women. The uneven distribution of material across these sections suggests that it is always difficult to divide the effects or processes of women's oppression into 'categories' of the public/ private, cultural/ institutional, and so forth.

However, this unevenness makes section four – men's personal war against women – look particularly sparse. It is always most difficult to imply forcefully and persistently, as French does, that men personally benefit from patriarchy, particularly in an era where men-blaming is regarded as particularly naive, even puerile. The late '80s and '90s have seen the increased production of writings by men anxious to disassociate themselves from patriarchy, or identify themselves as its casualties. There is also a trend for writings by women who feel obliged to remove the 'victim' label from women; writers such as Naomi Wolf in *Fire with Fire* (1993) and Katie Roiphe in *The Morning After* (1994) see second wave feminists as culpable in the construction of a notion of contemporary women as the necessary victims of a male power which renders them unable to change their lives. Not only is this a gross distortion of the feminist theory of patriarchal power, but 'victimhood' is replaced with a clear sense that women – and only women – are to blame for their own subordinate status.

In contrast, *The War against Women* has, as a whole, a welcome flavour of vanguardist '70s feminism about it, not least in its forceful affirmation that men invest in and benefit from patriarchy. Some of her assertions would be signally unpopular with the 'new feminists', for instance her claim that all men benefit by soaring rape figures and the resulting increase in fear among all women, which is not alleviated by any concerted legal response to such a threat. French, like Brownmiller and Millett (to name but two) before her, characterizes patriarchy and women's oppression as a war against women, and as the book progresses she suggests that crimes against women in the contemporary world amount to nothing less than genocide. Perhaps because she offers dates, numbers and specific geographical locations for her case studies, she avoids some of the pitfalls of '70s radical feminism; yet she revives the force of the original conceptualization and use of the term 'patriarchy' to connote a huge conspiratorial force within civilization as it has developed over thousands of years. Although the examples she offers are deliberately not universalized, she conveys a strong sense of the universality of patriarchy even though its effects differ in varying periods and locales. In fact, in her introduction, French characterizes civilization as having developed by a means which is entirely dependent upon female subordinacy: 'Women were probably the first slaves, and while elite women had considerable power in early states, they were subject to men of their class' (French 1992: 1).

According to French, the key aspects of women's oppression are the attempted control over female bodies (sexual and reproductive) and female labour; specifically, she cites statistics presented at the United Nations Conference on Women in Copenhagen in 1980 – that women do between two-thirds and three-quarters of the work in the world (French 1992: 24) – arguing that this state of affairs still persists. French's book is packed with examples of how the world appears to be essentially organized in male interests in such a way that women and men can remain blind to the input, value and needs of women; where, in fact, there is no vocabulary to quantify the value of female labour, or the viability of natural resources:

> Men's global accounting system reveals the profundity of male contempt for the necessity in human life, treating not just women's work but the environment as insignificant . . . . Consider: economic statistics calculate the value of 'undeveloped' rain forest in Brazil at $0. A standing tree offers shade and coolness, prevents erosion, and returns oxygen to the atmosphere. But it has no value in the GDP [gross domestic product] until it is cut down. (French 1992: 31)

With specific reference to the changing political climate since the increasing hegemony of right-wing and fundamentalist politics since the late '70s, she counters the popular wisdom that women have directly benefited from these systems of power, through the more regular emergence of female figureheads. Citing the examples of Margaret Thatcher, Indira Gandhi and Golda Meir, she cogently counters the usual argument that female leaders signify radical change, by arguing that this in fact does not disrupt the system of power or the meanings generated by it, nor does it in any way 'demasculinize' it:

> That is because where they can hold power, women rulers are women only incidentally seen as extraordinary, able to overcome the 'weaknesses' of their sex. Nevertheless, all are subjected to special attack because of their sex (the Chinese blamed emperors' concubines for the fall of dynasties). It may be ironic that a woman, Indira Gandhi, ruled a nation that more than any other kills its females, but the two factors are unrelated. That Indira Gandhi, Golda Meir, or Margaret Thatcher held power does not mean their countries have less contempt for women than others. Today, women usually come to power in countries with traditions of inherited elite rule: elite men may allow women of their own class to hold power if they have the potential to unify a country counting on their being malleable to male control. . . . Whether or not such women defer to male control, men can usually count on them to uphold class interests. (French 1992: 39–40)

French, therefore, interprets individual female 'success stories' in terms of men's broader political needs, and generally suggests that contemporary examples of female 'power' are contingent upon the vicissitudes of power relationships between men. For instance, French cites the example of a shift in the distribution of public political roles to women in Norway, and asserts that this seeming 'feminist' victory is a pyrrhic one: that women are gaining prominence in the political sphere because men are leaving it for more lucrative jobs in transnational corporations (French 1992: 41–2). In this respect, French is not simply pessimistic about the impact of feminism upon current social and economic realities: rather, she is attempting to be realistic about the size of the task still confronting women, as well as suggesting that these 'accidental' instances of female entry into networks of power can be capitalized upon. In this, she is set in direct polemical opposition to the likes of Wolf, who argue that women in the '90s are in the throes of a 'genderquake' (Wolf 1993: 29–39).

The New Right wing in politics is considered in tandem with the impact of fundamentalism and other dominant religious movements. This section is fascinating for its concentration on aspects of theology which focus on the control and even torture of women, but most cogent in the way in which religious power is linked to state/patriarchal power – so that in USA one witnesses the establishment of the power base of the moral majority, who in their advocation of 'natural' family values, can have a profound impact upon women's lives. The power of tradition is also evident in state domination of women's bodies, where ritual dictates the perpetuation of mutilation – for example footbinding in China, or genital mutilation in the Sudan – but also in dress codes which emphasize the status of women's bodies as sexual objects. Aimed at the kind of general audience that Wolf's work is being pitched at, French is mindful to collate instances of what her readers may construe as foreign 'barbarity' with the more prosaic – such as the fact that in most countries women and not men are forbidden by law from going into public without a shirt – to reflect the way the female body is the site of social and moral control.

Although her fourth section on men's personal war against women is relatively skimpy, it importantly reinforces her sustained and spirited defense of the 'unpopular' feminist view that all men benefit from patriarchy:

> As long as some men use physical force to subjugate females, *all* men need not. The knowledge that some men do suffices to threaten all women. Beyond that, it is not necessary to beat up a woman to beat her down. A man can simply refuse to hire women in well-paid jobs, extract as much or more work from women than men but pay them less, or treat women disrespectfully at work or at home. He can fail to support a child he has engendered, demand the woman he lives with wait on him like a servant. He can beat or kill the woman he claims to love; he can rape women, whether mate, acquaintance, or stranger; he can rape or sexually molest his daughters, nieces, stepchildren, or the children of a woman he claims to love. *The vast majority of men in the world do one or more of the above* (French 1992: 184)

As the above suggests, French at times reflects what might be seen as an unreconstructed radical viewpoint which universalizes the idea of man as a social grouping regardless of race, class or sexual identity, but I believe that this is wholly deliberate. The bottom line of her argument would be that women as a social class/caste are globally exploited and oppressed by men as a whole, and this is reiterated as a direct challenge to a wave of 'feminist' writings which anxiously attempt to exonerate 'men' as individuals to the point where an idea of patriarchal power has no currency, and generally concludes with attacks on female self-indulgent weakness. What is least satisfactory about French's work is her failure to link her own findings to the last two and a half decades of feminist thought, in that even though this failure might be regarded as a tactic to make her work more accessible to a 'general' reader, it gives the lie to the idea that her ideas are 'new', unsupported by the weight and authority of a feminist epistemological community. There is another danger that her insistence upon individual male accountability may be seen to lapse into straightforward essentialism,[6] but here I think French is a victim of the rhetoric of a backlash which, in attempting to remove all culpability from men, risks wholly undermining the feminist project. There is enough evidence to show that French does not naively cast women as saints in all this; but there is a clear danger that in casting conflict between men and women in terms of war, she might be assumed to be uttering a self-fulfilling prophecy, instead of a radical political statement of intent, where she claims more optimistically that 'women are fighting back on every front' (French 1992: 211).

BLAMING WOMEN? THE GUILTY FEMINISTS

It may still be questionable as to how far French's work develops beyond the compelling (but in the atmosphere of the '90s, politically inappropriate) '70s rhetoric of radical activist politics. Yet French's tenacity in detailing the past and current atrocities performed by men against women is a refreshing antidote to the kind of 'new feminist' rhetoric that hints that the only enemies of women in the '90s are their calorie charts, their tendency to cry 'rape' after an unsuccessful date, and themselves. Similarly, Faludi's work is an impressive contribution to feminism's rearguard action in a non-academic environment. But what neither writer offers us is an indication of how political and ideological change might be militated for, in a cultural environment which encourages individuals to see themselves as politically atomized, and where collective resistant political identities (anything from trade union membership to association with Left wing groups) are seen as nostalgic and politically regressive.

It is disappointing that both Faludi and French play down the feminist origins of their arguments, and in doing so acknowledge and possibly legitimate the increasing unpopularity of feminism as an identity. In addition some of the backlash myths Faludi exposes are a little too neat, and a little too redolent of the journalistic creative accounting that she attacks with such verve. Nonetheless such work does speak to women who thought feminism excluded them but who still felt freakish because they didn't conform to social norms or felt injustice at their treatment in the workplace or at home. Faludi's epilogue reminds us that women have consistently resisted patriarchal hegemonic forces, and that the role of the feminist of the '90s is to prove herself equal to demythologizing the powerful and ever-changing myths about the female self and nature perpetuated in the mass media and other state apparatuses. In opposition to Wolf in *Fire with Fire*, Faludi is clearly against the image of the individualist feminist of the '80s and outlines the pitfalls of attempting a struggle alone.

Yvonne Roberts' *Mad About Women* (1992) is a much shorter polemic, but one which relies upon the same investigative journalistic flair as Faludi's. This much less hyped British publication is in many ways a response to Neil Lyndon's *No More Sex War* (1992) which argued that men are currently more oppressed by women, and that the balance of power had tipped too far in the opposite direction. Perhaps its main flaw is that it is a response which is tailored to address Lyndon's accusations, and apart from anything else this tactic allows his ideas a degree of credence and legitimacy they probably never merited, given that his book is largely a very personal attack based on fairly shallow empirical 'evidence'. One result of Roberts's book being shaped in part as a response to the kind of anti-feminist vitriol represented by Lyndon and others – whom Roberts calls 'angry not-so-young men' (Roberts 1992: xiv) – is that she devotes a large amount of space examining feminist issues in relation to men. In this sense her scope is resolutely heterosexist, and within this framework addresses a clearly defined group of women – those who are in long-term relationships, and have or will have children. In common with other contemporary feminist commentators she identifies the means by which feminism has come to be blamed for the perceived personal and social cost of women 'having it all'. In this she identifies how feminist precepts can be turned against themselves, and women can be encouraged to blame feminism for the increased burden of entering careers while maintaining the home:

> Feminism is accustomed to opposition; no movement whose basis is radical change expects bouquets. It is used to the exhausted voices of complaint from women who blame it because they now carry the burdens of home *and* work: a strange kind of 'liberation'. The fault for this may lie with those

men who fail to provide adequate support, and a society that is still hugely ambivalent about the working woman, but feminism still carries the can. (Roberts 1992: ix)

Roberts describes feminism as 'neither dead nor dying, but – in Britain, at least – in need of some intensive care' (Roberts 1992: x). She begins from the premise that feminism has made some mistakes, but that the achievements of mainstream feminism are worth high-lighting, particularly in the means by which certain ideas have filtered down to 'ordinary' men and women. She is clear that there is a potential feminist 'ghetto'; but suggests that it is feminism's respon-sibility to widen its appeal, and acknowledge the extent of its current unattractiveness to 'ordinary' (white, heterosexual) women. In her assertion that feminism should also endeavour to make its precepts attractive to men, Roberts stance is slightly reminiscent of Janet Radcliffe Richards (discussed in Chapter One); in that she adopts a view of feminism as ideally a set of commonsense ideas that would, if correctly phrased, be transparently desirable to all concerned.

Roberts' text, in common with Faludi and French's, displays some of the schizophrenia inherited in a feminist context for the '90s, where feminism and 'p.c.' ideas are demonized at the same time that they are being quoted, misquoted and turned against themselves, by the media, parliamentarians, and the 'new feminists'. She describes feminism as being the site of one basic conflict, a war between those she terms 'radical separatist' feminists and more 'moderate' (pro-male) others; although she offers a backhanded tribute to radicals, arguing that, 'It was the separatists, the "man-haters", who acted as midwife to the movement as a whole, forcing it to give birth, I would argue, to a far healthier, far louder, for more bolshie baby' (Roberts 1992: 22). Despite her clear attempt to offer a 'rational' feminism with a cross-gendered appeal, Roberts seems aware of the pitfalls of adopting a stance which ignores the history and origins of feminism's second wave, its legacy in political disaffection with radical men. Yet she seems to feel that it is time to call some form of truce.

The bulk of her arguments circulate around issues of interest to men: there is practically a whole chapter on the Families Need Fathers organization about the inequities of visitation rights and custody,[7] whose purpose seems to convince us that men suffer injustice too. In a following chapter entitled 'Just wait until your father gets home' she suggests that feminists jealously guard their mothering rights, with the consequence that they deny men the opportunity to prove their competence as parents on equal terms. Again there is a

prevailing sense that Roberts, whilst defending the power of fundamental feminist arguments is simultaneously constructing an elaborate defence of the modern man against anticipated attacks. She
concludes that 'if men are to be "re-educated", perhaps feminism
now needs to accept that it must be less exclusive' (Roberts 1992:
234); this returns us to debates around the role of men in feminism
outlined in Chapter Eight, but also suggests that feminism and
women in general are largely to blame for the current dynamics
between the sexes.

Rosalind Coward's book *Our Treacherous Hearts* (1992) develops
this idea of women being culpable, if not for their own oppression,
then for letting men 'get their way'. Coward's reputation as an
important feminist theorist makes this book particularly poignant;
while she ironically charts the media's joyful sounding of feminism's
deathknell into the '90s, to some extent she seems to accept that
feminism may be irrevocably in a state of demise. In her introduction, Coward rather depressingly links the situation of women in the
1990s with that identified by Betty Friedan thirty years earlier: 'Why
is it that any conversation with any woman will reveal a 1990s equivalent of the female condition that Betty Friedan identified in the
1950s as "the problem that has no name"' (Coward 1992: 4). Coward
identifies the way that women in the 1990s face the contradictory
pull of the 'choices' feminism has helped to facilitate; with increased
access to the workplace but still a dearth of childcare facilities,
women are still constantly faced with the enormity of sacrifice rather
than the liberation of choice. In addition Coward recognizes that the
ideological cost of a rhetoric of social equality is that the onus is on
women to 'prove' their skills as carers as well as professionals; in the
wake of any sense of failure – the 'delinquent' child or the academic
failures – women receive the brunt of blame. Ironically, the injustice
of this situation has not provoked a renaissance in feminism during
the 1990s:

> Given such individual awareness of the new and additional
> pressures on women, it would have been reasonable to expect a
> resurgence of feminist protest. But there was nothing of the
> kind: the political visibility of women, *as women*, was nil.
> Organized feminism, which in any case had never won over the
> majority of women, disintegrated. . . . Apart from a few who
> risked mockery by the media for their dogged concern with
> 'wimmin's issues', most people agreed that these issues were a
> relic from the past. (Coward 1992: 5)

Whilst accepting that anti-feminist sentiments are an institutionalized part of Western culture Coward, in common with Roberts,
seems more concerned with turning the blame upon feminism itself.
Although she recognizes that a section of feminist thought during
the '80s acknowledged the need for men to change in order to ultimately improve women's lives, she suggests that feminism failed to
rise to this particular challenge: 'In crucial and important ways,
women – including once-active feminists like myself – backed off
from a confrontation with a system of values which gave certain men
real privileges. They fitted in, and found ways of justifying their deci-
sion to themselves' (Coward 1992: 8). This statement signals too easy
an acceptance of feminism's responsibility for the fact that a system of
ideas around the familial institution (a system that even Engels locates
as originating in 'prehistory') proved more tenacious than almost any
other system of beliefs. The wording of this statement is itself telling:
in speaking of feminists 'like myself', Coward threatens to reduce the
enormity of the struggle to that of a personal battle which she and
others proved 'unequal to'. The whole tenor of the book has a ring of
tiredness, a sense of the inevitability of defeat.

Her suggestion that women remain complicit in the traditional
family structure – a key theme in the book – endows women with the
power of individual agency and autonomy that they probably have
rarely had:

> In the last ten years women have appeared not just willing but
> positively eager to assume double responsibilities in the home:
> they have felt uneasy if their own achievements began to out-
> strip those of their male partners, and they have been almost
> frantic to retain male sexual approval. They have done all this
> in the full knowledge that feminism outlined the pitfalls of
> such strategies twenty years ago, even if it failed to offer any
> popular solutions. (Coward 1992: 12)

She is unhappy with Faludi's assertion that women remain complicit
purely because they remain socially and economically subordinate;
instead women are conceived as having a greater investment than
men in the status quo. She attempts to 'prove' her hypothesis that
women are complicit in the means of their own oppression by a series
of interviews with a number of women. From the outset she admits
to a middle-class bias in her select group of interviewees, but does
not appear to be concerned that an absence of considerations of race,
sexuality and even age might skew her findings.

On the whole the women she cites have, like her, had the luxury of an engagement with feminist ideas and a reasonable amount of good fortune in being able to pursue worthwhile careers. This acceptance of a bourgeois paradigm for female experiences of the '90s is on the whole accepted in this veritable cult of women blaming, a cult also fostered by Naomi Wolf and Camille Paglia. In terms of the development of a 'populist feminism' it marks a retrograde step, taking us back to the initial period of second wave expansion before black, lesbian and working class women transformed the existing model of feminist thought.

Not only does Coward pursue the kind of schizophrenic feminist viewpoint that one can identify in the work of Yvonne Roberts, she conflates prevailing feminist views of the social constructedness of gender with a notion of a deeply primitive female self. Nowhere is this more evident than when she speaks of her and her interviewees' responses to motherhood.

> I too had intended to share parenting equally. But the intention didn't stand a chance when challenged by something far more primitive and complex – the sense, perhaps for the first time in one's life, that it was *you* who was needed, and that you could do it well. (Coward 1992: 56)

Her interviewees on the whole suggest that their maternal responses – the attractions to the 'needy' child – become virtually pathological as compensation for alienation and feelings of lack of worth in other areas. It seems politically dangerous for women to evoke these kinds of responses without a thorough attempt at locating and identifying the legacy of many of these responses in the totally distinct social experiences of women from men. As it is, her statements risk affirming 'truths' about female nature long averred by anti-feminists – that the maternal instinct is both 'primitive' and irrational (like the female mind?) and possibly pathological. At the same time Coward accurately recognizes the ideological power of the image of the ideal woman, the model mother who must devote her whole being to the entertainment and especially the education of her child, and that 'most women recognize the impossibility of attaining this ideal – either consciously, or just by failing to do it – but it doesn't stop them feeling guilty' (Coward 1992: 83). Women's guilt is seen as a confusing mixture of their feelings of inadequacy in face of the dual role they feel required to perform, and guilt in the face of feminism's relative failure to offer parity across gender roles.

Coward identifies a major anxiety among these middle-class women who attempt success in career and domestic terms:

> This fear of being seen as anti-men or unfeminine – even
> among women sympathetic to feminism's general aims – attests
> to the deep sense of self that attaches to the construction of the
> feminine sexual being as one who is desirable to men. Rejecting
> this proved too uncomfortable for many, and there has been a
> retreat away from confrontational sexual politics and towards a
> more accepted notion of the feminine. Even among the most
> ardent of feminists, there has been a resurgence of personal
> adornment, but always justified as 'doing if for myself, not
> men'. (Coward 1992: 152–3)

There might in fact be more sophisticated reasons for the growth in
a 'lifestyle feminism'; but here Coward taps what seems to be the
central anxiety of the contemporary (white, heterosexual) woman as
represented by most of the writers discussed in this chapter. The
problem of the means by which one expresses a 'feminist' desire and
by which one politicizes the personal in the face of only modest
degrees of social change since 1968 is a thorny one; but it seems precipitate, to say the least, to blame those women who attempt to raise
their consciousness, as if failure is the inevitable result of attempting
a wholesale denial of the meanings and modalities of patriarchy.
Women, for all their political organization, are in Coward's concluding section the hopeless failures in all this:

> Women have let men get away with it. When it came to the
> crunch, most made it quite clear they didn't want conflict with
> men. Rather than have conflict, which they saw as a symptom
> of disturbed and angry people, they would prefer to keep the
> traditional structures of masculinity and femininity intact, even
> if it meant not coming to terms with themselves, even if it
> meant burying aspects of themselves in men and in children,
> even if it meant harder work and more pressures for women.
> (Coward 1992: 197–8)

This propensity for blaming women for the ills of patriarchy is a
tactic adopted by the 'new feminists' Camille Paglia and Naomi Wolf
with a view to discrediting 'old' feminism – although both their
agendas are quite different. Paglia's motive for launching fairly vitri-
olic attacks on feminism was, according to Susan Faludi, motivated
out of 'simple spite':

> Rival literary scholars who were feminists, she complained, had
> grabbed all the 'acclaim' and failed to be 'respectful' of her pro-
> digious talents, a situation that consigned her to the non-tenure

track at the unsung Philadelphia University of the Arts and allowed her book to be snubbed by seven publishers. It was then, as she told a *New York* writer later, that she began 'preparing my revenge' against feminist academics. (Faludi 1992: 353)

This account of her motivation is compelling[8] when one reads some of Paglia's more ludicrous claims such as that contained in *Sexual Personae* (1991) that 'if civilization has been left in female hands, we would still be living in grass huts' (Paglia 1991: 38). Paglia's utterances are soundbites in the making, declaring her manifest disaffection with the shape of second wave feminism itself. Her model of the 'true feminist' is Madonna, who is described as having 'taught young women to be fully female and sexual while still exercising control over their lives' (Paglia 1992: 4). What kind of control these young women exercise is not made clear, but Paglia identifies a fear of masculinity as one of feminism's problems, suggesting that for Paglia masculinity is an enduring and stable accompaniment to being male. Paglia likes to portray herself as a sexual radical of sorts, but her claim that woman's power has always lain in her sex is far from radical and her assertion that 'leaving sex to the feminists is like letting your dog vacation at the taxidermist's' (Paglia 1992: 50) is simply picking up on the popular consciousness that feminists are anti-sex and therefore tyrannical in their moral outlook.

Nowhere is Paglia more controversial than as an infamous sceptic about date rape. Believing that 'academic feminism is lost in a fog of social constructionism' (Paglia 1992: 50) and that sexual difference is rooted in biology she declares that it is the responsibility of women to avoid situations where they might be raped – for example if they happen to be drunk at a party – because 'college men are at their hormonal peak' (Paglia 1992: 51); in other words she concurs with the kind of responses that have been offered by judges and other men in power in perpetuity. These views are taken up and extended into an attack on the direction of contemporary feminism by the American Katie Roiphe. Roiphe depicts the US university campuses as promoting a climate of fear through what she sees as the over exaggerated dangers of date rape; like Paglia her final critique of modern feminism lies in her conception of its prudery:

> Feminists concerned with sexual harassment reproduce their own version of Charlotte Perkins Gilman's *Herland*, based on the absence of messy sexual desire. Although it takes some imaginative leaps to get there, their version of Herland is a land without dirty jokes, leers, and other instances of 'unwanted

sexual attention'. Whether or not visions of a universe free from 'sexual harassment' are practical, the question becomes whether they're even desirable. (Roiphe 1994: 111)

The scare quotes around the term 'sexual harassment' reminds us of Roiphe's scepticism of its existence: instead we are redirected to feminism's supposed lack of 'humour' as the source of the problem.

Not only does Naomi Wolf continue the trend of associating 'old' – what she terms 'victim' – feminism with tyranny and prudery, she also blames women for failing to recognize that they are currently at the epicentre of a 'genderquake'.[9] In *Fire with Fire*, feminism becomes perverted into a question of how women should use their power wisely rather than how they should continue their efforts to destabilize and confront patriarchal power. In this text Wolf is more keen to 'prove' her feminist credentials and, anticipating criticisms from her less charitable 'sisters', argues that her 'postfeminist' view 'is an act not of sacrilege but of love' (Wolf 1993: xiii). However, Wolf's message to her fellow women is a little more aggressive than this implies: if we don't beat the effects of a male backlash the fault is ours. We are encouraged therefore to seize the power which has fortuitously fallen into our hands; but the shape of this power appears strangely identical to the patriarchal power described by earlier second wave feminists – and the call to realize our strength seems to be a call to women who already have substantial social and material privileges (the white middle classes) to compete for the few glittering prizes in pro-democratic, high liberal fashion. In contrast, the main body of feminist thought, prompted in particular by writings from black, working-class and third-world women, has tended to avoid references to power and equality which do not scrutinize both these terms critically, particularly the question of what kind of 'power' feminists want to gain.

For Wolf the women-centredness of talkshows and daytime TV produced a platform to facilitate a female perspective on politics which politicians such as George Bush ignored at their peril. At the least this offers a rather two-dimensional account of television's relationship to the viewing public, leaving unscrutinized the possibility that the 'needs' of the viewing public are the constructed needs designated by commercial capitalism. Similarly President Bill Clinton's pro-feminism, in common with his pre-election pro-lesbian and gay stance, might be more cynically regarded as an obvious means to court the unrepresented voter.

Wolf technically accepts that there is an incipient backlash against feminism, but argues interestingly that the white male elite 'have lost their *authority* before they have lost their *power*' (Wolf 1993: 20), and that this necessarily foreshadows a loss of power which can be grasped by women. Wolf in opposition to the black American writer Audré Lorde seems to believe that the master's tools can dismantle the master's house and this gives a clear indication that her vision of female power is largely similar to the existing model of political power relationships based on a democratic model. The only difference is that women are not supposed to want to exploit and subordinate men in the process of gaining power. Rather, we are exhorted to reassure men that it is acceptable for them to drop their mask of dominance in exchange for the promise of an egalitarian future.

Wolf's conception of 'power feminism' seems to be a great deal about becoming streetwise to the new capitalist world order and very little about feminism in any of its past incarnations. Wolf states that 'power feminism' means learning from 'Madonna, Spike Lee and Bill Cosby'; (Wolf 1993: 108) without explaining the significance of this particular grouping containing two black men. 'Victim feminism' is, for Wolf, the definition of feminism as it has been developed in the second wave; and Wolf, in common with Coward, sees all characterizations of the lack of power for women as admissions of their weakness, rather than an attempt to analyse current social formations. At best Wolf's victim feminism accords with the worst parodies of radical feminism, whereas power feminism might be a rough approximation of modern liberal feminism – particularly in her assurance that power feminism 'hates sexism without hating men' (Wolf 1993: 150). Here we have come full circle: women-blaming 'feminism', self-consciously placatory to the imagined slights experienced by men, becomes unable to conceive of patriarchy as anything to do with individual men at all. In the absence of any other scapegoats women take on the burden of guilt.

Conclusion

> One of the sad conclusions I have reached in writing this
> book is that feminists have reinvented the wheel a number of
> times.
>
> (Donovan 1992: xii)

As this book has progressed it has charted the development of feminism from the realms of grass roots political issues, and reached into
more abstract areas of contemporary epistemology. Such a transition
mirrors the movement from activism to internal debate within
feminism, which many feminists have lamented over the years – such
sentiments appear in the British anthology *What is Feminism?*
(1986). Nonetheless, during the '90s there has been a tendency to
search again for feminism's 'lost' political edge, and the work of black
and lesbian feminists has been particularly important in their insis-
tent focus on the political and theoretical implications of the fact of
women's lived experience, without resorting to naive individualist
tendencies characteristic of earlier bourgeois feminism. Feminists
have learnt, too, that complacency can be dangerous – mainstream
matrices of power have the breadth and capacity to absorb and contain sites of resistance, to render opposition obsolete with ease and
rapidity. By the mid-'80s, feminism was mourning the increasing
stranglehold of the New Right in the West, and none of the dominant strands of socialist, liberal or radical feminism seemed equal to
face the challenge alone. As the '80s drew to a close the boundaries
which defined each strand increasingly became blurred. Such political and methodological distinctions were played out on the surfaces
of identity politics, which was either construed as an instance of
feminism's nascent humanism – its investment in the discrete individual subject self – or as a creative questioning of the status of
identity (in the singular) altogether.

In Britain, socialist feminism lost much of its initial investment in the Marxist Left. Indeed, Tessa ten Tusscher argues that the gender-blind political analyses of the British Left renders them unequal to challenging and understanding the nature of the New Right in America and Europe. Classic left-wing discourse, couched in economic and class-based terms, fails to account for the moral, traditional and familial aspects of current governmental policies and ideology. Tusscher asserts that the concept of individual freedom, fostered by Thatcherism, is a renewed freedom for men at the expense of women's newly-won economic and political freedoms (Evans et al. 1986: 69). The underlying themes of 'organic' Toryism are the family, duty, law and order, free economy and nationalism. Socialist feminism's emphasis on the pervasiveness of familial ideology highlights the moral and familial aspects of both the British and US New Right; and they began to place even greater emphasis on contextualizing the changing social and economic position of women since the 1950s.

During the capitalist boom of the '50s, and the resulting expansion of the labour market, more women took up full-time employment and participated in trade union activism; in addition, women gained freer access to higher education, leading to entry into the professions. Greater social freedoms themselves facilitated the conditions of existence of a new women's movement; and gradually the media began to characterize the 'new woman' as wielding unbridled power, with the potential to threaten the masculinist status quo. Tusscher suggests that feminism itself prompted a shifting of mainstream political agendas, arguing that, 'it was this crisis of patriarchy which prompted the birth of the moral right' (Evans et al. 1986: 75).

The conservative reaction against this supposed tidal wave of feminism and the rise of the so-called 'permissive society' strengthened in the wake of economic recession. Now the most widely publicized aspects of the 'Sexual Revolution' are the risks to society (or, more emotively, the 'family'), concentrating on disease (physical and moral), homosexuality and other forms of 'deviant' behaviour. As the '70s drew to a close, feminists, instead of being able to celebrate the 'victory' of having a woman at the head of the British government, have had to face the fact that women have suffered sustained attacks on their newly won economic and domestic freedoms. Unlike America's National Organization for Women, British feminists have been largely unsuccessful in effecting legislative changes: 'Instead British feminism has exerted pressure in a more vicarious manner, forcing the moral right to adopt more subtle and complex strategies to exert patriarchal relations' (Evans et al. 1986: 78). At the heart of this swing to the Right lies a certain conception of the family as a

natural unit as well as a morally desirable one, and therefore any
feminist critiques of current familial organization, are characterized
as antipathetic to the desires of human nature.

Of course a significant distinction made by feminists is the gap
between familial ideology and actual families, who are less and less
likely to conform to the perceived norm. 'Abnormal' families – such
as single parent households, or lesbian parent households are more
than likely to suffer when the state continues to tailor its legislation
and support facilities for the needs of the 'normal' minority. New
Right ideology assumes that women are functional for the maintenance of familial stability, and the labour market – equal opportunities
rhetoric aside – still operates along masculinist terms, subsuming
'female interests' within the family unit. This demonstrates that the
New Right has done much to reaffirm contemporary gendered
assumptions about women's place in society; moreover, the New
Right has reinscribed difference – especially in the cases of gender
and race/culture. It is not a new tactic to make reference to the natural to substantiate a preferred form of social order, but the New
Right has worked hard to give the category of the natural a more
urgent contemporary meaning. This is particularly evident in the
construction of a new ideology of the natural, where in seeming
legislatively to accommodate differing needs, otherness is an
entrenched part of political reality:

> For women, the New Right's political philosophy signals the
> undermining of many of the equal rights gains and freedoms
> won over the last decade. For Blacks, it provides the basis for
> an insidious form of racism, dressed up this time as common
> sense rather than science, which will undoubtedly be increas-
> ingly used against them. (Brittan and Maynard 1984: 152)

If we can identify a 'new racism' founded on the notion of irreconcilable cultural differences, rather than biological inferiority, perhaps
we need also to investigate a possible 'new sexism', which has gained
momentum by going 'underground'. The New Right cleverly favours
an indirect attack on feminism through ideological means, and
despite feminism's commitment to an interrogation of dominant
ideologies, feminism as marginal discourse has less access to forms of
communication which would enable them to counter such attacks.
Feminism is popularly portrayed as outmoded – media announce-
ments herald a 'post-feminist' climate where young women are
successful and independent, and less likely to espouse 'dangerous'
feminist ideals. Those women who doggedly insist on proclaiming

themselves feminist are lampooned as ugly, fat and undoubtedly lesbians who spend their time condemning men and tearing up pornography. An example of such a characterization appeared in Jaci Stephens's newspaper review of a BBC Omnibus programme which reported on the work of Andrea Dworkin. Stephens remarks:

> Why is it that the women who speak up most defensively about their own sex are such an unappealing bunch of creatures? I'm not suggesting that they should all be beautiful, nor that they should have the moles that seem to proliferate on their faces surgically removed; only that they make a bit of an effort on the presentation front so that viewers won't be tempted to think that they've accidentally tuned into a horror movie. ('The Big Issue for Large Ladies', *Daily Mail*, 26 October 1991: 30)

In opposition to this, the 'post-feminist' of the TV advertisements is resplendent in her executive suit and unruffled by her male colleagues. Both images are, of course, outrageous distortions, but serve their purpose well: the first is 'masculine'; the second retains a quintessential femininity, despite its inherent contradictions. Yet these images neatly summarize one of the most insidious threats for contemporary feminists: if young women are internalizing the post-feminist ideal and the assumption that feminist politics are therefore redundant, then 'consciousness raising' is again one of the most vital feminist activities – a consciousness raising that appeals to all women, whatever their background, but which avoids the pitfalls of divisive individualism. Here the legacy of radical feminist politics provides, perhaps, the strongest potential for both defence and counter-attack.

The idea of post-feminism has also been legitimized by a conservative backlash within feminist thought, typified by the later work of Germaine Greer and Betty Friedan, which announces a return to the sanctity of the 'private', and emphasis upon the family and childcare. Equality gives way to a celebration of difference and, in Greer's case, a utopian idealization of the extended family (see Greer 1984) – demonstrating that an awareness of the heterogeneity of female experience can lead to a celebration of individuality, rather than initiate feminist collectivity. Judith Stacey remarks that this new pro-conservative feminism discards 'the most significant contributions of feminist theory and, more alarmingly, provides in their place a feminism that turns quite readily into its opposite' (Mitchell and Oakley 1986: 235). Such women, who became public figures through feminism, continue to be received as feminists, and the feminist explosion of the 1960s and 1970s appears to risk implosion under the sheer weight of its contradictions. It is crucial, therefore, to focus upon contemporary issues which, depressingly, often turn out to be the 'old' issues in a new guise. The popular conceptions of feminist and Left-wing politics have suffered badly under the present government in Britain, and this must be largely attributed to a failure both to recognize the ideological impact of the New Right, and to devise a means of response. Feminists have always sought to avoid the 'star system' inherent in political manoeuvring, but recent developments in both politics and the media suggest a pressing need for a statement of intent, if not a mouthpiece for such intentions.

One of the central lines of attack of radical feminist politics – the anti-pornography movement, and the challenge against the continued sexual objectification of the female form – has itself been hijacked by New Right moralist agendas. I briefly discussed the paradox of the unholy alliance between activists such as Dworkin and moral purity campaigners, an alliance which clearly throws up wider ramifications for feminist coalitional strategies. The fusion of anti-porn with pro-censorship campaigners arguably dilutes the force of radical feminism's original attack, which was directed against a patriarchal ideology that utilizes the sexualized image of the female in all its cultural productions. Commentators such as Margaret Hunt have indicated that the moral crusaders' concept of obscenity and female degradation relies upon significantly different notions of 'appropriate' representations of women than does feminism:

> Feminists should be casting their nets both more carefully and more widely. It is madness to put new repressive tools into the hands of the state at a time when conservatism is riding high (perhaps at any time). A better strategy, which some feminists in both England and North America are already pursuing, is to infiltrate the TV and radio networks, develop alternative media, formulate subtler and better analyses of the intersections of power and representation, break straight white monopolies on all kinds of image production, not just pornography, and make coalitions with other groups traditionally excluded from the making of images. (*Feminist Review*, No. 34, Spring 1990: 42–3)

Hunt recommends coalitions, nonetheless, but only with groups that have themselves suffered exclusion at the hands of the mainstream; in addition, her recipe for change includes gestures towards offensive rather than defensive operations as an effective mode of resistance.

I believe that feminist academics, at least, are on the offensive in the '90s, particularly since the increasing sophistication of the 'men in feminism' debate has encouraged interventions by adversaries as well as allies. In 1992 Susan Faludi's *Backlash* was published in Great Britain: its title alone identifies the crux of the crisis in current feminism, a crisis which ought not to be attributed to a simple 'breaking of the ranks' among some of the most important feminist voices, but rather to the means used to undermine feminism's influence in society at large. Faludi tackles the dominant theme of apologists for 'post-feminism' – that feminism's battle for social and economic equality has made women depressed, susceptible to stress-induced illnesses, and even infertile. She incisively demonstrates that the biggest danger confronting feminism today is the meanings attributed to it by the media and politicians alike, and the way that it has accordingly become an effective scapegoat for society's ills.

Neil Lyndon's *No More Sex War* was also published in 1992, predictably accompanied by a blaze of publicity that overshadowed Faludi's work. Several months before the book's publication, Lyndon was given space in the 'quality' newspapers to outline the terms of his critique of feminism, which rest largely upon his conviction that 'modern feminism was rooted in the totalitarian attitudes of the late Sixties when, in its search for a "class enemy", the New Left in America and the rest of the West appropriated the axioms of Black Power about white "honky" culture and applied them to sexual politics' (Lyndon, 'Feminism's Fundamental Flaws', *The Independent*, 29 March 1992: 28). Such beliefs, which are being voiced with increasing regularity, are underpinned by conceptions of feminism as orthodoxy, and, as the above quote suggests, bolstered by a fear that outgroups such as blacks and feminists are undermining some of the most cherished features of 'our' culture. Responses to feminism's perceived threat are regularly cast in the language of nostalgia, which as Doane and Hodges point out, 'is not just a sentiment but also a rhetorical practice' (Doane and Hodges 1987: 3). In other words, the practice of 'nostalgic' writing often claims recourse to a pre-existent 'reality' and naturalness of a certain set of social relations that any radical discourse threatens to destabilize. It is a popular form of reaction, because it offers its readers the comfort of the myth of a past status quo which has been wrongfully swept away.

With regard to feminism, as I have suggested, there has been a steady stream of such work since the '70s. On the one hand this is itself a tribute to feminism's power to unsettle the popular consciousness. On the other, there are necessarily consequent dangers in that 'The popularity of nostalgic texts and the power of these texts to appropriate dissident voices must be read as a massive effort to discredit and control feminist and other radical writing' (Doane and Hodges 1987: 12). Anti-feminist work does not always come in predictable guises, and sometimes the most threatening and difficult to challenge is that which uses the discourse of feminism, or at least refers to it with an aura of scholarly knowledge. Camille Paglia's *Sexual Personae* (1992) is an example of this, where the writer situates herself as a disenchanted feminist, who now recognizes the pull of 'naturally' inscribed differences between the sexes and their contribution to men and women's predestined social roles. Even the phenomenon of the 'new man' – a term used to describe men who have acknowledged gender roles as oppressive, and have attempted to raise their own consciousness around the constraints of masculinity – is often ridiculed as an illustration of how feminism feminizes men. It is rare to find a positive appraisal of the new man that is not punctuated with scepticism and gloom;[1] yet its emergence as a term is at the least a backhanded tribute to feminism's power to infiltrate the popular consciousness – although as yet we have little control over the shaping of popular 'feminism'.

One of the reasons that I have chosen to devote a good deal of this work to a critical re-evaluation of shifting boundaries and transformation in the Women's Movement since the late '60s, is not to celebrate the evolution of feminist thought into the highly sophisticated academic business it has become. It is important to re-remember its origins in diversity, which in many ways explain its conceptual difficulties as well as its strengths. As the editorial in the Spring 1989 edition of *Feminist Review* put it, 'feminists have learned – often painfully – that women's liberation, indeed any social movement, has no single point of origin; it is born in a diversity of times and places' (*Feminist Review*, No. 31, Spring 1989: 2). Much of this diversity has been essential to the development of a feminist position which can take account of the heterogeneous subject identities women achieve in their specific ethnic/cultural and historical locations. Perhaps we might establish some common ground with postmodernist thought in arguing that feminism's chief successes have been when they have devoted their attention to the constellation of power relations that are perpetuated at local and immanent levels. Certainly in an environment where the most basic demands of Women's

Liberation have yet to be met – such as equal rights, equal pay, and the socialization of domestic labour – feminism must take heart from its origins in diversity, and use this as an object lesson in the necessity to keep shifting its focus, evading if not totally avoiding the absorption of a backlash.

Some readers will no doubt view my choice of dividing the first part of this book into a consideration of feminism's 'strands' with a degree of scepticism. For many contemporary feminists, the premises of such divisions have become stale already, and studies of points of conflict and comparison between opposing positions is the preferred critical stance (see Hirsch and Fox Keller 1990). To perceive feminism in terms of conflict and heterogeneity are workable points of departure for a feminism that now has to contend with an atmosphere of institutional absorption and political reaction. One of the most important intentions of this work was to link up the 'old' views of the 1970s and early '80s with the 'new' wave of more sophisticated feminist theory (and less sophisticated backlash), in order to argue that early second wave thinking is neither outmoded nor dispensable.

There are of course dangers in foregrounding feminism's conflicts without suggesting that they are positive and organic to the wider aims of feminist discourse, which constantly remakes itself in newer guises of resistance. In this light the work of recent black feminist theorists such as Patricia Hill Collins can be viewed as a salutary example of theory which places sites of conflict and internal debate in the background, favouring an emphasis upon the common roots and extra-theoretical supports for modern black feminist thought (see Collins 1990). Her account of the development of black feminist thought includes references to fiction, journals, blues lyrics; in addition she identifies a tradition among American black communities where mothers teach their daughters independence and self-confidence from an early age, in order to combat dominant ideological strategies which otherwise might convince black women of their continued cultural invisibility. Not all of these women, as mothers, singers or writers would conceive of themselves as feminists, but their special language of resistance created the conditions of existence for black women to conceive of themselves as feminists whilst simultaneously denying the centrality of the white feminist tradition.

Nonetheless, most black feminists are adept at identifying connections between their work and that of white feminists – unfortunately the reverse is rarely true. I think that white feminism could learn many lessons from black feminism – one of which would be to reconceive what is often perceived as black feminism's relative theoretical 'naivety'. What is often neglected when feminisms are judged in terms of their 'sophistication' is that an important function of black feminism has been to keep alive the vitality of the social and political environment from which it emerged, particularly evident in celebrations of past black female activism and epistemological radicalism. In general, white feminists have lost any sense of a tradition of feminist thought – even the legacy of the '70s is neglected. Much of it may seem naive, ill-conceived and contentious, but it is evidence of a moment of success for women, when many chose to identify themselves as feminists without fearing reprisals – such as being dubbed man haters – and endeavoured to develop a theory which had a bearing on the lives of ordinary women. This is not to undermine the importance of locating points of tension in such works – especially elements of blindness to other forms of oppression which shape women's lives.

Something that has struck me most powerfully in writing this work is that feminism as a site of contested meanings and strategies is increasingly problematized by the amount of feminist texts that emerge and sink rapidly out of print, while others survive and become landmarks in feminist thought. We need such 'landmarks' in order to communicate to others who wish to investigate the origins of second wave feminism. Yet their continued existence in the face of others' extinction gives the lie to the notion that a 'history' of feminist ideas is easily traceable and exists as a concrete phenomenon, whereas 'what is taken as history are some privileged and published histories of feminism, which have been all too quickly naturalized' (King in Hirsch and Keller 1990: 82).

It is important not to lose sight of the early aims of second wave feminism. No matter how simplistic some of their constructions seem today, early critiques made those important steps towards forging a language specific to the experiences of women, whilst simultaneously facilitating the articulation of such experiences as manifestations of oppression by gender. In the race for theoretical sophistication it is easy to forget feminism's main aim as a tool of communication available to all women who desired means to express the specificity of their own hardships. Buzz words such as 'patriarchy' and 'gender socialization' have been challenged for their over-simplistic universalism, and up to a point these criticisms are pertinent, particularly reconceptions of patriarchal power and gender divisions which deny women the simple 'luxury' of being victims to a huge anonymous system of power wielded by biological males. Yet these terms, contested from the moment they were coined in a feminist context, provided the beginnings of a language of resistance, even though it is often hard from our perspective in the '90s to recapture, for example, what was so earth-shattering about Germaine Greer's *Female Eunuch* or Kate Millett's *Sexual Politics*. Sheila Rowbotham echoes these sentiments when she recalls 'I remember when it was not obvious that housework was work – hence the initial excitement created by this assertion' (Rowbotham 1989: 294).

In tandem with the emergence of works of high feminist theory, there appeared publications such as Rowbotham's retrospective, *The Past is Before Us* (1989) and Michelene Wandor's *Once a Feminist* (1990), which attempt to offer personal and collective memories of the Women's Liberation Movement which are accessible and interesting to all women. There is no easy solution to the atmosphere of exclusionism endemic to a feminism which now does most of its maturing in universities, and where elements of cultural elitism are difficult to avoid. Nonetheless, it is worth recalling the writings of working-class women like Evelyn Tension, who entered feminism and attended conferences and meetings only to find that 'it's about hearing millions of words flying around our heads and it's not that we don't understand them, it's that they come from a different reality, a middle-class women's consciousness' (Tension, Feminist Anthology Collective 1981: 86). I would affirm the necessity for feminism perpetually to extend its scope, to interrogate its apparent past errors of judgement. Yet this widening of view should be supported by an awareness of why we continue to rejuvenate feminism in a semi-autonomous discursive field (yet remaining aware of its entrapment within dominant discursive practices), and specifically of the political reasons for this continuation. I have tried to look back, not to seek the origins of an authentic second wave consciousness in the interstices of our recent history, or to assert that there has been an evolution in thought in any simplistic sense, but to resist the 'sad conclusion' expressed by Josephine Donovan in the epigraph to this conclusion – that to lose the sense of what has gone before is to be burdened with the task of constantly reinventing the wheel.

Notes

INTRODUCTION

1. 'We must bear in mind that the word "feminist" only emerged in the early nineteenth century and "feminist" appeared for the first time in English to describe women campaigning for the vote in the 1890s' (Rowbotham 1992: 8).
2. It is difficult to give actual dates for the emergence of either the first or second wave of organized feminism, but Christine Bolt's *The Women's Movements in the United States and Britain from the 1790s to the 1920s* (Hemel Hempstead: Harvester Wheatsheaf, 1993) locates the origins of the first wave in the USA and Britain as around the 1840s and 1850s, and suggests that this period of intense feminist activity petered out during the 1920s after the First World War. As Bolt points out, however, feminist thought was produced from the eighteenth century until the present day.
3. As Alice Echols observes, in the USA the movement had informal beginnings in 1967 when small groups of radical women began to meet in the Autumn of that year (Echols 1989: 4).
4. In this context, 'movement' does not refer to the women's liberation movement, but to radical left political movements such as the SNCC (Student Non-violent Co-ordinating Committee), the American Student Democratic Society and the Draft Resistance Movement.
5. For an interesting account of women's postwar experiences in Britain, see Elizabeth Wilson, *Only Halfway to Paradise: Women in Postwar Britain 1945–1968*, London: Tavistock Publications, 1980.
6. It is well documented that many women in both the nineteenth and twentieth centuries have found feminine domesticity monotonous and ultimately clinically depressing. Elaine Showalter's *The Female Malady* (London: Virago, 1987) describes the categorization and treatment of mental illness among women from 1830 to 1980; Jane Ussher's *Women's Madness: Misogyny or Mental Illness?* (Hemel Hempstead: Harvester Wheatsheaf, 1991) pursues the historical contexts, treatment and diagnosis of women's mental illness in order to examine the extent to which institutionalized misogyny is a feature.
7. 'I went stickering with another woman; we would meet at, say,

five-thirty or six in the morning at Sloane Square underground station with our packets of these stickers. . . . We would get on the District Line and would ride along to Dagenham and beyond, getting off every once in a while and riding up and down the escalators putting stickers on the ads and trying not to get caught' (Lois Graessle, interviewed by Michelene Wandor, in *Once a Feminist: Stories of a Generation*, London: Virago, 1990, p. 130; see also p. 75).

8. 'De Beauvoir speculates that woman's identity as Other and her fundamental alienation derive in part from her body – especially her reproductive capacity – and in part from the prehistoric division of labour dictated by the child bearing and rearing functions. . . . Woman's mentality, her cultural outlook, and her religious world view are thus an expression of the fundamental role she has been cast in' (Donovan 1992: 123).

9. Later Freudian critics have on occasion taken a less generous view of Freud's psychoanalytical practices, and have analysed both essentialist and prescriptive tendencies especially as evident in the case histories. See, for example, C. Bernheimer and C. Kahane (eds), *In Dora's Case: Freud, Hysteria, Feminism*, London: Virago Press, 1985.

10. 'The Miss World demonstration was conceived as a propaganda action . . . As predicted, the media encouraged by Bob Hope's hysterical reaction, moved in – the screens of 7 million viewers erupted with streamers, leaflets and chaos for several minutes and the following day we were splashed all over the front pages of the popular press. We had indeed drawn attention to ourselves, but we had disastrously underestimated the ability of the press to "interpret" events . . . We had made, it seemed, yet another contribution to the bra-burning, man-hating horror image of Women's Liberation' ('Miss World', in Wandor 1972: 259).

11. If one glances through radical anthologies such as *Sisterhood is Powerful* or *Radical Feminism*, the ratio of lesbian writers to 'heterosexual' ones (writers who ignore women-to-women issues altogether) is very small.

12. Castro 1990: 63. Castro's description of second wave American feminism emphasizes discontinuities rather than consensus, and characterizes the movement as in the throes of a struggle for power between warring strands, but more particularly feminist 'stars'. Although her survey seems at times to delight in charting acrimony within the movement, she appears to regard such power struggles as inevitable: 'born out of powerlessness and lack of experience in holding power, internal dissensions thus are part of the pathology of oppression' (Castro: 1990: 64). Alice Echols reveals that it was the December 1970 issue of *Time* magazine which reported Millett's bisexuality (Echols 1989: 240).

CHAPTER ONE

1. I have chosen consistently to refer to liberal, lesbian, black and radical feminism in the lower case, whereas I have chosen to capitalize Marxism because it is common practice to do so. I feel that to capitalize 'liberal' is to create ambiguities (not least since this has been the title

of a parliamentary party). To leave liberal lower case is to encounter other kinds of ambiguities – not least to invite its more colloquial connotations of broadmindedness, unprejudiced, unrigorous and so forth. To some extent these diverse meanings serve my purpose well, which is ultimately to show cross-over points between strands, as well as to address the problem that male-oriented radical political thought often characterizes all feminisms as liberal – in other words as essentially reformist and obstructive to political (in a conventional sense) progress.

2. See Thomas Hobbes, *The Citizen* (1651), *Man and Citizen*, ed. Bernard Gert, Sussex: Harvester Press, 1978.

3. See, for example, Alison Jaggar: 'Liberal political theory emerged with the rise of capitalism, it expressed the needs of the developing capitalist class and the liberal values of autonomy and self-fulfilment have often been linked with the right to private property' (1983: 34).

4. This woman/slave analogy has been latterly criticised by black feminist commentators as both reductionist and offensive. It was an anthology wholeheartedly embraced by nineteenth-century American suffragists involved in the Abolitionist movement, even though its use effectively effaces the existence of black *women*.

5. 'Liberal feminists may be "personally" or "privately" revolted or titillated by pornography, but they have no "political" grounds for opposing it unless it can be shown to have a direct causal connection with the violation of women's rights' (Jaggar 1983: 180).

6. 'The ideals of the rational sphere give us a character model of the human which is masculine' (Val Plumwood, 'Women, Humanity and Nature', in Sean Sayers and Peter Osborne (eds), *Socialism, Feminism and Philosophy: a Radical Philosophy Reader*, London: Routledge, 1990, p. 212).

7. 'If we had no more than the name to go by we could not tell whether something calling itself Women's Liberation was trying to free women from the power of men, or conventional stereotypes, or political responsibility, or the lure of the unfeminine, or even the blandishments of the feminist movement' (Richards 1982: 88).

CHAPTER TWO

1. As Barbara Taylor asserts, 'The ideological roots of Socialist feminism lay in the popular democratic tradition of the late eighteenth century, and in particular in the radical egalitarianism of the 1790s' (Taylor 1983: 1).

2. 'Over 60% of the entire female workforce is concentrated in only ten occupations. These "top ten" jobs for women are headed by clerical work, which takes 17.5% of women workers, followed by shop assistants, typists and secretaries, maids, cleaners, nurses, teachers, canteen assistants, shop managers, sewing and textile workers' (Barrett 1988: 156).

3. Barbara Taylor's *Eve and the New Jerusalem* (London: Virago, 1983) is an illuminating survey of this phenomenon.

4. Of course, during the 1970s, feminists variously campaigned for paid

domestic labour. This was a landmark in feminist politics supported by liberals as well as socialists, but it is ambiguous: the danger lies in seeming to affirm that this is 'women's work' at all.

5. I do not wish to dwell upon a history of family forms here, but research has already confirmed the immense variation in the construction of the family system throughout history. For instance, Lawrence Stone argues that during the seventeenth century, all members of a household unit, including servants, were considered to comprise a 'family'. See Stone's *The Family, Sex and Marriage in England 1500–1800*, Harmondsworth: Penguin Books, 1979.

6. As Anna Coote and Beatrix Campbell state, 'British feminism was always more socialist than its counterpart in the United States' (1982: 23).

7. As Karen Hunt observes of nineteenth-century socialist politics, 'women were seen as a reactionary force in society. There was disagreement as to whether they were naturally or socially conditioned to be conservative, but there was a general fear that women constituted a threat to socialism' (in Evans et al. 1986: 56).

8. She specifically cites Ken Livingstone's engagement with Andrea Dworkin's position on pornography and male violence – one which is usually rejected, in part or whole, by socialist feminists (Segal 1987: 211).

9. '. . . white women cannot avoid the legacy of racism within feminism. This legacy has a long history which includes the dominance of eugenicism in both the early and more recent birth control movements, the eager acceptance by the majority of the suffragettes of imperialistic nationalism, and at best, the failure of anti-rape campaigns to challenge racist stereotypes of the sexuality of black men' (Bhavnani and Coulson, *Feminist Review*, Summer 1986: 82).

10. Both liberal and socialist feminists suffer to some extent from their links with male discourse, where they are often viewed as the supplement, and by extension as of lesser importance than their originary doctrine. At the risk of a further taint of male discourse, one might usefully appropriate the insights of two male poststructuralist thinkers – Michel Foucault and Jacques Derrida – and argue that a notion of supplementarity can be interpreted as something which further decentres the logic of a pre-existing originary 'truth' by denouncing its limits, and therefore destabilizing its claims to empirical hegemony.

Within both Marxist and liberal bodies of knowledge one opposition is deemed to lie at the origin of social formations and that is a divide between nature and culture – an opposition which Derrida claims, 'is congenital to philosophy' (Derrida 1978: 282–3). Of course feminist attempts to explode such a logic – in common with all forms of oppositional discourse – can only have recourse to the philosophy of such a logic itself, a double-bind which is both positive and negative. Positive in that feminism as supplement destabilizes the truth claims of such discourses, by analysing uninterrogated concepts such as 'nature'; negative in that 'we can pronounce not a single destructive proposition which has not already had to slip into the form, the logic, and the implicit postulations of precisely what it seeks to contest' (Derrida 1978: 280–1). Reason polices its own boundaries, so that a critique of the phallocentricity of reason can only occur from within: we therefore have 'only the recourse to stratagems and strategies' (Derrida 1978: 36).

CHAPTER THREE

1. For an interesting account of cultural feminism, see Josephine Donovan, *Feminist Theory: The Intellectual Traditions of American Feminism* (new expanded edition), New York: Continuum, 1992.

2. For instance, black feminists also address the problems of being lesbian within the black community and confronting instances of homophobia, just as they confront the dominant racist and (hetero)sexist ideologies perpetuated within society at large. See bell hooks, *Talking Back: Thinking Feminist Thinking Black*, London: Sheba Feminist Publishers, 1989, pp. 120–33; Jewelle Gomex and Barbara Smith, 'Talking About It: Homophobia in the Black Community', *Feminist Review*, No. 34, Spring 1990: 47–55; and The Combahee River Collective, 'A Black Feminist Statement' (1977), in Gloria T. Hull et al., *All the Women are White, all the Blacks are Men, But Some of Us are Brave*, New York: The Feminist Press, 1982, pp. 13–22.

3. Kate Millett and Ti-Grace Atkinson were members of the New York chapter of NOW, but Atkinson became rapidly disillusioned with the organization and she helped found the New York radical cell known as 'The Feminists' (see Echols 1989).

4. Alice Echols' *Daring to be Bad: Radical Feminism in America 1967–1975* (1989) is a fascinating account of radical feminism's heyday. Much of the material is confirmed by personal accounts – in many cases the only, albeit unreliable, method of reconstructing a history of radical feminist politics.

5. It is important to contextualize such a stance as likely to be a reaction to feminine norms seem as crippling to self-expression, rather than a feminist ploy to restrict individual choice. Such stances should be considered alongside Germaine Greer's ironic observation that 'the women who dare not go out without their false eyelashes are in serious psychic trouble' (Greer 1971: 324). Constructing the 'politics of appearance' was more about consciousness raising than intending to proscribe. For many radical feminists the challenge to the fashion and beauty industries was also a challenge to consumerism.

6. See, for example, Deborah Cameron, *Feminism and Linguistic Theory*, London: Macmillan, 1985.

7. MacKinnon is particularly critical of academic feminists' reluctance to champion the anti-pornography movement, although she concedes that, 'speaking about pornography is not like speaking about anything else. It is crazier. It has logic by Escher' (MacKinnon 1987: 221).

8. 'The people behind the Commission are some of the same people who are demanding the closure of shelters for battered women (because they

encourage women to abandon marriage), stringent crackdowns on lesbian and gay publications, social institutions, and civil liberties, ending teenagers' access to birth-control devices and information, and banning all abortions under any circumstances whatsoever.' Margaret Hunt, 'The De-eroticization of Women's Liberation: Social Purity Movements and the Revolutionary Feminism of Sheila Jeffreys', *Feminist Review* ('Perverse Politics: Lesbian Issues'), No. 34, Spring 1990: 36.

9. Indeed Echols asserts that many straight radicals were wary of allowing the movement to be dominated by issues relating to sex. She suggests that this is one reason why the group Radicalesbians defined lesbianism as primarily a political choice in 'The Woman Identified Woman' (1970).

10. 'It seems admissible in some contexts to refer to patriarchal ideology, describing specific aspects of male–female relations in capitalism, but as a noun the term 'patriarchy' presents insuperable difficulties to an analysis that attempts to relate women's oppression to the relations of production of capitalism' (Barrett 1988: 19).

11. 'Those awarded higher status tend to adopt roles of mastery, largely because they are first encouraged to develop temperaments of dominance. That this is true of caste and class as well is self-evident' (Millett 1977: 26).

12. Shulamith Firestone, on the other hand, accepts biological sexual difference as contributing to a 'natural' division of labour, and argues that an exploitation of the revolution in reproductive technologies is the only means by which women's social oppression can be eradicated – in the long term by means of artificial reproduction; in the short term spreading the child-rearing role as the responsibility of society as a whole:

> Women, biologically distinguished from men, are culturally distinguished from 'human'. Nature produced the fundamental inequality – half the human race must bear and rear the children of all of them – which was later consolidated, institutionalized, in the interests of men. Reproduction of the species cost women dearly, not only emotionally, psychologically, culturally but even in strictly material (physical) terms: before recent methods of contraception, continuous childbirth led to constant 'female trouble', early ageing, and death. Women were the slave class that maintained the species in order to free the other half for the business of the world – admittedly often its drudge aspects, but certainly all its creative aspects as well. (Firestone 1970: 192)

Although Firestone talks about the impact of Freudianism, the 'culture of romance' and so forth, the main thrust of her revolutionary agenda is towards a change in material social practices rather than ideological aspects.

13. See, for example, Paulina Palmer, *Contemporary Women's Fiction: Narrative Practice and Feminist Theory*, 1989; Carol Anne Douglas, *Love & Politics: Radical Feminist and Lesbian Theories*, 1990; Robyn

Rowland and Renate D. Klein, 'Radical Feminism: Critique and Construct' in Sneja Gunew (ed.), *Feminist Knowledge: Critique and Construct*, 1990.

14. There is a passage where the protagonist Ginny Babcock and her women-only commune friends decide to have a women's festival. In a series of episodes, Ginny's perceptions of the seminars that were taking place in various parts of the house are described:

> Eddie's group, called 'Women and Politics', went on a tour of the Free Farm, taking such inspiring sights as the manure-filled barn, the eggs we had neglected to collect, the un-pruned orchard . . . Laverne's group 'Women and Their Bodies', in Eddie's and my first-floor bedroom, was in a fascinated cluster around Laverne herself. She sat in a chair, her knees drawn up to her shoulders like chicken wings. With the aid of a complex arrangement of an inserted plastic speculum, mirrors, and a flashlight, Laverne was demonstrating to the intrigued gathering how it was possible, if one possessed the flexibility of an Olympic gymnast, to view the inside of one's vagina and the mouth of one's cervix . . . In the living room was Mona's group, the 'Women and Rage' set. A woman in a Sisterhood is Powerful T-shirt was lying on the floor. Tears were gushing from her closed eyes and down her cheeks. She was shaking with sobs. Mona and her group were lined up on either side of her, slowly massaging the entire length and breadth of her shuddering body.

Lisa Alther, *Kinflicks*, Harmondsworth: Penguin Books, 1977, pp. 353–4.

CHAPTER FOUR

1. Interesting accounts of the development of lesbian feminist politics include, Margaret Cruikshank, *The Gay and Lesbian Liberation Movement* (1992) and Lillian Faderman, *Odd Girls and Twilight Lovers* (1992).
2. See also Chapter Three, note 8.
3. 'Revolutionary feminists have indeed turned decisively away from the early radical feminist principle of sexual freedom, as is indicated both by their hostility to heterosexuality as a personal choice and their growing antipathy to birth control, not to mention their loathing for any kind of sex they consider "incorrect".' Margaret Hunt, 'The De-eroticization of Women's Liberation: Social Purity Movements and the Revolutionary Feminism of Sheila Jeffreys', *Feminist Review*, No. 34, Spring 1990, p. 41.
4. During the '70s she was part of the Leeds Revolutionary Feminist Group, who advocated 'political lesbianism' as an essential feminist requirement.

CHAPTER FIVE

1. This statement was allegedly made at a meeting held in November 1964, when a paper on the position of women had been tabled (see Echols 1989).

2. Although black feminism has recently more visibly fragmented into more diverse groups of women of colour and ethnic origins, black feminism seems to have initially emerged among African-American women in dual recognition of the potential of women's liberation and its endemic racism.

3. Sandra Gilbert and Susan Gubar's *The Madwoman in the Attic* (Yale University Press, 1979) is an early example of such exclusions; the situation has improved marginally since the mid-1980s, when most anthologies of feminist literary critical work include an article by a black woman, or consider the work of black women writers. This is not so true of feminist theoretical anthologies, however.

4. 'The history of black women in this country is the history of a labour force. Almost every black woman living in the United States has as her past the accumulated work of all her female forebears' (Susan Willis, *Specifying: Black Women Writing the American Experience*, London: Routledge, 1990, p. 6).

5. See, for example, Diana Fuss, *Essentially Speaking* (1989); *Differences* Vol. 1, No. 2, Summer 1989; Judith Butler, *Gender Trouble*, 1990.

6. As I write this (September 1994), the UN International Conference on Population control is taking place in Cairo; one of the major controversies is questions of abortion and contraception, and decisions which will have a profound effect on women's control over their bodies.

7. OWAAD, The Organization of Women of Asian and African Descent, is one notable exception. This organization lasted four years, its break up heralded by the chosen theme of its final conference – 'Black Feminism' (Lovenduski and Randall 1993: 82).

CHAPTER SIX

1. For critics like Toril Moi, for example, the act of producing a feminist reading of a text is a political act in itself:

> The radically new impact of feminist criticism is to be found not at the level of theory or methodology, but at the level of politics. Feminists have politicized existing critical methods and approaches. If feminist criticism has subverted established critical judgements it is because of its radically new emphasis on sexual politics. (Moi 1985: 87)

2. This is not to say that I believe that the differences between feminisms can be simply obliterated at the level of theory. For example, I do not agree with Toril Moi that 'a lesbian and/or black feminist criticism have presented exactly the same *methodological* and *theoretical* problems as the rest of Anglo-American feminist criticism' (Moi 1985: 86). On the contrary, the introduction of factors of race and sexual orientation are

examples that profoundly affect feminism precisely at a methodological level – as I hope my own argument shows.

3. In the light of my concluding chapters, one might be tempted to add a fourth dimension – that of 'backlash' – although that would be to put an altogether negative construction on feminist theory. Feminism, in common with other radical discourse, constantly lives under the threat of backlash.

4. 'At the deepest level of "Western knowledge", Marxism introduced no real discontinuity; it found its place without difficulty, as a full, quiet, comfortable and, goodness knows, satisfying form for a time (its own), within an epistemological arrangement that welcomed it gladly ... and that it, in return, had no intention of disturbing and, above all, no power to modify, even one jot, since it rested entirely upon it. Marxism exists in nineteenth century thought like a fish in water: that is, unable to breathe anywhere else' (Michel Foucault, *The Order of Things*, London: Tavistock Publications, 1970, pp. 261–2).

5. See, for example, hooks 1989; Gayle Green, 'The Uses of Quarreling', in Kauffman 1989b; L. Jeffries et al., 'Painting the Lion: Feminist Options', in Thompson and Wilcox 1989.

6. Several years after the publication of *Feminist Literary Studies* (1984), some of the assertions made by its author, K. K. Ruthven are still strikingly symptomatic. Firstly, he rapidly dispenses with all the questions of the political impact of feminist literary criticism by describing it as 'just one more way of talking about books' (Ruthven 1984: 8); and then sporadically throughout the book he vents his spleen on feminist 'terrorists' who would perhaps receive his work with trepidation, by a series of cheap shots that seem designed to reinforce current stereotypes of feminism:

> Even in its milder forms, feminist discourse strikes men . . . as being accusatory, as it is meant to do; and in its . . . most uncompromising manifestations it is unrelentingly intimidatory.
>
> Feminist terrorism is the mirror image of machismo. Unregenerately separatist – men are the problem, so how could they possibly be part of the solution? – it offers the vicarious satisfactions of retaliation and reprisal in a war of the sexes for which the only acceptable end is unconditional surrender of all power to women. Terrorism polarises the sexes in such a way that men must either ignore feminism or attack it . . . (Ruthven 1984: 10)

7. See, for example, Hull et al., 1982, and James and Busia, 1993.

8. Rosemarie Tong's *Feminist Thought: A Comprehensive Introduction* (1992) was first published in 1989 and has become a useful reference book for students and scholars of feminism. Yet this volume does not address black feminist issues in any explicit way, and only discusses lesbian feminism as a separatist wing of radical feminist thought.

9. One important focus for disagreement lies in whether or not the family should be perceived as the central site of women's oppression;

indeed how one defines 'the family' is a point of contestation. See Collins 1991: 43–66.

10. It is perhaps scarcely necessary to point out too that this form of 'feminism' is advocated solely by white middle-class, educated females, with little regard or knowledge of true material hardship.

11. Although Wolf herself, in classic self-contradictory fashion, later states that 'there is no feminist version of Casaubon's key to all mythologies. And admit it: you wouldn't want to read it if there were' (Wolf 1993: 129).

12. For this reason, I have made it a policy to limit, as far as is possible, direct references to male-oriented theories and criticisms, when a woman-centred one can serve my purposes equally well. In an academic environment where feminists often have to retreat two paces in order to move forward, I hope a little theoretical 'skipping' will be accepted.

CHAPTER SEVEN

1. 'I cannot explain the opposition which is raised in this way by little girls to phallic masturbation except by supposing that there is some concurrent factor which turns her violently against that pleasurable activity. Such a factor lies close at hand. It cannot be anything else than her narcissistic sense of humiliation which is bound up with penis-envy, the reminder that after all this is a point on which she cannot compete with boys and that it would therefore be best for her to give up the idea of doing so' (Freud 1977: 340).

2. 'Sex penetrates the whole person; a man's sexual constitution is a part of his general constitution. There is considerable truth in the dictum: "A man is what his sex is"' (Havelock Ellis, cited by Weeks 1985: 62).

3. 'Sexuality is something men have: problems are what women have, according to *Forum*' (Jackson in Coveney et al., 1984: 103).

4. By Radicalesbians and reprinted in Koedt et al. 1973: 240–5.

5. See Snitow, Stansell and Thompson 1983: 30.

6. An early example of such a critique is Anne Koedt's essay 'Lesbianism and Feminism', in Koedt et al. 1973.

7. 'This separation of the public and private is a fundamental premise of sexual liberalism. In the short term it was helpful for gay liberation. But the idea that whatever takes place between consenting adults in private should be seen as exempt from politics has led to a sexual libertarianism in the 1980s which is in direct opposition to feminism' (Jeffreys 1990: 112).

8. 'Sexology has never been straightforwardly outside or against relations of power; it has frequently been deeply implicated in them' (Weeks 1985: 79).

CHAPTER EIGHT

1. A cursory glance at the contents of *The Achilles Heel Reader* confirms

this sense of an absence. Although the writers valiantly scrutinize masculinity in the context of fatherhood, men's groups, the workplace, and socialist theory, there is a marked reluctance to speak personally. In one case 'Pregnant Fatherhood – 2 years on' by Paul Morrison, the writer talks of his feelings about caring for his daughter and attempts to separate this from details of his relationship with his partner, 'L'. While one can see the intention behind this – to treat his partner as a discreet individual with her own separate life, the elision struck a false chord; tensions around the division of childcare were alluded to but not foregrounded. Such unwillingness really to write the personal is apparent in much feminist writings too – particularly around the same sphere of heterosexual relationships and responses to parenthood.

2. With regard to forms of exclusion, it should be noted that Jardine and Smith acknowledge the dearth of gay and lesbian or black contributors to *Men in Feminism* stating that 'this is largely a reflection of a serious institutional problem' (Jardine and Smith 1987: viii).

3. Harry Christian's *The Making of Anti-Sexist Men* (1994) is an interesting volume in its endeavour to provide some empirical case studies of British anti-sexist men, through interviews and autobiographical narratives.

4. In the opening of his introduction he cites the fact that more men than women commit suicide, as if this proves a *prima facie* case against the contention that women in Western society suffer systematic material and ideological forms of subordination.

5. See Jill Radford and Diana E. H. Russell (eds), *Femicide: The Politics of Woman Killing*, Buckingham: Open University Press, 1992.

CHAPTER NINE

1. Jean-François Lyotard's 'grand narratives of legitimation', as discussed in Fraser and Nicholson's essay in Nicholson 1990: 21–2.

2. Such criticisms are not restricted to anti-feminists: Shelagh Young, a feminist cultural critic, declares that 'many feminist women do perpetuate a sort of alternative puritanism which can be very boring indeed' (Gamman and Marshment 1988: 178).

3. There are several interesting texts on utopian writings and feminist criticism. See, for example, Sarah Lefanu, *In the Chinks of the World Machine: Feminism and Science Fiction*, London: The Women's Press, 1988; Anne Cranny-Francis, *Feminist Fiction*, Oxford: Polity Press, 1990; and Rosemary Jackson, *Fantasy: The Literature of Subversion*, London: Methuen, 1981.

CHAPTER TEN

1. It is interesting to note that Marjorie Ferguson charts the way in which 'old' issues are constantly being rehashed into the 'new' in women's magazine publishing (See *Forever Feminine*, London: Heinemann, 1983). It seems to me that Wolf, Katie Roiphe and Camilla Pagila adopt the same tactics as those utilized in contemporary magazine

journalism and refashion the 'old' feminist precepts to their own (often anti-feminist) image.

2. 'The backlash is not a conspiracy, with a council dispatching agents from some central control room, nor are the people who serve its ends often aware of their role; some even consider themselves feminists' (Faludi 1992: 16).

3. 'If women are more intelligent, stronger and more independent than the men they associate with, and if they refuse to be governed by those inadequate men, they are deemed in law to be responsible for their own deaths. Female strength and independence are construed as wilful acts of provocation which diminish men's responsibility for their violence' (Radford in Radford and Russell 1992: 232). Jill Radford and Diana H. Russell in the collected writings which comprise *Femicide: The Politics of Woman Killing* 'have illustrated that femicide, far from comprising only random or isolated incidents of sexual terrorism, is extensive. Femicide has cost the lives of thousands of women . . . Femicide is a phenomenon that patriarchal interests have taken pains to deny' (Radford in Radford and Russell 1992: 351).

4. 'Politically correct is an idea that emerges from the well-meaning attempt in social movements to bring the unsatisfactory present into line with the utopian future, in fact, to make the "revolution" happen. Although ideas about what is acceptable behaviour develop in any political organization, left or right, the express phrase, politically correct, seems to be associated with the left. The phrase is charged, because the left, in its conception of itself, stands for freedom, yet finds itself telling people how to behave and therefore interfering with their freedom' (Dimen in Vance 1992: 138–9).

5. Perhaps one of the most famous examples of fallacious 'trends' of the '90s was accompanied by the 'fact' that forty-year-old single women are more likely to be killed by a terrorist than find a husband. Faludi reveals this trend to have been initiated as a joke among *Newsweek* staff; it ended up as a truism which reached millions through the highly successful film *Sleepless in Seattle*.

6. Here is an example of French's position which might be regarded as highly contentious:

> While men strut and fret their hour upon the stage, shout in bars and sports arenas, thump their chests or show their profiles in legislatures, and explode incredible weapons in an endless contest for status, an obsessive quest for symbolic 'proof' of their superiority, women quietly keep the world going. Women know that men will not do this, that either they do the job or it will not be done. They grow or buy, they carry and prepare food for the essential, inevitable, necessarily female-prepared dinner: they give birth to the children and feed them and bathe them and hold them and teach them and hope they will survive. They encourage their men, nurture them, soothe them, nag them, hoping they too will survive and help the children to survive. They

do not – as a caste – want the same things men want, and so different are the motivations driving the two sexes that men shake their heads wondering 'what do women want?' Women know what men want – but they too shake their heads. (French 1992: 202)

7. Roberts's book predates the establishing of the Child Support Agency, set up in April 1993; but one assumes she would have broached this subject here. It seems important to remark that such organizations as 'Families need Fathers' are not necessarily pro-feminist in their purview, and some critics of the CSA resort to quite extensive women-blaming.

8. The appendices of *Sex, Art and American Culture* themselves shows Pagila's flair for self publicity, even when she depicts herself as a hapless subject of a media tidal wave. The first appendix details her history as a media phenomenon, the second collects some cartoons depicting her, and the third offers extensive further reading of articles about her.

9. The genderquake is alleged by Wolf to have been started by Anita Hill's charges of sexual harassment against Clarence Thomas in 1991–2. Other landmarks include 'the election of the pro-feminist President Clinton' (Wolf 1993: xiv) – rather a disappointing feature of this 'quake' being that victories for male-dominated political mainstreams who pay some token regard for women, is seen as monumental. In general, the image of a 'genderquake', which conjures up impressions of total, revolutionary and irreversible change is not substantiated in Wolf's book. Her gigantic claims never seem to be realized in the text of her work: it is difficult to see how Clinton's election or Australia's re-election of the socialist Paul Keating, and the election of Canada's first female Prime Minister gesture towards the conclusion that 'women have become the political ruling class' (Wolf 1993: xiv), but they just don't know it yet. Her British example – that Alison Halford's 'courageous stand against sexual discrimination in the police force opened the door for other women' (Wolf 1993: xv) – is frustratingly oblique: what door?

CONCLUSION

1. See, for example, *The Guardian*, 'Women', 21 June 1990: 38.

Bibliography

Alcoff, L. and E. Potter (eds), *Feminist Epistemologies*, London: Routledge, 1993.

Althusser, L., *Essays on Ideology*, London: Verso, 1984.

Assiter, A., *Althusser and Feminism*, London: Pluto Press, 1990.

Assiter, A. and C. Avedon, *Bad Girls and Dirty Pictures: The Challenge to Reclaim Feminism*, London: Pluto Press, 1993.

Bammer, A., *Partial Visions: Feminism and Utopianism in the 1970s*, London: Routledge, 1991.

Barrett, M. and M. McIntosh, *The Anti-Social Family*, London: Verso, 1982.

Barrett, M., *Women's Oppression Today: Problems in Marxist Feminist Analysis* (rev. edn), London: Verso, 1988.

Barrett, M. and A. Phillips (eds), *Destabilizing Theory: Contemporary Feminist Debates*, London: Polity Press, 1992

Bly, R., *Iron John: A Book About Men*, Shaftesbury, Dorset: Element Books, 1991.

Boone, J. A. and M. Cadden (eds), *Engendering Men: The Question of Male Feminist Criticism*, London: Routledge, 1990.

Brittan, A. and M. Maynard, *Sexism, Racism and Oppression*, Oxford: Basil Blackwell, 1984.

Brownmiller, S., *Against Our Will: Men, Women and Rape*, Harmondsworth: Penguin Books, 1976.

Brownmiller, S., *Femininity*, London: Paladin, 1986.

Butler, J., *Gender Trouble: Feminism and the Subversion of Identity*, London: Routledge, 1990.

Carr, H. (ed.), *From My Guy to Sci Fi: Genre and Women's Writing in the Postmodern World*, London: Pandora Press, 1989.

Castro, G., *American Feminism: A Contemporary History*, trans. E. Loverde-Bagwell, New York: New York University Press, 1990.

Campbell, B., 'A Feminist Sexual Politics: Now you See it, Now you Don't', *Feminist Review*, No. 5, 1980, pp. 1–18.

Chapman, R. and J. Rutherford (eds), *Male Order: Unwrapping Masculinity*, London: Lawrence & Wishart, 1988.

Christian, H., *The Making of Anti-Sexist Men*, London: Routledge, 1994.

Collins, P. Hill, *Black Feminist Thought: Knowledge, Consciousness and the Politics of Empowerment*, London: Routledge, 1990.

Coote, A. and B. Campbell, *Sweet Freedom: The Struggle for Women's Liberation* (2nd edn), Oxford: Basil Blackwell, 1987.

Coveney, L. et al., *The Sexuality Papers: Male Sexuality and the Social Control of Women*, London: Hutchinson, 1984.

Coward, R., *Patriarchal Precedents: Sexuality and Social Relations*, London: Routledge, 1983.

Coward, R., *Female Desire: Women's Sexuality Today*, London: Paladin Books, 1984.

Coward, R., *Our Treacherous Hearts: Why Women Let Men Get Their Way*, London: Faber & Faber, 1992.

Cruikshank, M., *The Gay and Lesbian Liberation Movement*, London: Routledge, 1992.

Dahlerup, D. (ed.), *The New Women's Movement: Feminism and Political Power in Europe and the USA*, London: Sage Publications, 1986.

Daly, M., *Gyn/Ecology: The Metaethics of Radical Feminism*, London: The Women's Press, 1979.

De Beauvoir, S., *The Second Sex* (first pub. 1949), trans. and ed. H. M. Parshley, Harmondsworth: Penguin Books, 1972.

Derrida, J., *Writing and Difference*, trans. A. Bass, London: Routledge, 1978.

Differences, 'The Essential Difference: Another Look at Essentialism', Vol. 1, No. 2, Summer 1989.

Doane, J. and D. Hodges, *Nostalgia and Sexual Difference: The Resistance to Contemporary Feminism*, London: Methuen, 1987.

Donovan, J., *Feminist Theory: The Intellectual Traditions of American Feminism* (new expanded edn), New York: Continuum, 1992.

Douglas, C. A., *Love and Politics: Radical Feminist and Lesbian Theories*, San Francisco: ism press inc, 1990.

Dworkin, A., *Letters form a War Zone: Writings 1976–1987*, London: Martin Secker & Warburg, 1988.

Echols, A., *Daring to be Bad: Radical Feminism in America 1967–1975*, Minneapolis: University of Minnesota Press, 1989.

Ellmann, M., *Thinking About Women* (1969), London: Virago, 1979.

Engels, F., *The Origin of the Family, Private Property and the State* (1884), Harmondsworth: Penguin Books, 1985.

Evans, J. et al., *Feminism and Political Theory*, London: Sage Publications, 1986.

Faderman, L., *Surpassing the Love of Men: Romantic Friendship and Love Between Women from the Renaissance to the Present*, London: The Women's Press, 1985.

Faderman, L., *Odd Girls and Twilight Lovers: A History of Lesbian Life in the Twentieth Century*, Harmondsworth: Penguin Books, 1992.

Faludi, S., *Backlash: The Undeclared War Against Women*, London: Chatto & Windus, 1992.

Feminist Anthology Collective, *No Turning Back: Writing from the Women's Liberation Movement 1975–80*, London: The Women's Press, 1981.

Feminist Review, 'Socialist Feminism: Out of the Blue', No. 23, Summer 1986.

Feminist Review (eds), *Sexuality: A Reader*, London: Virago, 1987.

Feminist Review, 'The Past Before Us: Twenty Years of Feminism', No. 31, Spring 1989.

Feminist Review, 'Perverse Politics: Lesbian Issues', No. 34, Spring 1990.

Figes, E., *Patriarchal Attitudes: Women in Society*, London: Faber & Faber, 1970.

Firestone, S., *The Dialectic of Sex: The Case for Feminist Revolution*, London: The Women's Press, 1979.

Foster, H. (ed.), *Postmodern Culture*, London: Pluto Press, 1983.

Foucault, M., *The Order of Things: An Archaeology of the Human Sciences*, London: Tavistock Publications, 1970.

Foucault, M., *The History of Sexuality – Volume One: An Introduction*, trans. R. Hurley, London: Allen Lane, 1979.

French, M., *The War Against Women*, London: Hamish Hamilton, 1992.

Freud, S., *On Sexuality*, trans. A. Richards, Harmondsworth: Pelican Books, 1977.

Friedan, B., *The Feminine Mystique* (first pub. 1963), Harmondsworth: Penguin Books, 1965.

Fuss, D., *Essentially Speaking: Feminism, Nature and Difference*, London: Routledge, 1989.

Gallop, J., *Around 1981: Academic Feminist Theory*, London: Routledge, 1992.

Gamman, L. and M. Marshment (eds), *The Female Gaze: Women as Viewers of Popular Culture*, London: The Women's Press, 1988.

Greene, G. and C. Kahn, *Making a Difference: Feminist Literary Criticism*, London: Methuen, 1985.

Greer, G., *The Female Eunuch*, London: Paladin Books, 1971

Greer, G., *Sex and Destiny: The Politics of Human Fertility*, London: Picador, 1984

Griffiths, M., and M. Whitford, *Feminist Perspectives on Philosophical Traditions*, London: Macmillan, 1988.

Grimshaw, J., *Feminist Philosophers: Women's Perspectives on Philosophical Traditions*, Brighton: Wheatsheaf Books, 1986.

Gunew, S. (ed.), *Feminist Knowledge: Critique and Construct*, London: Routledge, 1990.

Hagan, K. L. (ed.), *Women Respond to the Men's Movement*, San Francisco: Pandora, 1992.

Haug, F. (ed.), *Female Sexualization*, London: Verso, 1987.

Hirsch, M. and E. Fox Keller (eds), *Conflicts in Feminism*, London: Routledge, 1990.

Hite, S., *The Hite Report: A Nationwide Study of Female Sexuality*, London: Summit Books, 1977.

Hobbes, T., *Man and Citizen*, ed. B. Gert, Hemel Hempstead: Harvester Press, 1978.

hooks, b., *Ain't I a Woman: Black Women and Feminism*, London: Pluto Press, 1982.

hooks, b., *Feminist Theory: From Margin to Center*, Boston: South End Press, 1984

hooks, b., *Talking Back: Thinking Feminist – Thinking Black*, London: Sheba Feminist Publishers, 1989.

hooks, b., *Yearning: Race, Gender, and Cultural Politics*, London: Turnaround, 1991.

Hull, G. T., P. Bell Scott and B. Smith (eds), *But Some of Us are Brave: Black Women's Studies*, New York: The Feminist Press, 1982.

Jackson, M., 'Sex Research and the Construction of Sexuality: A Tool of Male Supremacy?', *Women's Studies International Forum*, Vol. 7, No. 1, 1984.

Jaggar, A. M., *Feminist Politics and Human Nature*, Hemel Hempstead: Harvester Press, 1983.

James, S. M., and A. P. A. Busia, *Theorizing Black Feminisms: The Visionary Pragmatism of Black Women*, London: Routledge, 1993.

Jardine, A. and P. Smith, *Men in Feminism*, London: Methuen, 1987.

Jeffreys, S., *Anticlimax: A Feminist Perspective on the Sexual Revolution*, London: The Women's Press, 1990.

Jeffreys, S., *The Lesbian Heresy: A Feminist Perspective on the Lesbian Sexual Revolution*, London: The Women's Press, 1994.

Kaplan, C., *Sea Changes: Essays on Culture and Feminism*, London: Verso, 1986.

Kaplan, E. A. (ed.), *Postmodernism and its Discontents: Theories, Practices*, London: Verso, 1988.

Kauffman, L. (ed.), *Gender and Theory: Dialogues on Feminist Criticism*, Oxford: Basil Blackwell, 1989.

Kauffman, L. (ed.), *Feminism and Institutions: Dialogues on Feminist Theory*, Oxford: Basil Blackwell, 1989.

Koedt, A., Levine and A. Rapone (eds), *Radical Feminism*, New York: Quadrangle Books, 1973.

Kuhn, A. and A. Wolpe (eds), *Feminism and Materialism: Women and Modes of Production*, London: Routledge & Kegan Paul, 1978.

Lovell, T. (ed.), *British Feminist Thought: A Reader*, Oxford: Basil Blackwell, 1990.

Lovenduski, J. and V. Randall, *Contemporary Feminist Politics: Women and Power in Britain*, Oxford: Oxford University Press, 1993.

MacKinnon, C. A., *Feminism Unmodified: Discourses on Life and Law*, Cambridge, Mass: Harvard University Press, 1987.

Marx K., *The Revolutions of 1848: Political Writings Volume One*, ed. D. Fernbach, Harmondsworth: Penguin Books, 1973

Millett, K., *Sexual Politics* (1st pub. 1971), London: Virago, 1977.

Mitchell, J., *Woman's Estate*, Harmondsworth: Penguin Books, 1975.

Mitchell, J., *Psychoanalysis and Feminism*, Harmondsworth: Penguin Books, 1975.

Mitchell, J., *Women: The Longest Revolution*, London: Virago, 1984.

Mitchell, J. and A. Oakley (eds), *What is Feminism?*, Oxford: Basil Blackwell, 1986.

Modleski, T., *Feminism Without Women: Culture and Criticism in a 'Postfeminist' Age*, London: Routledge, 1991.

Moi, T., *Sexual/Textual Politics: Feminist Literary Theory*, London:
   Methuen, 1985.
Morgan, R. (ed.), *Sisterhood is Powerful: an Anthology of Writings from the
   Women's Liberation Movement*, New York: Vintage Books, 1970.
Morris, M., *The Pirate's Fiancee: Feminism, Reading, Postmodernism*,
   London: Verso, 1988.
Nestle, J., *A Restricted Country: Essays and Short Stories*, London: Sheba
   Feminist Publishers, 1987.
Newton, J. and D. Rosenfelt, *Feminist Criticism and Social Change* London:
   Methuen, 1985.
Nicholson, L. J., (ed.), *Feminism/Postmodernism*, London: Routledge, 1990.
Nye, A., *Feminist Theory and the Philosophies of Man*, London: Croom
   Helm, 1988.
Oakley, A. and J. Mitchell, *The Rights and Wrongs of Women*,
   Harmondsworth: Pelican, 1976.
Paglia, C., *Sexual Personae: Art and Decadence from Nefertiti to Emily
   Dickinson*, Harmondsworth: Penguin Books, 1991.
Paglia, C., *Sex, Art, and American Culture*, Harmondsworth: Penguin
   Books, 1992.
Radford, J. and D. H. Russell, *Femicide: The Politics of Woman Killing*,
   Buckingham: Open University Press, 1992
Richards, J. Radcliffe, *The Sceptical Feminist: A Philosophical Enquiry*,
   Harmondsworth: Penguin Books, 1982.
Rich, A., *On Lies, Secrets and Silence: Selected Prose 1966–1978*, London:
   Virago, 1980.
Rich, A., *Blood, Bread and Poetry: Selected Prose 1979–1985*, London:
   Virago, 1986.
Roberts, Y., *Mad About Women: Can There Ever be Fair Play Between the
   Sexes?*, London: Virago, 1992.
Robinson, L. S., *Sex, Class, and Culture*, London: Methuen: 1978.
Roiphe, K., *The Morning After: Sex, Fear, and Feminism*, London: Hamish
   Hamilton, 1994.
Rowbotham, S., *Woman's Consciousness, Man's World*, Harmondsworth:
   Penguin Books, 1973.
Rowbotham, S., L. Segal and H. Wainwright, *Beyond the Fragments:
   Feminism and the Making of Socialism*, London: Merlin Press, 1979.
Rowbotham, S., *The Past is Before Us: Feminism in Action Since the 1960s*,
   London: Pandora Press, 1989.
Rowbotham, S., *Women in Movement: Feminism and Social Action*, London:
   Routledge, 1992.
Rowe, M. (ed.), *'Spare Rib' Reader*, Harmondworth: Penguin Books, 1982.
Sawicki, J., *Disciplining Foucault: Feminism, Power, and the Body*, London:
   Routledge, 1991.
Sayers, S. and P. Osborne (eds), *Socialism, Feminism and Philosophy: A
   Radical Philosophy Reader*, London: Routledge, 1990.
Segal, L., *Is the Future Female? Troubled Thoughts on Contemporary
   Feminism*, London: Virago, 1987.
Segal, L. and M. McIntosh, *Sex Exposed: Sexuality and the Pornography
   Debate*, London: Virago, 1992.

Segal, L., *Straight Sex: The Politics of Pleasure*, London: Virago, 1994.

Seidler, V. J. (ed.), *The Achilles Heel Reader*, London: Routledge, 1991.

Seidler, V. J., *Recreating Sexual Politics: Men, Feminism and Politics*, London: Routledge, 1991.

Sheridan, S. (ed.), *Grafts: Feminist Cultural Criticism*, London: Verso, 1988.

Snitow, A., E. Stansell and S. Thompson (eds), *Powers of Desire: The Politics of Sexuality*, New York: Monthly Review Press, 1983.

Taylor, B., *Eve and the New Jerusalem: Socialism and Feminism in the Nineteenth Century*, London: Virago, 1983.

Thomas, D., *Not Guilty: In Defence of Modern Man*, London: Weidenfeld & Nicolson, 1993.

Thompson, A., and H. Wilcox, *Teaching Women: Feminism and English Studies*, Manchester: Manchester University Press, 1989.

Tong, R., *Feminist Thought: A Comprehensive Introduction*, London: Routledge, 1989.

Vance, C. S. (ed.), *Pleasure and Danger: Exploring Female Sexuality*, London: Pandora, 1992.

Wandor, M. (ed.), *The Body Politic*, London: Stage One, 1972.

Wandor, M. (ed.), *Once a Feminist: Stories of a Generation*, London: Virago, 1990.

Weed, E. (ed.), *Coming to Terms: Theory, Feminism, Politics*, London: Routledge, 1989.

Weedon, C., *Feminist Practice and Poststructuralist Theory*, Oxford: Blackwell, 1987.

Weeks, J., *Sexuality and its Discontents: Meanings, Myths and Modern Sexualities*, London: Routledge, 1985.

Weeks, J., *Sexuality*, London: Routledge, 1986.

Wilkinson, S. and C. Kitzinger, *Heterosexuality: A Feminism and Psychology Reader*, London: Sage Publications: 1993.

Wilson, E. (with A. Weir), *Hidden Agendas: Theory, Politics, and Experience in the Women's Movement*, London: Tavistock Publications, 1986.

Wittig, M., *The Straight Mind: And Other Essays*, Hemel Hempstead: Harvester Wheatsheaf, 1992.

Wolf, N., *The Beauty Myth*, London: Chatto & Windus, 1990.

Wolf, N., *Fire with Fire: The New Female Power and How it will Change the 21st Century*, London: Chatto & Windus, 1993.

Wollstonecraft, M., *Vindication of the Rights of Woman* (1792), Harmondsworth: Penguin, 1975.

Woolf, V., *A Room of One's Own* (1929), London: Triad Grafton, 1977.

Index